Dynamism in Islamic Activism

The Netherlands Scientific Council for Government Policy (WRR) was established on a provisional basis in 1972. It was given a formal legal basis under
the Act of Establishment of June 30, 1976. The present term of office runs up
to December 31, 2007.

According to the Act of Establishment, it is the Council's task to supply, in
behalf of government policy, scientifically sound information on developments which may affect society in the long term, and to draw timely attention to likely anomalies and obstacles, to define major policy problems and to
indicate policy alternatives.

The Council draws up its own programme of work, after consultation with
the Prime Minister, who also takes cognisance of the cabinet's view on the
proposed programme.

*Dynamism in Islamic Activism. Reference Points for Democratization and
Human Rights* is a translation of the Council's report *Dynamiek in islamitisch
activisme. Aanknopingspunten voor democratisering en mensenrechten*,
Reports to the government nr. 73, Amsterdam: Amsterdam University Press,
2006 (ISBN-13: 978 90 5356 827 9). The report was translated from the Dutch
by Kate Delaney.
This report was completed under the responsibility of the seventh Council
(2003-2007), which at the time had the following composition:

Prof. dr. W.B.H.J. van de Donk (chairman)
Prof. mr. dr. L. Hancher
Prof. dr. P.A.H. van Lieshout
Prof. dr. P.L. Meurs
Prof. dr. J.L.M. Pelkmans
I.J. Schoonenboom
Prof. dr. J.J.M. Theeuwes
Prof. dr. P. Winsemius

Executive director: dr. A.C. Hemerijck
Deputy-director: dr. R.J. Mulder

Lange Vijverberg 4-5
P.O. Box 20004
2500 EA 's-Gravenhage
Tel. + 31 70 356 46 00
Fax + 31 70 356 46 85
E-mail: info@wrr.nl
Internet: http://www.wrr.nl

WRR

SCIENTIFIC COUNCIL FOR GOVERNMENT POLICY

Dynamism in
Islamic Activism

REFERENCE POINTS FOR DEMOCRATIZATION
AND HUMAN RIGHTS

Amsterdam University Press, Amsterdam 2006

Cover illustration : ANP / Robin Utrecht

Cover design: Studio Daniëls, The Hague
Layout: Het Steen Typografie, Maarssen

ISBN-13   978 90 5356 918 4
ISBN-10   90 5356 918 9
NUR   741 / 717

CONTENTS

SUMMARY

Background
Since the 1970s, Islam has become an increasingly important political factor. The various manifestations of this phenomenon of 'Islamic activism' have led to considerable tensions and violent conflicts, not only within the Muslim world itself, but also in (relations with) the West and the Netherlands. The interrelatedness of what occurs outside and inside national borders means that what takes place elsewhere may also have consequences for the internal relationship between segments of the population. A climate of distrust and fear has arisen between Muslims and non-Muslims, and also within the Muslim community itself. Communication about 'Islam' now only takes place through intemperate images and inflated words, such as a 'clash of civilizations' or an 'irreconcilability of Islam with democracy and human rights.'

Research question
This report investigates the characteristics and dynamics of Islamic activism. It poses the question of whether, and in what respect, the manifestations of this activism since the 1970s offer reference points for democratization and the improvement of human rights. It also investigates which policy perspectives for the Netherlands and Europe can contribute to a reduction of tensions surrounding Islamic activism in the longer term and can support processes of democratization and the improvement of human rights.

Goal
With this report, the Council intends to formulate a policy perspective that will contribute to reducing the tensions with and within the Muslim world on issues of Islamic activism. The Council considers it essential that this perspective be based on factual knowledge of the developments and characteristics of this activism. At the same time, this report does not intend to be a description and analysis of *all* facets of Islamic activism, including its well-known negative manifestations. The research concentrates on positive reference points for policy directed towards democratization and human rights in Muslim countries.

This report is directed towards the Dutch government. However, by their nature, the international developments discussed, demand efforts of international policy. For this reason, the report primarily explores the policy options available to the EU. It is precisely within this larger context that the Netherlands can exert influence. However, reference points for the EU's external policy also have implications for approaching Islamic activism within the Netherlands.

Approach
The relationship between Islamic activism and democracy and human rights is examined along three dimensions, namely:
- Islamic political thought,
- Islamic political movements, and
- Islamic law.

Reference points
The report concludes that Islamic activism does indeed offer reference points for democratization and human rights. Each of the three investigated dimensions shows, in this respect, great diversity and promising dynamism. Even though these are only tentative reference points and much uncertainty still exists, it is inaccurate to assume that 'Islam' in a general sense is at odds with the acceptance of democracy and human rights.

On the level of *Islamic political thought* there are indeed many thinkers who reject important principles for the polity of the state, such as the separation of church and state, democracy, constitutional government, and human rights, as incompatible with Islamic principles and the supremacy of Islamic law. Yet, alongside these opinions, which shape much of the image of Islam, there are increasingly more thinkers who strive for these same principles precisely on Islamic grounds. They turn away from dogmatic approaches that claim that the precepts of the sacred sources should be followed to the letter. Rather, they are more concerned with the spirit and expressive power of these sources in relation to current circumstances. Thinkers holding such views can now be found in many Muslim countries – Indonesia, Malaysia, and Egypt, for example. This modernizing mode of thought can even be found in Iran, a country that has now had a quarter century of experience with Islamic theocracy.

The recent history of *Islamic political movements* in the Muslim world also reveals a large degree of diversity and dynamism. Such movements do not form a homogenous, unalterably radical, and always violent threat. Transnational terrorism that concentrates on jihadist actions is, of course, threatening. Alongside this, however, there are a number of Islamic movements with very diverse aspirations, including groups seeking reforms within the existing political systems. Moreover, Islamic political movements in many Muslim countries have abandoned their initially radical attitude in favor of a pragmatic political standpoint. The movements most strongly oriented towards the *political arena*, such as the Muslim Brotherhood in Egypt, have shifted the most in the direction of accepting democratic principles and norms. In doing so, they distance themselves from absolute truths and become familiar with the positive workings of democratic principles and human rights.

In the last few decades many Muslim countries have been exposed to the pressure of introducing elements of *Islamic law* in national legislation. The views on what Sharia contains, however, are quite divergent, ranging from very general guidelines to concrete codes of behavior. Thus there are large differences not only in the laws based on Sharia, but also in how these laws should be put into practice. The Islamization of law since the 1970s has had limited scope in most countries; exceptions are countries like Iran, Pakistan, and Sudan. Additionally, the first wave of Islamization has not been not followed by a second; rather, there has been a decline in the influence of strict interpretations of Sharia on national law in the last fifteen years. Even when Sharia plays a formal role, it seems that this does not exclude gradual modernization of law. Thus the reform of marriage laws has gone forward in most countries despite activism. In reaction to *universal* human rights, ideas about *Islamic* human rights have been developed in the Islamic world. In addition to sharing similarities, these two concepts also demonstrate important fundamental differences. Nevertheless, here, too, there appears unmistakably a tendency towards gradual rapprochement.

Policy perspective
The member states of the EU cannot permit themselves to stand aloof. An inwardly focused Union which renounces external ambitions only creates an illusion of security that does not remove the existing vulnerability. Furthermore, aloofness means that Europe fails to make use of its opportunities for supporting promising developments in the Muslim world. For this reason, the WRR argues for an active and, wherever possible, constructive attitude on the part of EU member states. This policy encompasses the following points:

- taking into account the diversity of Islamic activism;
- recognizing Islamic activism as a potentially constructive political and legal factor in the development of Muslim countries;
- engaging with endogenous development processes and trajectories that promote democracy and human rights;
- investing in an informed public opinion in Europe on Islamic activism and on the main European and Dutch policies in this area.

Diversity
Between and within Muslim countries there are many different interpretations of the way in which Islam relates to politics, democracy, and human rights. Whether Islam and democracy can coexist, and whether Islamic legislation is at odds with human rights, cannot be established in any general sense but differs according to particular views and/or practices of Islam or Sharia, and may also change over time. The Netherlands and the EU will have to invest in knowledge of these different views and practices as a foundation for a policy towards Muslim countries.

9

Constructive or not

In the past, the EU, in its advocacy of democratization and the improvement of human rights in neighboring Muslim countries, primarily put its hopes on non-religious movements and parties, even if these groups had little political support within the local population. It becomes increasingly apparent, however, that ignoring the political and legal agendas of religious activism offers no solution and may even be counterproductive. Not only does such a stance discourage Islamic groups with substantial followings who are prepared to pursue gradual political liberalization from *within* the existing system, but it also fuels the widely-held view amongst ordinary citizens in the Muslim world that secularism and (Western) democracy, by definition, serve anti-religious interests. This will only fan the demand for Islamization, either because radicals will receive more support from the population for their religious views, or because political rulers themselves will play the conservative 'Islamization card' in order to maintain political legitimacy.

The EU and the Netherlands should no longer rule out in advance Islamic movements as potential interlocutors, but should be guided by the concrete political actions of these groups. They should strongly support groups moving towards the acceptance of democracy and human rights and condemn groups which move away from this goal. In addition, they must develop more positive incentives to be able to encourage and reward reforms. Furthermore, they must be prepared to levy sanctions in the case of serious violations of human rights. In the case of Euro-Mediterranean policy, this may amount to the (temporary) suspension of a partnership agreement. In this way, the Union allows space for different courses of democratization and the progressive realization of human rights, while at the same time maintaining its own values in this area.

Endogenous dynamism

Democracy and human rights cannot be permanently imposed from outside. The Netherlands and the EU should influence without lecturing and accept the fact that within an Islamic frame of reference democracy and human rights may sometimes (temporarily) be worked out in a manner different from that which is customary in Western countries. In many respects, Muslim countries do not satisfy contemporary international standards regarding democracy and human rights. In this, for that matter, they do not differ from many (other) developing countries. Precisely because of this, the question of whether and how they wish to aim for *improvement* is crucial. Serious reforms in the direction of international standards deserve support, including those which proceed from an Islamic discourse. Progressive improvements of human rights in many Muslim countries are simply easier to accept if they can be imbedded in the local tradition and culture. This is illustrated by the new family legislation in Morocco; considerable improvement in women's rights has taken place under the banner of Sharia.

Implications for the Netherlands

Internal European and Dutch relations also demand attention to diversity and dynamism. This, however, will require a cultural shift. To date, political and public debate in the Netherlands lacks sufficient knowledge of Islam and the many Islamic political movements and schools of thought. Governments should support active and especially structural initiatives which broaden the supply of information about these themes among Muslims and non-Muslims. Structural contributions may serve as an excellent counterbalance to the one-sided information and influence mechanisms, such as that of 'web Islam' practiced by radical factions.

In the Dutch situation, the formation of parties (partially) based on Islam or Muslim identity can offer a constructive contribution to political debate. Political parties inspired by Islam can give voice to those who do not feel themselves to be represented in the Muslim representative bodies. Such parties attest to the aspiration for participation in the existing institutions and according to the pertaining democratic rules.

Conclusion

A climate of confrontation and stereotypical thinking does not create stable conditions for security, democratization, and increasing respect for human rights. The only advisable alternative is to engage the reference points for democracy and human rights in Islamic activism itself. The analyses presented in this report demonstrate that these reference points, indeed, exist.

PREFACE

This report has been prepared by an internal project group of the Netherlands Scientific Council for Government Policy (WRR), comprising staff member W. Asbeek Brusse and Council member I.J. Schoonenboom.

The analyses in the report are based, in part, on studies conducted by externals at the request of the Council. These studies were published simultaneously with the original Dutch version of this report. They concern the following titles:

- J.M. Otto (2006) *Sharia en nationaal recht. Rechtssystemen in moslim-landen tussen traditie, politiek en rechtsstaat,* WRR-Verkenning nr. 11, Amsterdam: Amsterdam University Press.
- J.M. Otto, A.J. Dekker, L.J. van Soest-Zuurdeeg (red.) (2006) *Sharia en nationaal recht in twaalf moslimlanden,* WRR-Webpublicatie nr. 13, Amsterdam: Amsterdam University Press.
- N. Abu Zayd (2006) *Reformation of Islamic Thought. A Critical Historical Analysis,* WRR-Verkenning nr. 10, Amsterdam: Amsterdam University Press.
- M.S. Berger (2006) *Klassieke sharia en vernieuwing,* WRR-Webpublicatie nr. 12, Amsterdam: Amsterdam University Press.

The WRR assumes full responsibility for its "Report to the Government". The authors of the commissioned studies are entirely responsible for their own views.

13

1 INTRODUCTION

1.1 BACKGROUND

Over the last few decades, Islam has become an increasingly important political factor. The 1979 Islamic revolution in Iran marked the sensational start
of a period in which Islamic activists gained increasing currency as political
players (see box 1.1). Initially their influence appeared to be mostly limited
to countries with a Muslim majority ('Muslim countries').[1] Terrorist attacks
such as those in New York, Madrid, and London, however, have made it
unambiguously clear that non-Muslim countries in the West also are a part
of the image of the enemy for some Islamic groups. Indications of this have
been around for much longer; the Iranian revolution, for instance, had a
strong anti-Western motivation at its core. This understanding led writer
Samuel Huntington to predict in 1993 that after the disappearance of the
opposition between East and West, new conflicts would take place more
often between 'Western' and 'Islamic' civilizations (Huntington 1993).

The last two decades of the twentieth century are the pre-eminent years of
the third wave of democratization and an increased focus on human rights
(Diamond 2003; UNDP 2002:14-16).[2] This trend, however, appears to have
left major parts of the Muslim world almost untouched (Fish 2002). Only
four of the seventeen Arab countries have an electoral system which allows
competition among multiple parties through regularly recurring elections
(UNDP 2002: 15). Additionally, in a number of Muslim states in sub-Saharan Africa and in Central and South Asia, political liberalization seems to
have stagnated since the middle of the 1990s. Insufficient civil and political
liberties, bad government (which continues to exist in the Arab region
thanks in part to oil income), lack of a proper constitutional state, and great
economic and social inequalities contribute to the increasing unrest and
hopelessness which help create a breeding ground for violent Islamic radicalism (UNDP 2005; Rabasa 2005). The violence is, in part, directed at the
people of the region. It is also partially directed at the West, which in the
Arab world is seen as another force maintaining the status quo for its own
(energy) interests, despite all the Western rhetoric about human rights and
democracy.

There are also other factors which contribute to tensions around Islam and
the Muslim world. The practices of 'Islam in power' in countries where the
pursuit of Islamization results in the reintroduction of Islamic law (Sharia),
or in theocracies such as Iran and Saudi Arabia, are at odds with universal
human rights. The sometimes far-reaching segregation and inequality of
men and women, cruel punishments, animosity towards homosexuality,

and limitations on the freedom of expression in these countries are far removed from what many in Europe and other parts of the West consider important (though in some cases fairly recent) achievements. The same holds for phenomena such as the practice of honor killings and female circumcision which are likewise often associated with Islam. These phenomena manifest themselves increasingly closer to home due to the large number of Muslims currently living in Europe. Tensions surrounding Islam have thus also become European and national political issues, which often generate fierce debate and conflict within society.

Box 1.1   Political mobilization under the banner of Islam

There is already substantial literature available regarding the characteristics and backgrounds of the recent revival of Islamic activism.[3] This literature emphasizes a complex of underlying factors and catalysts, a few of which we list below:

- the protracted decline of the great Islamic civilization and the rise of the Western powers, resulting in the fall of Islamic empires and colonial domination;
- parallel to this, aroused feelings of humiliation, powerlessness, and lost identity, which prevailed also after independence;
- the policy carried out by postcolonial governments directed towards the consolidation of the (mostly secular) state, economic planning, and modernization. Through this policy, large segments of the population for whom Islam was an important reference point were, at the same time, placed culturally outside the system;
- international political events, such as the Six-Day War, the Arab oil boycott, the long, drawn-out confrontation between Israel and the Palestinians, and, recently, the war against Iraq, which functioned as catalysts of discontent with the failed domestic policies and Western presence in the Middle East;
- the mobilizing effect of the Islamic revolution in Iran and the jihadist struggle of the Taliban in Afghanistan;
- Saudi Arabian attempts to spread the doctrine of conservative Islamic Wahhabism through the rest of the world with the help of 'petrodollars'. This doctrine should serve as a Sunni counterweight to Shiite revolutionary zeal;
- the increasingly manifest political failures of postcolonial governments in many Muslim countries against a background of growing international economic competition, rapid population growth, substantial migration to large cities, and rising expectations of the population as a consequence of higher levels of education;
- the emergence of political movements which – after the relaxation of tensions between 'East' and 'West', the decline of communism, and the worldwide pressure for political liberalization since the start of the 1990s – treat Islam as a frame of reference for political legitimization; many strive toward the 'Islamization' of politics, the state and law;
- the use of terrorism by radical, often transnationally operative, activist groups and networks who charge geopolitical conflicts (such as the Gulf War, the Balkan War, the

conflicts in Kashmir and Chechnya, the Palestinian conflict, and the war in Iraq) with 'Islamic' and primarily anti-Western overtones;
• Muslims' experience of exclusion and discrimination in the economic, cultural, and political arenas in Western countries.

The connection between what happens outside and inside our borders involves not only concrete facts, but also images. Terrorist actions carried out by Muslims elsewhere in the world may suddenly cause Muslims in the Netherlands to be seen as potential terrorists and their religion as intrinsically antidemocratic and violent. The reverse also holds true: Muslims living in Europe and the US may interpret the wartime actions of Western countries against Muslim countries as new 'evidence' that the West is targeting Islam. International tensions and conflicts thus no longer affect only the international and foreign political relations between countries, but also greatly influence internal relationships between population groups via events and images. Even if our relationships with the governments of the Muslim world are stable, tensions and violent conflicts within and between Muslim countries can have significant consequences in Europe and the Netherlands, both for Muslims and non-Muslims. This accentuates the importance of more relaxed relationships between and within Muslim countries.

1.2 GOAL, KEY QUESTIONS, AND DEFINITIONS

Goal and key questions

The report aims to provide insight into the dynamics of Islamic activism in the Muslim world, and to formulate a policy perspective for reducing tensions surrounding Islamic activism and supporting processes of democratization and the improvement of human rights in Muslim countries. The central questions are outlined below:

• *What insights can be derived from the development of Islamic activism since the 1970s in relation to democratization and the advancement of human rights?*
• *What reference points does Islamic activism offer for rapprochement with the concepts of democracy and human rights?*
• *What policy perspectives for the Netherlands and Europe can, in the long run, reduce the tensions related to Islamic activism within the Muslim world and also support the processes of democratization and the advancement of human rights?*

These questions are naturally based on the assumption that democracy and human rights represent *universal* values, and that the active support of

these values should not be limited to certain regions or (religious) population groups. Put undiplomatically: even if the Arab region is rich in oil and
terrorist Islamic activism, that is no reason to view the systematic violations of human rights by repressive Arab regimes as an acceptable 'price'
for political stability in the region. Even if many authoritarian regimes
inside and outside the region are only too grateful to use the American
'war' on terror to label their Islamic activist opponents as terrorists, Western democracies should not ignore the justified democratic wish of Islamic
political parties to take part in the normal political process of their country.

The questions asked in this report are expressly focused on *reference points*
within Islamic activism for *democratization and the advancement of human
rights*. This report is thus not concerned with providing a representative
image of all facets of this activism, including all its aberrations. This selective approach has been chosen consciously. *The primary assumption of this
report is that precisely because of the mutually interrelatedness of foreign
and domestic politics, the West has an enlightened, long-term self-interest in
helping countries in parts of the Muslim world to break out of the political
and economic stagnation.* Lack of opportunities for development, bad
government, lack of regular institutional channels for expressing political
discontent, and repression form a dangerous mix which can easily encourage (violent) radicalism within the Muslim world. Violent radicalism is also
increasingly easily directed towards population groups outside the Muslim
world, certainly in relatively open societies. However, policies directed
towards the structural support of democratization and human rights in
the long term can counteract radicalism. Democratization and respect for
basic human rights enable people to mandate political parties that are
responsive to the voter's interests and respect democratic procedures and
institutions. They also offer people opportunities to send away political
leaders who neglect the agenda of development for their country. Without
these opportunities present, radical groups will maintain their appeal since
they are the only ones in the position to challenge the established order,
yet without having to account to the population for their actions. In these
circumstances, radical Islamic groups can easily obtain the lead over other
competing political groups since they primarily spread their message
through mosques, religious welfare organizations, and other religious
networks which, thanks to the protection of the banner of Islam, are less
quickly exposed to direct government repression (Gambill 2004).

Breaking through the cycle of repression and extremism in parts of the
Muslim world and allowing real political competition in elections *can*
contribute to the moderation of Islamic extremism in the long run, but
there are, of course, no certainties. In the short term, processes of democratization may even be destabilizing, because in new democracies with a long

history of authoritarian control, for instance, democratic institutions are still weak, the people have little trust in democratic procedures, and the newly chosen political elite plays on nationalist or populist sentiments to overcome domestic political differences. The critics of policies for democratization even believe that the short term risks of a take-over by Islamic extremists with the attendant chaos and instability are not compensated for by the possible chance of successful democratization in the long run. The Council, however, emphasizes the importance for the Netherlands and Europe of developing a strategic policy that will take into account not only such short-term dilemmas and risks, but will also be equipped in the long run to exploit opportunities whenever and wherever these arise.

Definitions

How the processes of democratization will take place and what form democracy will finally take may vary from country to country and also over time.[4] It is clear, however, that the concept of democracy assumes more than periodic (free) elections alone. Democracy must ultimately also be based on the rule of law, respect for basic individual human rights, such as human dignity, freedom of expression, association, assembly, and religion, the right to education, constitutionally guaranteed oversight of government decisions by chosen representatives of the people and civilian control of the army and police.

The Council will use the term *Islamic activism* to refer to the revival of 'Islam' as a political factor in the Muslim world. This refers to the endeavors of people for whom Islam is an important source of inspiration in the organizing of contemporary politics and society (Fuller 2003: xi). Here Islamic activism is an umbrella term for various possible objectives and demands, from the pursuit of a (worldwide) Islamic state to its antithesis – namely the separation of mosque and state based on Islamic principles. The word 'Islamic' emphasizes that Islam functions as a common vehicle and idiom for raising the political and social consciousness of large groups of Muslims. 'Activism' indicates that many different kinds of efforts may be included and that these may be highly susceptible to change. Understanding this requires interpreting the *symbols, rhetoric, and idiom* of Islam as well as *the actions and behavior* of the Muslims concerned.

Along with other concepts such as Islamism, fundamentalism, extremism, and political Islam, the term 'Islamic activism' in the current context sometimes evokes associations with violent, extremist action in the name of Islam. This is not surprising; it is always the extreme and violent manifestations which attract attention these days. Much of the turbulence which manifests itself under the name of Islam, both within and outside the Muslim world, is concerned with expressions of self-awareness raising and

19

militancy. This is something which should not be ignored, of course. This militancy, however, is not solely expressed in violent forms; it covers the whole spectrum from peaceful, playful, and provocative actions to those that are violent, terrorist, and intimidating. It is also expressed in various political, social, and cultural arenas and through various forms such as political movements and parties, non-governmental organizations (NGOs) and individual, and collective scholarly research into Islamic political thought.

The concept of *Islamization* refers to the founding of politics, the state, law, and society on Islamic principles. This concept is not entirely unambiguous since these principles and their meanings can be interpreted in very different ways. Thus the view that Islam cannot relate positively with democracy, the constitutional state, and human rights has come to be held not only by many in the West, but also by many in the Muslim world (Huntington 1993 and 1996). Don't the experiences in Iran, Sudan, and Afghanistan teach us that the relationship is more likely to be a negative one? This relationship, however, can also vary according to time and place. By focusing on developments that have taken place since the 1970s we can see what implications Islamic activism has had for politics and law and whether any changes have arisen with regard to the Islamization advocated. Have Islamic movements and groups maintained their original goals and instruments or have these changed over time? It is plausible that Islamic-political groups that originally presented themselves as violent or anti-system forces may, in the end, play a constructive role within the existing political system and increasingly orient themselves toward democratization and the advancement of human rights (Fuller 2003). Conversely, one can also imagine that movements and groups that first aimed to function within the existing systems could later formulate increasingly extreme demands in terms of the Islamization of the state and law.

This report uses the term *fundamentalism* to mean the pursuit of political reforms based on guidelines set down in the sacred sources (the Quran and the Sunna, the acts of the Prophet Mohammed). *Radicalism* is defined here as the pursuit of sweeping changes in the political and social order. The terms radicalism and extremism are used synonymously in this report.

1.3   LIMITATIONS

To be clear, the Council stresses that this report will not conduct a discussion about 'the (in)compatibility of Islam with democracy and human rights' in a *general* sense. While this question has occupied many (Muslims and non-Muslims) in the West for the last few years in particular, this discussion is seldom fruitful. Seeking an answer by relying solely on the sacred texts does not help. In the end it is not so much the texts, but primarily their interpretation and the concrete actions of the adherents which determine whether or not their religion is compatible with democracy and human rights. The many diverse interpretations and forms of conduct are, in turn, dependent on a range of different factors such as the cultural norms of the religious population in question and economic and political development trajectories – factors which are strongly linked to time and place. Therefore the proposition that Islam, democracy, and human rights are (in)compatible as such can neither be confirmed nor denied. The Council deems it more productive to investigate under which circumstances and in which places in the Muslim world Islamic activism creates opportunities for, or impediments to democratization and the advancement of human rights.

Likewise, the theme of this report is not 'development' (of democracy, human rights, etc.) in Muslim countries in a general sense. The focus is on Islamic activism in relation to (further) democratization and advancement of human rights in these countries. By limiting itself to this religious political factor, we aim to shed light on an extremely relevant line of approach. We do recognize, however, the risk of over-emphasizing this factor and ascribing more importance to it than is justified. With the focus explicitly on *Islamic* activism, the impression may easily arise that all the behavior of individual Muslims, Islamic movements, and governments is motivated by their religion, while in actual fact other factors might be more important. Yet also in cases where Islam as a religion does play an explicit role, it may serve as a vehicle for completely different goals, such as the underlining of identity, resistance against corrupt regimes or foreign domination, nationalistic aspirations, or ethnic dominance. This report will attempt to do justice to these nuances.

The analyses of this report do not refer all the time to *all* Muslim countries. That would require a much larger research project than the present one. Some information here does indeed concern all Muslim countries – as far as it is available – but for more 'in-depth' information, a selection has to suffice. This primarily concerns Chapter 4, which draws on the research into comparative law in twelve Muslim countries commissioned by the WRR and conducted by J.M. Otto, professor and director at the Van Vollenhoven Institute for Law and Administration in Non-Western Countries at the University of Leiden. For Chapter 2, which deals with developments in modern Islamic political thought within the mainstreams of Sunni and Shiite Islam, the WRR similarly commissioned research by Nasr Abu Zayd, Ibn Rushd Professor at the University for Humanistics and professor at the University of Leiden. Both studies have been published simultaneously with the Dutch version of this report (Otto 2006; Abu Zayd 2006).

1.4 ELABORATION OF THE RESEARCH QUESTION AND STRUCTURE OF THE REPORT

The development of Islamic activism in the Muslim world in relation to democratization and human rights is studied in terms of three dimensions:
- Islamic political thought within the Sunni and Shiite mainstreams,
- Islamic political movements, and
- Islamic law.

These dimensions are dealt with in Chapters 2 through 4 in the order indicated above. This order, however, does not suggest any causal progression or sequential connection in the sense that renewal starts on the intellectual level, is subsequently translated into political activism, and then finally settles into law. Changes *can* take place in this order, but different sequences are also conceivable, while, at the same time, renewal may also finds its origin outside these areas. Furthermore, other approaches may plausibly be used to view the development of activism, such as that of Islam as 'lived' in practice. Because of this report's focus on the relationship between Islamic activism and democracy and human rights, the public dimensions noted above have been chosen.

The development of *Islamic-political thought* is the focus of Chapter 2. There is a broad spectrum of views with regard to the organization of the state and society, and the relationship of Islam with democracy, the constitutional state, and human rights. The schools of thought researched here can be found within the Sunni and Shiite mainstreams. First we will examine the authors who are considered the intellectual fathers of the movements that have dedicated themselves since the 1970s to the establishment of an Islamic state and the introduction of Islamic law (sec. 2.2). They are also designated as fundamentalists since they pursue political reform on the basis of the original sources of Islam: the Quran and the Sunna. Many look to the early days of Islam for inspiration to break out of the stagnation in the Muslim world. Next to be considered are thinkers who distance themselves from following these sacred sources literally. These thinkers are inspired by the intention and expressive power of these sources when applied to modern questions (sec. 2.3). Subsequently, the chapter addresses the question of dynamism within viewpoints and a possible rapprochement with concepts of democratization and universal human rights (sec. 2.4). Finally, conclusions are drawn in section 2.5.

Chapter 3 deals with the development of *Islamic political movements*. Section 3.2 describes the most prominent characteristics of activist political movements that sprung up in the 1970s. In some countries they have succeeded in taking power (sec. 3.3). In most other countries they have not been successful, or, if so, only temporarily. These groups are, however, emphatically present in the political and social arenas in these countries (sec. 3.4). Interaction with the state greatly influences the dynamism and radicalism of this activism. Section 3.5 outlines this dynamism and assesses the opportunities for (further) democratization and advancement of human rights.

The *development of Islamic law* in Muslim countries is the subject of Chapter 4. This chapter investigates the scope of the Islamization of national law (sec. 4.2) and the relationship between universal and Islamic human rights (sec. 4.3). An important question here is whether these legal structures are at odds or if they permit rapprochement. Section 4.4 interprets the legal dynamics, after which conclusions are drawn (sec. 4.5).

This report is primarily directed toward the Dutch government. However, several of the proposed policy guidelines demand cooperation at the European level; it is precisely within this larger context that the Netherlands can exert influence. Chapter 5 investigates which policy options the Netherlands (working in conjunction with the EU) has at its disposal for reducing potential tensions within the Muslim world around the issue of Islamic activism and for supporting processes of democratization and the advancement of human rights. It begins by characterizing the context of contemporary world politics in which this policy must be carried out (sec. 5.2). Next it briefly sketches the findings of the previous chapters on the reference points within Islamic activism for rapprochement with the concepts of democracy and human rights (sec. 5.3). These sections offer a prelude to the policy perspective: a guiding framework with general starting points for constructively dealing with Islamic activism and, where possible, supporting democratization and human rights in the Muslim world (sec. 5.4). Section 5.5 throws light on the relevance of these general points of departure by exploring concrete options for the Dutch government to shape its constructive involvement with Muslim countries on European and bilateral levels. Finally the WRR briefly discusses the implications of this policy perspective for dealing with Islamic activism within the Netherlands itself, also given the increasing interrelatedness between external and internal developments (sec. 5.6). The last section will be used to formulate final conclusions (sec. 5.7).

NOTES

1   This report uses the term 'Muslim countries' to denote countries where over fifty percent of the population is Muslim. There are 48 such countries (see the appendices at the end of this report). An overview of countries with a Muslim majority can be found in Karatnycky 2002, amongst others. In this report the adjective 'Islamic' is used to refer to the religion of Islam.

2   The worldwide increase in the number of democracies has been relatively recent. Circa 1900, there was no nation that could be designated an 'electoral democracy' – what would today be considered a very minimalist and inadequate interpretation of democracy based on universal suffrage and competitive multi-party elections. Only a handful of nations (about 19 percent of all countries and 12.4 percent of the world's population) had democratic characteristics, but even the most democratic of these had no female suffrage and, in the case of many states in the US, blacks were prevented from voting. The overwhelming majority of countries in this group had political systems in which a dominant party controlled political power and could exert a disproportionately large influence on the media and the course of elections. Of the 130 states, no fewer than 55 were colonies and another 20 were protectorates. Most of these would only obtain independence during the process of decolonization which took place in the two decades after World War II. Illustrative of this is the fact that in 1950, 33 of the current 57 member states of the Organization of the Islamic Conference (OIC) still had the status of colony or protectorate. The number of electoral democracies in the world increased rapidly only from 1974 onwards; there was a jump from 27 to 43 percent in 1987, and by the end of the twentieth century this finally reached about 62 percent (Freedom House 1999).

3   For more recent analyses, see, amongst others, the RAND report (Rabasa et al. 2005), the *Arab Human Development Reports* of the UNDP (UNDP 2003, 2004, and 2005), Roy 2004, as well as publications by the International Crisis Group (ICG), such as ICG 2005a.

4   There is substantial literature regarding the characteristics and qualities of democracies and processes of democratization. For recent investigations and discussions see, for instance, the many contributions in the *Journal of Democracy*, such as Diamond and Morlino 2004. For a debate on democratization and democratic deficiencies in Muslim countries see, amongst others, Karatnycky 2002; Stepan and Robertson 2003 and 2004; Fish 2002; Lakoff 2004, and Nasr 2005.

2   THE DEVELOPMENT OF ISLAMIC POLITICAL THOUGHT

2.1   INTRODUCTION

This chapter investigates which insights can be gained from the development of Islamic political thought since the 1970s and its relations with
democracy and human rights. Are there reference points which could in
the longer term reduce tensions regarding Islamic activism, and which
could reinforce processes of democratization and the improvement of
human rights within Muslim countries?

It will be evident that Islamic thought on the design of the state, politics,
and law offers a varied image. The thinkers presented here have sought, or
continue to seek, new powers of expression for Islam within public life.
They take part in Islamic activism and can all be seen as reform-minded.
Nevertheless, there are great differences in the directions of the reforms
they champion. To make these differences more apparent, the thinkers will
be divided into two categories. The first group includes thinkers who look
for inspiration in the utopia of the foundation period of Islam, and who
follow the *letter* of the Quran and the Sunna as guidelines. This group will
be discussed in section 2.2. These thinkers exert great influence; many
Islamic movements – including militant ones – that have made themselves
felt strongly since the 1970s were established or influenced by them. It is
primarily their views which feed the fear that Islam is at odds with democracy and human rights.

There are, however, also thinkers who emphasize a positive connection
between Islam, democracy, and human rights; given the research question
of this report, attention will be paid primarily to their views (section 2.3).
Unlike the former group, they employ a modern epistemology and
emphasize the inherent relativity of human interpretations of the sacred
sources (Filali-Ansary 2003). They distance themselves from the literal
texts through their emphasis on the *spirit* of the Quran and the Sunna and
in this way create space for the appreciation of democracy and human
rights. The choice of which thinkers to present here is not based on their
influence or following, but on their substantive contribution to the freeing
of Islam from a traditionalist and legalistic interpretation. The selection is
limited to thinkers within the two mainstreams of Islam, namely Sunni
and Shiite. That is not to say, however, that there are no relevant views
on democracy and human rights within other groups such as the Alewite,
Ahmadi, and Sufi movements. The selection is further concentrated on
thinkers from a limited number of countries. In this way it is possible to

take into account the context of those countries along with the ideas and their dynamics.

Section 2.4 deals with the issue of the dynamism of opinions and potential rapprochement with concepts of democratization and the strengthening of human rights, while section 2.5 draws conclusions from the insights that have been presented. This chapter is based to a significant extent (particularly section 2.3) on a study conducted for the WRR by Nasr Abu Zayd, professor at the University of Leiden and the University for Humanistics in Utrecht. This study, titled *Reformation of Islamic Thought: A Critical Historical Analysis,* has been published simultaneously with this report (Abu Zayd 2006). Abu Zayd's publication will be referred to for literature on the thinkers discussed below.

2.2   REFORM BY RETURNING TO THE SOURCES

Current thinking about reform is strongly inspired by views which were developed at the end of the nineteenth and the beginning of the twentieth century. The context of intensive confrontation with the West and with Western thought at that time led to a great need for reform within the Muslim world. Whether caused directly by colonization or indirectly through the influence of Western thought on the indigenous regimes, the West strongly left its mark on states and nations. This usually meant that Islam was relegated to the private sphere. Western dominance led to a profound crisis of identity within the Muslim world. The dominant question throughout the Muslim world was: why is the West so powerful and the Muslim world – once a great power – so weak? The abolition in 1924 of the caliphate of the Ottoman Empire – the former Muslim empire that appointed itself as ruler of the whole Muslim community (*Ummah*) – was a traumatic event which many in the Muslim world viewed as yet another defeat for 'Islam' by the dominant West. This led to an intensive debate on the caliphate. At the same time, the debate on 'Islam and politics' was born, a debate in which the two categories of reform thinkers take such very different positions (Abu Zayd 2006).

Muhammid Rashid Rida (1865-1935) defended the caliphate as an authentic Islamic political system. While it was not explicitly stated as such in the sacred sources of the Quran and Sunna, the caliphate was viewed by Rida as necessary to prevent Muslims from reverting to a state of heathenism, *jahiliyya.* For this reason he saw the reinstatement of the caliphate as an essential strengthening of Islamic law and order that could counter the existing decadence brought about by Western influence. This view was shared by Hasan al-Banna (1906-1949). He blamed the decline of the Muslim world on the loss of the religious fervor so characteristic of its foundation era – the time of the Prophet and the so-called 'rightly guided caliphs', the first four caliphs who ruled after the Prophet's death. Al-Banna was strongly opposed to the practices of faith of his time, which were traditionalist and unconcerned with worldly affairs, as well as to the *ulama* who supported these practices. His ideological message was that Islam, which was based on divine revelation, is an unequaled system that should permeate all aspects of human life. Muslims should return to the pure faith of the devout forefathers of the *Ummah*, a faith that had not yet been 'contaminated' by foreign influences. The faithful will only be able to know Allah through the description that He personally and via His Prophet has given. Everything else is heathenism. For this reason, all Western influences, such as codes of law, social customs (clothing, greetings, working hours, languages), ideas and institutions should be removed, and Sharia (Islamic law) should be instituted across the board (Abu Zayd 2006).

In 1928, al-Banna set up the Egyptian Muslim Brotherhood to implement his ideas. His strategy was to use the Brotherhood to first Islamize Egyptian society. This example was meant to be followed elsewhere in the Muslim world as a necessary step towards ultimately achieving a caliphate. Because of these concepts, al-Banna is viewed as the father of the idea of 'the Islamic state' (Fuller 2003: 9), which was to be gradually built from *the bottom up* and ultimately result in a caliphate. He viewed Islam as the universal solution for all the major issues and as the ideological alternative to capitalism and communism (Buijs 2002: 68). From the very start, the movement was directed under his leadership towards – what would be considered in modern terminology – humanitarian goals and social work amongst the poorer layers of the population, and employed peaceful means of Islamization. In this way the Brotherhood created an extensive network of Islamic schools, professional associations, youth associations, and so on. Al-Banna, who was assassinated in 1949, also argued for participation in the political process; after all, the Islamization of the state was an important intermediate step towards the ultimate goal of recreating the caliphate.

The Egyptian Muslim Brotherhood is seen as the mother of the many movements that have appeared up to the present time with the demand for the Islamization of the state and society. This role certainly concerns the Sunni world, although it extends even beyond. Hasan al-Banna was strongly influenced by both Salafism and Wahhabism. Salafism is derived from the ideas of Jamal al-Din al-Afghani and Muhammed Abdu, thinkers known as important reformers. This movement initially directed its efforts chiefly towards modernization. The objective was to overcome the large gulf between the Sunni and Shiite sects as well as between the four Sunni schools of law. By calling for 'the utopia of the early days' and for following the example of the early *Ummah*, it appealed to the authentically Islamic in reaction to Western political and cultural domination, as well as to activism in reaction to tradition and quietism. In this way the existing discord and rigidity could be overcome. Al-Banna's pursuit of the restoration of the caliphate, however, gradually led him and the Brotherhood in the direction of the very conservative and intolerant Wahhabism (Abu Zayd 2006). This doctrine, which is also the faith of present-day Saudi Arabia, is based on the views of Muhammed Ibn 'Abd al-Wahhab (1703-1792). He preached absolute theocracy and an extremely puritanical, 'true' Islam based on a literal interpretation of the Quran and imitating the life of the Prophet as faithfully as possible. Backed by petrodollars, this belief system, which also preaches a very strict separation of the sexes, has gained great influence throughout the Muslim world as well as in the West, including the Netherlands (AIVD 2004). It should be noted that external influencing is primarily occurring under the banner of Salafism, the contemporary mainstream of which is now linked to Wahhabism. This puritanical movement emphasizes transnational Islamic identity and community (*Ummah*) and is strongly opposed to Western influence (ICG 2004a).

In the course of its history, the Brotherhood has had periods of radicalization, and more radical splinter groups have emerged in reaction to oppression by the Egyptian government. These groups include, for instance, explicitly revolutionary movements, such as Jama'a al-Islamiyya and the Egyptian Islamic Jihad, which flourished primarily in the 1980s in Egypt and, like the Brotherhood, have been imitated elsewhere in the Muslim world. The inspiration with respect to content for this radicalization was primarily supplied by Sayyd Qutb (1906-1966), who led the Muslim Brotherhood in the early 1950s.

Qutb is known as the theoretician of militant Islamic activism. He mainly developed his ideas while imprisoned. Like al-Banna, he described Egypt as being in a state of jahiliyya (pre-Islamic heathendom). This diagnosis was not only directed towards the majority of the population, but, more particularly, towards the established political order and the religious establishment. According to Qutb, since the Quran is the source of all true knowledge and thus also the absolute standard for judging knowledge, philosophy, social science, and political systems must therefore be seen without exception as manifestations of heathenism. Using the concept of the absolute and exclusive sovereignty of God (*hakimiyya*: all power belongs to God and only God should be obeyed), he divided society into two camps: those who obey God and those who do not. This Manichaean view of the absolute opposition between good and evil served as an important justification of rebellion and struggle. While al-Banna placed his emphasis on (peaceful) Islamization from the bottom up, Qutb focused his attention specifically on the Islamization of the state. In his view, anti-Islamic governments and neocolonialism had led to a corrupt and unreligious society; Islam stood on the edge of the abyss. For him, all secular governments were godless and had to be overturned so that a true Islamic regime could be established (ultimately throughout the world). He called for the formation of a vanguard organization which would engage in this struggle. He viewed this 'jihad' against the existing powers as an urgent and legitimate duty. According to Buijs (2002) – whose work forms the basis of this description – this does not necessarily entail armed struggle. Qutb saw the choice of means as dependent on the concrete situation and goal in question. With this vision of jihad-as-liberation-struggle, he broke out of the traditional Islamic juridical belief that favored stability over the justice and legitimacy of the state. At the same time, he argued for the reopening of 'the gates of *ijtihad*' (the right to a legal interpretation of the concrete implications of religious doctrine) which had been declared closed by the religious scholars since the tenth century.

The Indian – and later Pakistani – al-Mawdudi (1903-1979) also contributed significantly to the shape and content of what would eventually come to be known as political Islam. He greatly influenced Qutb, but lacked the latter's militant radicalism. Instead he took part in the political institutions of Pakistan. Unlike al-Banna he was an outspoken advocate of Islamization from the top down (Kepel 2002: 34). But like al-Banna and Qutb, he emphasized Islamic identity (in terms of religion, philosophy, culture, the political and economic systems, and education). Much more than the other two thinkers, however, al-Mawdudi strongly emphasized the superiority of Islamic civilization over what the (materialistic) West had to offer. In his view, there was no need to 'borrow' anything from the West. The earthly representation of the all-encompassing universe, in which all power belongs to Allah, is found in 'the state of Islam'. Only two authoritative sources exist for the necessary Islamization, namely the Quran and the Sunna, and, according to Mawdudi, these should be taken literally. They are, after all, sacred texts: the Quran is the 'uncreated' – and therefore eternal – revelation of the word of God, and the Sunna contains Mohammed's God-inspired utterances that have been passed down (Arkoun 1992).

Al-Mawdudi played an important role in the Jamaat-i-Islami movement (organization for Islamic revival) he set up in 1941 in what was to become Pakistan. He was an outspoken pan-Islamic thinker and was opposed to nationalism. Indeed, he saw Muslim identity as universal and the national state as antithetical to this universality. In this sense, the concept of the nation-state is dangerous, both in terms of theology and in practice: theologically, because it can never be an authoritative object of identification between God and man, and practically because it threatens the unity of the

Muslim community (*Ummah*). For this reason, he rejected the idea of Pakistan as a *Muslim* state; Pakistan must instead become an *Islamic* state. For him, the return to Islam derived from hakimiyya; Islam is thus an all-encompassing ideology for the individual and the community, for the state and society. The faithful, and not the religious scholars (ulama), are the guardians of God's legacy. Strict and thorough submission to God's word and following the example of the Prophet are what makes a good Muslim; everything else is an expression of unbelief. It is precisely the subordination to God's authority that gives people freedom. The establishment of one's own laws is an expression of arrogance since the Sharia contains all the necessary precepts. Rulers must not only be competent but pious, and they must refrain from pursuing their own self-interests. They are obligated to consult with the faithful (the Quranic principle of *shura*) to reconcile interests and bring about a state of universal harmony amongst the faithful (Buijs 2002: 68-70).

Al-Banna, Qutb, and al-Mawdudi had great influence in the Sunni world, in particular, but they also served as an important source of inspiration for the leaders of the Islamic revolution in Shiite Iran (Abu Zayd 2004: 60). The offspring of their views make themselves felt today, including in the particularly fierce forms so well known in the West after 9/11. The Palestinian Abdullah Azzam is a major source of inspiration for extremist groups that support armed jihad. He is also the teacher of Osama bin Laden, the pre-eminent symbol of armed conflict. Azzam was deeply influenced by Qutb and the *Salafiyya jihadiyya*, the extremely conservative and violent movement that arose in the context of the war against the Soviet-backed regime in Afghanistan (ICG 2004a). While Qutb can be seen as the father of Islam as ideological resistance to repressive regimes at home, Azzam extended this to jihad against external enemies of Islam, which he viewed as besieging the Muslim world and wished to tackle one by one. He opposed the nationalist orientation of many movements and viewed the nation state as a product of colonialism and imperialism. Following the Muslim theologian and jurist Ibn Taymiyyah (1263-1328), he claimed that "the Muslim countries are equal to a single country". Osama bin Laden has extended Azzam's armed conflict over the entire world (Buijs 2002: 76-80). His views are precisely in keeping with Huntington's concept of a 'clash of civilizations' (Huntington 1996).

As will become evident in the next chapter, many of the movements that have arisen from the ideas of the authors discussed have only partially succeeded in the Islamization of state and society. This is due to the fact that they not only found the government against them, but often the religious establishment as well, which, according to the authors – incidentally, all laymen – formed a part of the problem by selling out to the regime

(Kepel 2002). Islamic activism achieved great political success in Shiite Iran, however. The intellectual inspiration was provided by Ali Shariati (1933-1977), who would greatly influence Ayatollah Ruhollah Khomeini. Shariati was primarily influential among students; Khomeini had substantial authority in the religious world and amongst loyal segments of the religious population. It was precisely this collaboration that allowed the Islamic revolution to succeed in Iran.

Shariati was strongly influenced by leftist intellectuals such as Jean-Paul Sartre and revolutionaries such as Ernesto 'Che' Guevara and also found inspiration in the Algerian fight for independence. In addition, he rejected the idea that the third world could benefit from a Western ideology such as Marxism in the struggle to free itself from corruption, stagnation, and economic and cultural domination. Liberation would only be possible if countries rediscovered their indigenous identity. Islam contained all the theoretical qualifications for a radical doctrine and at the same time provided spiritual sustenance which modern materialistic ideologies were incapable of providing. For this Third Way, Islam had to recover its original revolutionary zeal. He accused the mullahs (clerics) of turning Shiism into an 'old women's' religion. This Shiism ascribed significance to the martyrdom of Imam Hussein, the son of the fourth caliph Ali (son-in-law of the Prophet), who was defeated and killed in 680 by the Sunni caliph of Damascus. This event, which Shiites commemorate annually, had for long been interpreted as an encouragement to turn away from the world of politics and power. Shariati attacked this political quietism; in his view, the events of 680 should be seen as encouragement to resume the struggle Ali engaged in against the injustices of the state of his day. The fundamental message of Islam must be resumed and the established political order be challenged. With his emphasis on 'the underprivileged', Shariati added Marxist connotations to his interpretation of Islam.

Ayatollah Khomeini adopted this revolutionary activism, both in terms of the idea of revolution in the name of the underprivileged and Shariati's ideas regarding the taking over of state power. The difference was that while Shariati envisioned the revolution being led by a vanguard of enlightened intellectuals, Khomeini saw this as the role of the clerics. Khomeini also elaborated on how an Islamic state should be formed. Influenced by French constitutional thought, he envisioned a 'theo-democracy' (Mawdudi's term for the system he strove for in Pakistan): a combination of theocracy and democracy. The Quranic principle of shura (consultation between the ruler and an assembly; sometimes seen as the equivalent of a parliament) would be retained, but the president and members of parliament were to be chosen by general suffrage. Both organs were nevertheless subordinate to a Council of Guardians and the Supreme Leader who would inspect the Islamic caliber of the candidates of these organs as well as the decisions made. The important role Khomeini assigned the clerics ensured that in Iran a literal interpretation of the Quran and Sharia would, at least formally, set the tone.

The thinkers discussed here have all had great influence on the politiciza-tion of Islam. Their efforts at reform were primarily directed towards rais-ing Islamic awareness and no longer accepting *a priori* the authority of the state and traditional religion. Together they supplied the components of an activism that has manifested itself in a number of movements, especially from the 1970s onwards. These components include: the literal interpreta-tion of the Quran, using Sharia as the only valid legal source (particularly in the Sunni world), turning against the religious establishment, theocracy, rejecting worldly authority, anti-secularism, Jihad (in the sense of 'holy war'), authenticity, and a strongly anti-Western disposition. This activism is at odds with democracy and universal human rights. Against the concept of popular sovereignty, these thinkers posited the sovereignty of God in such a way as to exclude inalienable human rights.

2.3   REFORM BY REINTERPRETATION OF THE SACRED SOURCES

2.3.1   THE PIONEERS

The authors discussed in the previous section sought a revival of Islam by returning to the *letter* of the Quran and the Sunna. They set themselves against the human traditions (with a small t) by returning to what they considered the holy Tradition (with a capital T) laid out in these sources: the foundation era of Islam. At present, however, many authors are also concerned with seeking the *spirit* of these sources, using this as inspiration to answer questions about the organization of society. These authors are of great interest for this report. For the most part, they have developed their political thought in the twentieth century, but the groundwork was laid out in the nineteenth century. At that time, a number of significant dogmatic obstacles that were blocking the development of this political mode of thought were removed. For this reason, we will address the pioneers of this mode of thought first.

These pioneers' ideas of reform were also developed in reaction to the identity crisis which stemmed from Western dominance in the Muslim world. Like the first category of reform thinkers, they focused on the idea of the *decline* of the Muslim world. Their reaction, however, was not a call for a renewed Islamization of society and state following the example of the foundation era, but for modernization of Islam itself. The causes of the decline were sought in the traditionalism which in the Muslim world had

reached an almost dogmatic character. They were thus opposed to the
'deterioration' of Islam into a religion solely concerned with what was
compulsory and not allowed.

Classical Islam's fixation on rules is based on four sources of knowledge
(listed in decreasing order of importance):
1   The Quran as the literal word of God, whose message applies to all of
    humankind and is thus independent of place and time.
2   The prophetic Tradition (Sunna): the pronouncements and actions of
    the Prophet, based on revelation. For the jurists, this source of knowl-
    edge gradually became as important as, or perhaps even more important
    than the Quran.
3   The doctrine of the 'consensus of the ulama' (religious scholars) for
    cases that were not settled by the first two sources.
4   Syllogism (via analogy) for all other cases.

The last two sources mentioned do not serve as autonomous sources of
legal interpretation , but are methods of interpreting the first two textual
sources. There existed a right to interpretation (ijtihad) since not all the
rules in the Quran and the Sunna were clear and therefore had to be
worked out with the help of human intellect. This theory of judicial
construction was developed in the first centuries of Islam. The law was
considered completed by the tenth century. After this, the ulama closed
'the gates of ijtihad' again. From this century on, all the rules had been
established and the period of 'imitation' began (Berger 2006).

To release Islam from the straitjacket of such a dogmatically grounded
status of the traditions, and even from the Tradition, some very basic steps
had to be taken. It is thus not surprising that reformist thinking started
with an attack on one of the least sacred foundations, the denial of the right
to new interpretations, and ended by discussing the most sacred, the
Quran itself. The different layers of dogmatic traditionalism thus had to be
peeled away like the layers of an onion in order to reach the core: the intentions of the Quran and the Sunna. Only then would there fully be a basic
appreciation of democracy and human rights. The authors discussed in
section 2.2, who were similarly opposed to traditionalism, sometimes
argued for a renewed right to ijtihad, but never went so far as to question
the status of the Quran and the Sunna. On the contrary, the thinkers and
movements that followed them wanted only to remove the historically
grown misfits (human traditions) to re-establish the original prescribed
codes of behavior – the Tradition.

Discussions of whether the classical ulama had a monopoly on the interpretation of the Quran and the Sunna (the consensus) took place early on,

in the eighteenth century. The Indian Sufi, Shah Wali Allah (1702-1762), defended the right to ijtihad as the outcome of personal effort also undertaken by those other than the ulama. He emphasized the spirit of the law. Since this is always applicable, the form of the law can be adjusted to the circumstances of time and place. In this way he distanced himself from the indiscriminant use of the old codes of behavior. According to the Egyptian Al-Tahtawi (1801-1873), the religious scholars were more than just the guardians of an established and fixed tradition. Like Wali Allah, he argued for a re-opening of the gates of ijtihad. Through a renewed use of reasoning, the principle of consensus could be opened up and Sharia could be adapted to new circumstances. He even suggested that there was little difference between the principles of Sharia and the natural law which forms the basis of European law. This also legitimized the idea that under certain circumstances the faithful could accept laws from sources other than Islamic law books. Thus Al-Tahtawi paved the way for introducing Western legal codes into Egyptian law. Likewise, attacks began on the principle of consensus and on the related hegemonic authority of the traditional ulama throughout the Muslim world – a process which has continued and intensified to the present. Thanks to rising levels of education and modern means of communication, this traditional authority has sharply diminished and many, even those outside the circle of ulama and intellectuals are now involved in the interpretation of the precepts.

Thus after the dogma forbidding human interpretation of the sacred sources was breached, there emerged intellectual room for new reflection on the two sacred sources themselves. Important pioneers in the reinterpretation of the Sunna and the Quran include Jamal al-Din Al-Afghani (1838-1897), Sayyed Ahmed Khan (1817-1898) and Muhammed Abdu (1845-1905). The position that they took regarding these two sacred sources has remained controversial in the Muslim world up until today.

Al-Afghani sounded the clarion call for this renewal. Like the later Rashid Rida, discussed in the previous section, he was an outspoken supporter of the pan-Islamic idea. He also supported the caliphate as a counterbalance to European domination with the caveat, however, that Islam – the unifying factor – modernize. In his view, the backward situation Muslims found themselves in was due not to Islam as such, but to an incorrect understanding of Islam by Muslims. Al-Afghani saw Islam as a religion more in harmony with the principles of scientific reason than was Christianity. Islam could even serve as an engine for science and progress. He did not use the foundation era of Islam as his source of inspiration, as Rida did, but was inspired by the tenth to fourteenth centuries when philosophy, sciences, and free-thinking flourished. This period provided evidence for the compatibility of Islam with rational science. Radical social, political, and intellectual changes were necessary for a revival of this kind of Islam; only then could it rediscover its role as moral compass.

Building upon this, the Indian Sayyed Ahmed Khan and the Egyptian Muhammed Abdu wished to free Islam from the dogma of the Tradition, as embodied in the Sunna. In the classical teachings, the prophetic Traditions had the same authority as the Quran itself, despite their difference in form. The Traditions did not deal with the word of God, but with the utterances, actions, and revelations of the Prophet passed down orally and recorded by people much later. Over time, however, the Sunna increasingly came to be accepted as the correct explanation of the Quran, which could not be properly understood without the Sunna. It was even held that the Quran could not exist without the Sunna, but that the Sunna could exist without the Quran. Khan contested this by emphasizing the universality of the Quran as opposed to the historicity, and thus the accidental nature and fallibility, of the Sunna. Using the analogy of Western biblical criticism to show how much the Sunna was influenced by prevailing views, he also attempted to free exegesis of the Quran from the Tradition; the Quran was, after all, interpreted through the Sunna. He claimed that the Quran was completely self-sufficient and that it could be understood by enlightened minds using the principles of 'reason' and 'nature'. It is precisely this universality that makes it possible for each generation to derive relevant significance from the Quran for the prevailing situation. Unlike Khan, Abdu did not dismiss virtually every *hadith* as unreliable, but he did want to place the Quran in the center of Muslims' attention once again. In the early twentieth century, these views led to fierce polemics in India and Egypt between movements that rallied around the competing slogans 'Ahl-i-Quran' ('follow the Quran') and 'Ahl-i-Hadith' ('follow the *hadith*').

With the exegesis of the Quran freed from the heavy burden of the Tradition, the Quran found itself in a central position. Thus the way was paved for a more modern interpretation of the Quran itself. In the Muslim world, (Western) modernity was mainly identified with scientific discoveries and rationalism. Khan proposed the task of reconciling the Quran with the spectacular discoveries of Western science. His position was that these manifestations relate to God's promises in *reality*, while the Quran presents God's promises in *words*. Thus the wonders and supernatural phenomena mentioned in the Quran should not be understood literally, but should be taken as metaphors, allegories, or other indirect forms of expression. Based on the thesis of harmony between 'promises in words' and 'promises in reality', his central point was that the Quran and modern science were not in conflict. In this Khan prepared the groundwork for authors and movements that are also influential now, such as those who attempt to demonstrate the scientific inimitability of the Quran (all knowledge is already present in the Quran), as well as the current trend towards the 'Islamization of knowledge and science'. Unlike the thinkers discussed in section 2.2, he did not simply dismiss knowledge as a product of modernity, but attempted to see it in an Islamic light.

Muhammed Abdu was similarly concerned with the relationship between Islam, modern knowledge, and rationality. Unlike Khan, however, he did not attempt to achieve reconciliation by regarding all modern knowledge as principally 'Islamic', filtered through Islam and the Quran, but by employing modern sources to fundamentally research the Islamic heritage, including the Quran itself. This was the first attempt made to contextualize the Quran, in this case by projecting it against the historical and cultural background of the seventh century. In this way he freed the Quran from claims of being without historical and scientific equal. The Quran, he argued, should not be understood literally, but rather as a literary text whose message is conveyed in a language which reflects the Arab worldview and intellectual climate of the time in which it was written. Thus the stories need not be taken literally; they are meant to serve ethical, spiritual, and religious purposes and, as such, may also serve an important function for other times and places. With his contextualizing, Abdu came close to demythologizing the Quranic story as well as the sanctity of the text itself. However, he believed this did not detract from the importance of religion. Religion would remain an essential part of human existence; precisely for this reason, real societal reform would only be possible through a reformation of Islamic thought.

These views made Abdu the leading pioneer, paving the way for later reform thinkers. He and his predecessors had freed Islam from its identification with traditions and Tradition and from the sacred power of the letter and a resulting dogmatic obsession with what is commanded and forbidden. Thus the mental space was created for challenging the identification of Islam with power and the state, and for coming to appreciate democracy and human rights.

Reform thinkers in many Muslim countries have continued to build upon this foundation. The next section will concentrate on a selected number of these. After all, while it is the intention of this report to research whether there are conceptual reference points in the Muslim world for the development of a democratic constitutional state, it is not necessary to review all the thinkers associated with this reform movement. The elaboration of their concepts is influenced by the specific political contexts of the countries within which the thinkers concerned operate. Taking this into account, the focus will primarily be on thinkers from two important Sunni countries, namely Egypt (the intellectual core of the Arab world) and

Indonesia (the country with the greatest number of Muslims), as well as thinkers in Shiite Iran, a country with 25 years experience with theocracy, including a classical Islamic legal system. Finally, a few prominent thinkers from outside these three countries will be discussed. Some attention will also be paid to the very active school of feminist hermeneutics, which is rethinking the position of women in Islam.

2.3.2 CONTEMPORARY REFORMERS

Egypt

The contextualization of the Quran – initiated by Abdu, amongst others, using the right for renewed interpretation which had earlier been fought for – has been carried on by many thinkers in the twentieth century. In the early twentieth century, Abdu's pupil 'Ali' Abd al-Raziq (1888-1966) defended the abolition of the caliphate with the argument that there is no such thing as one specific Islamic political system. Based on research, he concluded that a system such as the caliphate cannot be deduced from the Quran, the Tradition, or the consensus of the ulama, whether from the foundation period of Islam or since. If Islam is without a political theory, Muslims have freedom of choice. Using argumentation from within Islam he showed himself to be a great advocate of the separation of mosque and state.

The idea – supported by many Muslims – of the Quran as the literal word of God had been challenged by Taha Husayn, Amin al-Khuli, and Ahmad Khalafalla using methods of literary and historical research. They focused on the Quran as a – human – 'text', a text that should primarily be seen as a literary product. Taha Husayn (1889-1973) saw the Quran as an independent literary category. He demonstrated that the stories told within it existed long before the Quran; they were used in the Quran to situate Islam vis-à-vis the Judeo-Christian tradition and to confirm its monotheistic character. Amin al-Khuli (1895-1966) elaborated on this by proposing that the Arabs accepted Islam precisely because of the literary qualities of the Quran. According to the modern theory of rhetoric, the emotional impact is not unrelated to the esthetic qualities of the text and the esthetic awareness of the reader. Only through methods of modern literary theory can the meaning of the Quran be (re)discovered. Khalafalla (1916-1998) collected Quranic stories, reordered them chronologically, and analyzed them by relating them to their original contexts. He viewed all the stories as self-contained, even if they were concerned with the same event, in order to discover their meanings and intentions. He thus concluded that the Quranic texts should be seen as allegories and not as historically authentic descriptions. The writers of the many stories used these to clarify ethical and spiritual questions. Through this literary and contextualizing approach, Khalafalla intended to free the Quran of the burden of being seen as the ultimate book on history, science, political theory, or law.

These authors' opinions have remained controversial up until today because they take away from the uniqueness and sacredness of the Quranic stories and therefore also drastically relativize the Quranic commandments and prohibitions. They have thus been met with fierce opposition. This holds true for the views of Nasr Abu Zayd (born 1943) as well. Using the idea of the Quran-as-text, he tries to show its human dimensions. In his view, this applies foremost to the completion of the final text itself. While the revelations themselves took over twenty years to be completed, it took the Prophet's companions until after his death to record them all on paper. It actually took several centuries for the vocalized version to reach completion. All the phases of this realization involved human contributions, such as the determining of the recitation order of the verses that sharply depart from the revelations themselves. Furthermore, Abu Zayd demonstrates that, from the beginning, all the methods used by religious scholars to determine codes of behavior from Quranic texts have been based on often controversial *choices*, made by the scholars themselves. The final result, the Sharia, including the differences set down in the schools of law, does not, then, rest on 'objective' interpretation, but is completely man-made; there is nothing sacred about it. It is also evident that the punishments for offences mentioned in the Quran itself or by the jurists are not authentically Islamic, but date from earlier or later times. It is thus very presumptuous, Abu Zayd argues, to consider these man-made and historically determined codes sacred and therefore compulsory for every place and time.

Similarly, he dismisses as mistaken or apologetic attempts to model contemporary desirable concepts, such as democracy, on the Quran. The current appeal to democracy, which is also heard in the Muslim world, has been parried by both incumbent regimes and Islamic movements by references to 'Islamic' democracy, namely the Quranic concept of shura (the obligation of the ruler to consult his subjects). This, however, was a pre-Islamic practice, according to Abu Zayd, used in the earlier autocratic tribal societies. The concept of shura naturally also suits today's autocratic rulers well, yet, despite the claims of the rulers, it has nothing to do with Islam. Neither can it be contended that this concept forms the embryo of the current understanding of democracy. Thus the conclusion must be that contemporary Muslims are not relegated to shura, even if this is mentioned in the Quran. Islam in no way whatsoever limits the freedom of Muslims to choose their political or legal systems.

Abu Zayd does not limit himself to the conclusion that the Quran is a cultural product which gives a new articulation to pre-Islamic culture and concepts and must be analyzed in order for its intentions to be revealed. In his view, it is not enough to show that, on closer inspection, historical and literary contextualizing often reveals many 'sacred' dogma to be the work of humans. Every form of hermeneutics creates its own central point from which an interpretation can be developed; just as history can be read in 'any' way, so can the Quran when it is seen as simply a text. What one reads in the Quran thus depends on one's ideological stance; both the fundamentalist and the liberal can find justification within it.

Abu Zayd argues that within the structure of the Quran there is not only a vertical dimension, but also an implicit horizontal, communicative, and humanistic dimension which can be revealed through 'humanistic' hermeneutics. Conceptually, the Quran should be seen not only as a text, but also as a collection of discourses; it is a polyphonic rather than a mono-phonic (God is the only voice) text. According to Zayd, it is precisely this dialogue between different voices full of argumentation, role reversal, rejection and acceptance of earlier assumptions and assertions that makes the Quran relevant for current questions about meaning on all levels of life. The internal discrepancies which are found regarding many points in the Quran should not be explained away through all sorts of rules, then, but should be seen as positive qualities since they allow for a diversity of options. Thus the Quran invites active interpretation and the further development of the spiritual and ethical dimensions of our existence (Abu Zayd 2004).

Indonesia

The plea by thinkers such as al-Afghani and Abdu for a new interpretation of the Quran has also been echoed in Indonesia. Just like these thinkers, Nurcholis Madjid (1939-2005) attributes the stagnation of religious thought not to Islam itself but to Muslims' inaccurate understanding of Islam. The masses do not make a distinction between transcendent and worldly values. All values derived from the traditions are seen as transcen-dent and therefore as sacred, without exception. As a consequence of this, Islam becomes identical with tradition. Breaking through this traditional-ism demands secularization first and foremost. This should not be seen as an ideology, but as a process in which practices and articles of faith may go in two ways. In the downward trajectory, to which secularization is usually limited, an article of faith is stripped of its former sacredness. There is also an upward trajectory, however, in which something that is actually transcendent and holy is made sacred. In Madjid's view, many codes of behavior should take the first path, and therefore should be recognized as merely traditions. The second path, however, should also be traveled. This may be applied to 'plurality' for instance, a concept that many Muslims have difficulty with. The positive regard for difference is firmly established in the Quran. In order to differentiate between these two paths, a reopening of the right to ijtihad is essential, and, accordingly, so is intellectual freedom without any restrictions. Madjid developed these views during the Suharto era. Thus he placed emphasis on a renewal of Islamic thought through culture, strongly focusing on education. Under Suharto's New Order, room for political Islam to deliver actual renewal would remain limited.

Abdurrahman Wahid (born 1949), president of Indonesia from 1999 to 2001, similarly propagated 'cultural' Islam. Specifically through the *pesantrens*, the Indonesian system of Islamic boarding schools, he hoped to stimulate Islam by emphasizing positive values and replacing negative ones. Dynamism can arise by giving priority to the spirit of the law, the inner truth. Through rational efforts, it is possible for Islam to take up the challenge of modernity. By rediscovering the humanitarian message of Islam, which is expressed in tolerance and concern for social harmony, Muslims have no need to fear the plural nature of modern society and can, in fact, view this positively. The same holds for democracy, for which he also led a fervent campaign throughout Suharto's rule. There is no distance between Islam and democracy; when democracy is a process focused on realizing a better society, both are in harmony. Respect for human rights is thus inherent in this process, since this is precisely what democratization is about. The texts of the Quran deal with human dignity, which contains three aspects: individual, social, and political dignity.

In Indonesia, not only is democracy a sensitive issue, but so is religious plurality. Religion – the belief in one, almighty God – is part of the *Pancasila*, the five pillars of the state defined in the constitution of 1945. Formulated in this way, this pillar formally accommodates religious diversity. However, since independence a segment of the large Muslim majority has sought the introduction of an Islamic state. For this reason, Wahid has put great emphasis on the positive significance of democracy and plurality drawn from a specifically Islamic perspective. This focus can also be found in the work of other contemporary reformers. Syafii Maarif, for example, argues that important components of democracy can be found explicitly in the Quran, including justice, equality, the recognition of different views, and plurality.

What these thinkers have in common is that they do not wish to remodel contemporary actuality based on the letter of the Quran and Sunna, but, conversely, wish to accept contemporary actuality and seek inspiration from the Quran for its improvement. They hope to reinvigorate the signifi-cance of Islam within a modernity that is, in principle, accepted and valued. Thus Ahmad Wahib (1942-1974) sees freedom of thought as neces-sary for renewal; free-thinking is not only a right, but a religious obligation. In his view, modernity cannot be avoided and demands a positive response. Religious renewal is therefore a *conditio sine qua non*. Mohammed is the preeminent role model as an innovator; he altered the social and intellectual world of his time. This example calls for imitation, naturally in a different context than in Mohammed's day. The obligation of ijtihad is not reserved for the elite, but applies to everyone. Munawir Sadzali (born 1925) also calls on ijtihad to make Islam more responsive to the needs and requirements of the contemporary Indonesian situation. Thus he argues for a change to the law of inheritance; the Quranic rule that male heirs receive twice the share of female heirs is at odds with current notions of justice. The argument is that justice in contemporary relationships between men and women demands another form of expression than it did at the time in which the Quran came into existence. Here, too, the religious text is contextualized and the pressure for a literal interpretation is removed; the intention is privileged. Likewise, Sadzali – whose approach is analogous to that of al-Raziq discussed earlier – dismisses the idea, popular in radical circles in Indonesia, of an Islamic state. He does this not merely because none of the sources command this, but also because Indonesia's pluriform reality benefits by maintaining the *Pancasila* principle.

Iran

The 1979 revolution in Iran is without a doubt the most spectacular example of the Islamization of the state and the political and social establishments in the last few decades. While elsewhere Islamization was the result of civil war (Afghanistan) or coups (Sudan and Pakistan), the Islamic revolution in Iran took place with comparatively little bloodshed and was broadly supported. The great majority voted in a referendum for the establishment of the Islamic Republic. The constitution was unambiguous: the aim was to create a model society based on Islamic norms. All elements of the movements arguing for a 'return to the sources' discussed in section 2.2 were synthesized in the new ideology: totalitarian theocracy, Sharia, anti-Westernization (in response to the so-called *westoxication*), anti-Western and armed struggle for ideological jihad (aimed towards the worldwide establishment of the sovereignty of God).

It is precisely this widely supported Islamic revolution as well as the chance Iran then had to realize this model society in relative freedom over a period of more than 25 years that make this 'experiment' exceptionally interesting. This holds for Muslims and Muslim movements elsewhere pursuing a similar form of theocracy as well as for those who believe that democratization and respect for human rights, rather than Islam, offer the solution for the large problems with which many Muslim countries wrestle. Thus the developments in Iran have been followed everywhere with great interest.

In 1979 the Iranian state quite explicitly defined itself as anti-Western. The constitution states that the revolution purged the country of its heathen past and of foreign ideological influences, through the return to the authentic intellectual standpoints and philosophy of Islam. From this basis, it is implied that values commonly associated with the West, such as democracy and human rights, would have to be vehemently rejected at first. Khomeini himself was very clear about this: in the relationship between man and God, only the latter has rights. People have no rights and certainly none which are inalienable, as is implied in the concept of human rights. Humans merely have obligations to God. God can grant rights to human beings, but can also take them away. Additionally, the rights and interests of the Islamic community have priority over those of the individual. Khomeini viewed human rights as the work of the devil; there was no such thing as the rights of the individual as distinct from the – Islamic – state. He thus also accused the West of having developed an anthropocentric system.

This anti-Western attitude affected not only politics, but certainly also the cultural sphere. It is interesting to note that this continual harping on 'the decadent West' is something Islamic thinkers shared with Western cultural critics. Thus Heidegger's critique of modernism is popular with many Iranian writers. The crisis in the West is so large, Reza Davari claims, that decline and fall are inevitable; Islam shall then triumph (Davari 1980, in Abu Zayd 2006). In the black-and-white mentality after the revolution, every attempt at making subtle distinctions was *a priori* suspect, and a call for more freedom and democracy could easily be suppressed with the argument that these represent 'Westernization' or 'Western decadence'. For this reason it is all the more striking that a large and very active reform movement emerged in Iran. Many Islamic thinkers now reject both the theocratic principles and the fervent anti-Western stance. This even includes thinkers who contributed to the conceptual foundations of the Islamization of the Iranian state and society. In the Iranian theocratic context, where every debate must be framed in terms of Islam, the views of the so-called 'new theology' movement are especially radical. Important proponents include Abdolkarim Soroush and Mohammed Mojtahed Shabestari.

After more than 25 years experience with the daily practices of Islamism and the apparent inability of this dominant interpretation of Islam to solve societal problems, Soroush (born 1942) – originally an enthusiastic participant in the revolution – argues for a constructive involvement with the West and its values. The West's scientific progress – rather than its political-imperialist behavior – offers much inspiration, also in the areas of philosophy and social sciences. Learning is not the property of the West;

there are no property rights to ideas. Philosophical concepts can be adopted without having to share the corresponding intellectual and historical context. Similarly, Soroush is not convinced by Shariati's plea (see section 2.2) to return to indigenous sources: "what our heart and mind is willing to accept, belongs to us" (Soroush 1993: 121, in Abu Zayd 2006). After all, in Iran returning to the sources could also mean abandoning Islam. He argues that a culture is always heterogeneous, and so why shouldn't people borrow each others best ideas?

Soroush, who studied in England and was influenced by Popper's 'open society', views the Quran as an 'open' text inviting interpretation. Since human understanding is always dependent on the time period and state of knowledge, religious understanding may also be changeable. He thus makes a distinction between first- and second-order values. Second-order values concern the details religions use to distinguish themselves from one another (dress codes, punishments), but they do not form the essence of religion; they may change under the influence of new perceptions. Values of the first order, such as justice, however, are constant; their importance is common to all religions and to human reason. A value such as justice is a religious value, but at the same time, a universal value.

In Soroush's opinion, Islam, human rights, and democracy may be very compatible. His argument, however, is not historical ('look at the tolerance Islam had for Jews') or hermeneutic ('if you contextualize and interpret a text from the Quran in a specific manner, a respect for human rights is evident'). According to Soroush, human rights are a requirement of human reason in our contemporary world, and they do not contradict values of the first order; the rights of God remain fully intact. The fact that they have been developed outside the religious domain is no reason to exclude them from an Islamic form of government. He thus argues that people have inalienable natural rights, even if this is not actually stated as such in religion.

What is the use of religion, however, if not for serving as the exclusive basis for importance values? Here Soroush adopts a pragmatic position: human rights may be inherently independent of religion, but religion is important for passing these values on to the masses. Soroush views the democratic state as the best system for realizing both human rights and religion. Totalitarian states destroy both humanity and sanctity. In these systems, religion is damaged by the abuse of power by 'men of God'. Through respecting human rights, including the freedom of religion, democracy protects religion against the abuse of power. The ideal government is not only democratic but also religious when it creates the conditions under which people can live their faith. Such a system is more religious than a system in which 'only' the Sharia is carried out. Freedom of

43

religion, including the freedom to choose *against* religion, is a necessary condition for a truly religious society. Forced faith is no faith at all. Based on this reasoning, Soroush argues for a separation of mosque and state in order to restore religion as individual belief, rather than a collection of dogma's.

The Islamic revolution was inspired by the desire to give the Quran a central position in daily life once again, rather than being collected just on holidays from the *tachtsche* (the place where the Quran is kept: the highest place in the house). Soroush has experienced the implications of this; it did not lead to improvements compared to the previous regime. In theocratic Iran, thousands have been killed in the name of Allah, and the country is marked by large-scale corruption, mismanagement, and nepotism. Soroush wishes to clear Islam of all blame for this. For precisely this reason, the Quran should return to the *tachtsche*, where it can again serve as an inspiration for arts and science and for the personal relationship between man and God.

Unlike the philosopher Soroush, the reformer and theologian Shabestari (born 1939) is difficult for the clerical elite to ignore. Like Soroush he is schooled in both Western philosophy and Christian theology. His approach is a hermeneutic one, in which he is inspired by Gadamer, Dilthey, and, most of all, Habermas. How does one achieve the most objective knowledge possible, especially when interpreted through the 'epistemological interest' (Habermas) that the interpreter has in any given explanation? Any text, including the Quran, only answers the questions posed; anyone may find the answer he or she is looking for. When a text cannot be fully understood, however, a democratic explanation is possible. Analogous to modern Christian theology, Shabestari seeks an answer to the question of what role faith can play in the modern world. This demands actual modernization of Islamic theology – something far different from simply putting the Quran onto a cd-rom. The modern condition is one of uncertainty in human thought. The traditional security of religion no longer offers a solution for this condition. A new role for faith can only be found through exchanging new experiences of faith. All the great Christian reformers, such as Thomas Aquinas, Martin Luther, and Friedrich Schleiermacher have formulated new definitions of and functions for religion and theology. Essential in determining this new role is not only the enriching of theology with insights from, for instance, philosophy, methodology, and sociology, but also the search for a connection with the practice of faith. The convictions and emotions in the practices of faith form a different, yet no less important, category than the revelations to the Prophet. A new understanding of religion can thus only come about in an open climate in which criticism of and competition between ideas are encouraged.

Shabestari sees such initiatives for renewal; the politicization that Islam is undergoing everywhere demonstrates that it is reaching out to the world and to daily life. He finds it desirable, however, that the experimentation and struggle that takes place in practice be translated into a theology that will exchange dogma for faith and will start from religious experience.

Shabestari's views are also fueled by negative experiences with theocracy; to prevent Islam from falling into discredit, he argues for the necessity of a democracy. The Quran demands only a just political system without tyranny and oppression – nothing more than that. Contrary to what the leading clerics claim, a statist philosophy cannot be derived from this ethical imperative. This being the case, people have freedom in the arrangement of the political system. Like Soroush, Shabestari believes this should be a democratic system since this is best equipped to secure the principle of religious freedom. Only a faith based on free choice is a true faith.

Soroush and Shabestari are not the only thinkers advocating democracy and human rights, and many of the other critics of theocratic theory and practice are, like Shabestari, Islamic clerics. It is precisely for this reason that the Iranian discussion is equally important for other Muslim countries with movements pursuing theocracy based on the Quran. In Iran, more than anywhere else, a theological discussion is being conducted about what Islam or the Quran does and does not dictate. In the meantime, large segments of the population have come to the conclusion that there is no one single explanation based on Quranic imperative (i.e. Bayat and Baktiari 2002, and Bayat forthcoming). The posture toward the West is directly at issue here. This is due not only to the scientific input – people in Iran are extremely well informed about scientific progress in the West – but also because of Iranian reformers' obvious affinity with Western political 'software'. The enormous religious pressure of the theocratic system leads these reformers to emphasize religious freedom. Abdallah Nuri (born 1949), who is also a cleric, claims that if people are forced into religion, it is no longer religion. For this reason he is a great proponent of religious and political pluralism. He sees Europe as a political example for Iran to imitate. The European democracies of today carry on the tradition of pluralism and democracy found in the Islam of the Middle Ages. This re-assessment of Western thought finds even more far-reaching expression in Mohsen Kadiwar (born 1959). Based on extensive analysis, he concludes that Islamic law is incompatible on a number of important points with the Universal Declaration of Human Rights. Since modern humanity wants to live according to humanistic principles, however, it is not the concept of human rights, but *Islam* that should adapt. Traditional, legalistic Islam should give way to the development of a spiritual Islam that can be used to address modern questions.

With these views, reformers have distanced themselves from the theocratic ideology and the anti-Western attitude still cultivated by the regime.
They demonstrate that there are many ways in which to interpret Islam in
a modern way. The religious thought of the reformers goes much further
than rethinking the tradition and the Quran. The humanistic interpretation of the Quran and Islam has led to a complete acceptance of the principles of human rights, democracy, freedom of religion, separation of
mosque and state, and individuality.

Elsewhere in the Muslim world

The list of thinkers who use hermeneutic freedom to liberate Islam from
the dogmatic straitjacket of traditions is extensive, both in terms of people
and countries (of origin). They do not represent a specific school; what
they share, however, is that their thinking is based on modern epistemological premises and is set in opposition to the ahistorical essentialism of
the thinkers described in section 2.2 (Filali-Ansary 2003). To illustrate this,
two authoritative writers, namely Abdullah An-Na'im and Mohammed
Arkoun, will be discussed below along with a field of application that is of
particular interest to the Western image of Islam, namely feminist
hermeneutics.

Abdullah An-Na'im, from Sudan, aims at achieving an integration of
Islamic heritage and Western thought. Against the background of internal
decline, disorder, political powerlessness, economic frustration, and Western dominance, he finds it unsurprising that the Muslim world seeks an
answer by drawing on the power of its own, authentic sources. Muslim
peoples have a legitimate right to self-determination in terms of an Islamic
identity, including Islamic law. At the same time he emphasizes the failure
of Islamization in countries such as Iran, Pakistan, and Sudan, where
attempts have been made to use pre-modern Islamic law in the modern
context. That theme serves as the basis for the search for an alternative. In
An-Na'im's view, the question of whether Islam is compatible with political development in the Muslim world is an erroneous one. The question is
not about 'Islam', but about which form of Islam. The concept of the nation
state is not a product of the indigenous history of the Muslim world. At the
same time the nation state is a fact and therefore demands legitimacy in
Islamic terms and reconciliation with the principles of Islamic law.
However, precisely because public law has not been strongly developed in
Islamic theories of law, the advent of the nation state also brought with it
secular public law.

The task, therefore, is to Islamize public law without losing the benefits of
secularism. These benefits include constitutionalism, with its principles of
the rule of law, representation, separation of powers and human rights.

That this constitutionalism has best been articulated and applied in the West is no reason to forgo it, but rather it should be regarded as a valuable contribution to the total of human experiences available to everyone. The necessary Islamization of these achievements cannot happen by using classical Sharia, which is hopelessly obsolete, for instance, in regard to the position and rights of women and non-believers. Since historical research shows that the Sharia deals for the most part with the work of humankind and rules that are determined by historical context, re-interpretation is possible and necessary. This should be based on the fundamental sources and thus be consistent with the essential moral and religious precepts. Following his teacher Mahmud Taha (executed for dissidence in Sudan in 1984), An-Na'im makes a distinction between the 'first' and 'second' messages of the Quran. The first message concerns the revelation Mohammed received in Mecca and the second that of Medina. The first concerns spiritual values, such as justice, freedom, and equality and is gradually surpassed or replaced by the Medina message which emphasizes law, order, and obedience. Because they were meant for Medina, the precepts are context-specific and must be re-interpreted according to the contemporary context. The first message is the most fundamental one; due to the emphasis on inherent human dignity, the equality of man and woman, and freedom of religion, it contains the basis for a revision of the Sharia that is compatible with international law and the concept of human rights. An-Na'im further elaborated this basic assumption for important areas of law.

Mohammed Arkoun (born 1928), originally from Algeria but a long-time resident of France, is much less programmatically inclined than An-Na'im. His interest is more methodological and epistemological and is primarily aimed towards including Islam in a general development of knowledge. It is precisely the strangling of this development by both the orthodoxy as well as the state authorities, who in alliance with it, placed (orthodox) Islam and the ulama under state authority, that has made any form of critical thought impossible. Because of this, Islam has remained purely an object of theology and Islamic legal scholarship, rather than of the human and social sciences. This 'dogmatic closedness' of Islam can only be opened up by confrontation with scientific thought. It is all the more necessary because Islam has never gone through the learning process (of secularization, erosion of the mythic world view, the rise of the bourgeoisie) that the West, including Christianity, went through in the eighteenth century.

By denouncing dogmatic closedness, Arkoun goes much further than re-applying ijtihad according to the classic juridical-epistemological model. He is not concerned with a new exegesis of the Quranic statements, but with a reinterpretation of the Quran as such and the implications of this for

'Islamic reason'. In this reinterpretation, the mechanisms of the conferral of meaning are central, starting with the 'Quranic fact', namely the Revelation itself: the spoken words that Mohammed attributed to God. This fact must be distinguished from the 'closed official corpus', namely the final version of the written text. The phenomenon of 'Revelation', its language, the historical context, and the mythic and symbolic forms of expression cannot escape research. The same applies to what took place between that Quranic fact, the final book, and the processes of selection, interpretation, and 'canonization'. The dynamic mechanisms of the production of meaning through classical Islamic reason, which ultimately led to orthodoxy and dogmatic closedness, contrast greatly with the openness and unending possibilities for interpretation of the original text. These processes and selection mechanisms, looked at through a number of disciplines (semiotics, linguistics, history, sociology, anthropology, hermeneutics, the comparative study of religions), throw light on both the 'unthought' and the 'unthinkable', namely that which is excluded from Islamic thought due to dogmatic closedness. Arkoun's aim is to make these excluded concepts and issues, such as rule of law, civil society, and the equal status of men and women, visible so that they can be included in a radical reconstruction of Islamic reason and Muslim societies.

While dedicated to another idea himself, Arkoun does not dismiss the apologetic reasoning which attempts to demonstrate the compatibility of Islam with modernity. In the 1981 Declaration on Human Rights in Islam, for instance, it is stated that Islam as a religion not only accepts and wishes to defend human rights, but that these rights are described in the Quran itself, thus long before the revolutions in the West led to the codification of human rights. Aside from the historical accuracy of this proposition, Arkoun considers this effort to lay claim to human rights as beneficial, because the cause of human rights can use the support from religious authorities to its advantage. According to Arkoun, similar reasoning is used in Judaism and Christianity. At the same time, however, a critical historical study of the content of the sacred texts of all monotheistic religions in relation to the development of modern human rights is urgently needed. Such a study can help these religions recognize that even the most developed religious teachings, as well as the Revelation itself, cannot escape their historicity and thus the inadequacy of traditional religious representation (Arkoun 1992: 142-144).

Like most of the thinkers cited earlier, Arkoun wants to make it possible for Muslims to discover the spiritual side of Islam. More than the cited authors, however, he does this by deconstructing the hallmarks and foundations of the orthodox 'episteme' – in Foucault's terms – rather than by offering alternative readings or interpretations.

Feminist hermeneutics

All of the authors discussed are relevant for the renewal of Muslim views on the organization of the state and the relationship between Quranic principles and democracy and human rights. Their ideas are therefore also relevant for the position and rights of women. In addition, however, an active school of (mostly women) thinkers has emerged explicitly oriented towards the theme of Islam and women: feminist hermeneutics, a term which certainly does not imply that these thinkers would embrace a Western form of feminism. As in other religions, the position of women in Islam is problematic, certainly if the interpretation follows the letter of the sacred sources and wishes to restore relationships to the patriarchal model of the past, as in the case of the salafiyya movement. According to Khaled Abou El Fadl, it even seems as if some movements, such as those discussed in section 2.2, translate all of their theology into the restriction of women's freedom of movement (El Fadl 2003).

As in the West, reformers in the Muslim world initially placed emphasis on emancipation and equal rights, both at the conceptual level and at the level of social action. In his investigation for the WRR (2006), Abu Zayd reported that as early as 1909 a feminist women's union was established in Egypt that fought for equal rights both in the public sphere (primarily education) as well as in the realm of the family (polygamy, marriage, divorce). According to Abu Zayd, the Tunisian Tahir Haddad was the first, in 1930, to point out the historicity of the Quranic provisions regarding women's rights. In respect to the pre-Islamic situation, these provisions formed a huge step towards granting equal rights, according to Haddad. The Quranic strategy was precisely to use values such as justice and equality to bring about improvements in this situation by subjecting polygamy to limitations, by including women in the law of inheritance, and so on. These new rights must not be made sacrosanct; in the contemporary situation the principles deserve a different interpretation.

Emancipation in the sense of granting equal rights is still a very topical and controversial issue in the Muslim world, evident in the laws pertaining to the family in most Muslim countries and the granting of the vote to women in Kuwait only in May 2005. Contemporary Islamic feminist hermeneutics goes beyond equal rights, however, and additionally concentrates on the broader gender problematics of power inequalities between men and women and social injustice. The basic assumption is, of course, the rejection of the exclusive right that men have appropriated to define Islam, and therefore to legitimize and perpetuate patriarchal relationships. Gender distinctions must be exposed and fought.

49

Feminist hermeneutics assumes that the fundamental ideas of the Quran cannot be negated by its parts. For this end, three steps are taken: firstly reinterpreting all those verses in the Quran which have been seen by men as the basis for inequality, secondly, pointing out the verses that indicate equality, and, thirdly, deconstructing verses that indicate differences between men and women (Abu Zayd 2006).

To illustrate the first step: Riffat Hassan, amongst others, points out that no indication can be found in the Quran that Eve should be held responsible for Adam's sin; both ate the forbidden apple. Therefore no difference between the rights of men and women can be derived from this incident; the only norm for the difference between people is the awe before God. Hassan subsequently shows – the second step – that, alongside the verses that emphasize the equality of men and women, significant verses of the Quran focus on *people*, which men are often inclined to read as 'men'. In the same spirit, Aziza al-Hibri analyzes the Quranic concept of *tawhid*, which she interprets not only as monotheism, as is customary, but as a principle of unity and equality. Men have unjustly appropriated the doctrine of *khilafa*: God's deputy. Where the Quran does differentiate between men and women, as in regard to polygamy, marriage, divorce, obedience, and rebellion, the proponents of feminist hermeneutics point out – the third step – the historical context (Abu Zayd 2006). The concern is with the intentions behind the concrete codes of behavior; the current situation demands other codes of behavior based on the same intentions. In the seventh century, when women were completely without rights, the Quran implied a great leap forward. Thus the intention of the Quran is the improvement of the position of women. The current context once again calls for great steps forward based on the principle of equality (Kugle 2003).

2.4 INTERPRETATION OF THE DYNAMISM IN ISLAMIC THOUGHT

The ideas examined in this chapter reveal an extremely varied picture of the relationship between Islam and the organization of the state and society. This is evident not only in the two successively discussed categories of thinkers; a broad spectrum of views also exists within both categories. Within the first category, for instance, opinions vary regarding the role of violence, the question of whether the called-for Islamization should be brought about from above or below, and whether this can be achieved through participation in political institutions. The thinkers in the second category reveal important differences regarding the way in which Islam, democracy and human rights are linked. Some appropriate the concepts of democracy and human rights by grafting them to their own intellectual heritage, in other words, by arguing that these are Islamic values. In addition to this 'Islamization of modernity', there are other thinkers such as Soroush, Abu Zayd, and Wahid who instead support a 'modernization of Islam'. In this way of thinking, democracy and human rights are accepted as products of human reason and the expressive power of the Quran is proven in answering questions arising from these issues. Between these two extremes are attempts, such as that of An Na'im, to encourage Muslims to accept secular values such as democracy and human rights through a revised view of the Quran, or of feminist hermeneutics to revise the relationships between men and women using new interpretations of the Quran. These cases involve new interpretations of the sacred scriptures as well as a selective approach to modern existence.

Given this plurality of views, it is unfair to view 'Islam' as one undivided quantity. That is to say, Islam should not be identified with qualities about which Islamic thinkers now have such widely varying views. This insight about internal plurality is relevant not only for non-Muslims, but also for Muslims themselves. As Safi notes, the market in the West is being flooded with brochures and Internet postings with titles like 'the status of women in Islam', 'the concept of God in Islam', and so on. He calls this 'pamphlet Islam' and 'web Islam'. These information streams give Muslims looking for something to hold on to in their religion the idea that there is only one true explanation and that complexity is excluded: 'Islam is the answer' (Safi 2003: 22). The preceding sections show, however, that there are many authors who have reservations about this idea and who contest the absolute claim of one, 'true' Islam.

From the foregoing findings it also appears that the view that 'Islam' is *in principle* irreconcilable with democracy and human rights is not tenable; both concepts are part of the Islamic discourse, not only as negative points of disconnect but as goals worth striving toward. Nevertheless, the idea of irreconcilability has gained great currency due to the influence of 'clash thinkers' in both the West and the Muslim world. Governments in the Muslim world also use this argument to discourage democratic experiments, in which Islamic-inspired formations could gain more political influence. This fear is fed, to a large extent, by the image-defining movements that make absolute claims and are based on the thinkers discussed in section 2.2. Indeed, these interpretations of Islam do not conceptually tolerate democracy and human rights. The presence of thinkers who positively emphasize the relationship between Islam, democracy and human rights, however, refutes this supposedly fundamental irreconcilability. At the same time, it should be recognized that the mere existence of this type of thought provides no prognosis for compatibility in political and legal practice. The authors discussed in section 2.3 are treated in coordination with those in section 2.2; their possible societal or political influence or support was not a criterion of selection. Thus their views may only (continue to) occupy a marginal or isolated position. The perspectives of political movements and law, discussed in the following chapters, may also supply important supplementary indications for judging the actual relationship between Islam, democracy and human rights.

There is, however, no reason to trivialize the importance of new modes of reform thought due to limited, or limitedly visible, support at this time. Renewed thinking must start somewhere and can gradually gain depth and influence, for instance, when changed political circumstances or developments in the individual behavior of Muslims bring about a need for views that can support and theoretically build on these changed conditions. Section 2.3 makes it clear that during the evolution of reform thought, important dogmatic obstacles to the acceptance of democracy and human rights were gradually overcome. The fact that positive views about democracy and human rights now shelter under the banner of Islam means that, in principle, there is more support conceivable for these ideas. The obstacles to the dissemination of these ideas, however, should not be underestimated either. In many Muslim countries, free thinking and debate are seen as dangerous by the orthodoxy, radical Islamic movements, and governments; it is in the interest of all these groups to disqualify these ideas as apostate. That these views are often so vehemently opposed and lead to 'clashes within' indicates their potential attraction.

In Iran in particular, intellectual thought and debate about Islam, democracy, and human rights has grown exponentially. This not only concerns views directed towards Islamic democracy and Islamic human rights; a category of intellectuals who argue the desirability of democracy and human rights on purely humanistic grounds has emerged (Jahanbegloo 2005). The identification of Islamic thought with anti-democratic ideas and antagonism to human rights by writers like Samuel Huntington (1996) and Bernard Lewis (1990), the fathers of 'clash thinking', seems to have been sharply influenced by the ideas behind the militant activism of the 1970s and 1980s. The Islamic revolution in Iran in 1979, in particular, and the original response to this throughout the Muslim world, have made a strong impression. It is precisely this experience with over 25 years of theocracy, however, that has brought many intellectuals in Iran to the view that religion and power should be separated, that power should be controlled by democracy and that human rights should aim at offering protection from the state. This also applies to authors like Soroush who contributed to the theoretical foundations of the Islamic republic. In the 1970s and 1980s, the 'Islamic utopia' was seen by many Muslims as a beckoning perspective. As long as it remained a dream, the negative sides remained in shadow. The best way to become aware of the downsides was through the actual realization of this 'ideal state'. Recent research shows that the 'lessons' have not been limited to intellectuals. While in 1974 a large majority of the population wished for religion to play a larger role in public life, in 2004 a large majority, including youth, wished for a decrease of religious influence (Asadi et al. 1976; Goedarzi et al. 2004). On these grounds it is likely that the outcome of the presidential elections of 2005 was not determined by religious considerations. Additionally, the lessons of Iran have not remained limited to that country; the experiment has been followed with great interest across the Muslim world. According to Bayat and Baktiari, the influence of proponents of theocracy has not disappeared, but has decreased, and the Iranian experience has contributed to a gradual modification in the doctrine employed by Islamic movements, namely from a revolutionary to a more democratic persuasion (Bayat and Baktiari 2002: 322-323). This offers an important reference point for democratization. It is after all a known fact that democracy cannot be imposed but can only succeed when it stems from endogenous dynamics (WRR 2001).

Thus we have arrived at the possible future dynamism in the support of democratic ideas. Is a further shift from revolutionary to democratic views indeed a possibility? Just as previously the revolutionary ideas spread quickly, this could also be the case for the ideas discussed in section 2.3. Through the current means of communication, thinkers can be expelled from their country, but their ideas cannot be easily expelled. In addition, the dynamics of situations may increase the need for a different 'reading' of religion, as seems to be the case with Iranian thinkers. The problem is that the people's appreciation of this dynamics is difficult to determine. Thus far in most Muslim countries the existing democratic mechanisms for measuring preferences have not been strongly developed. Elections are held sparsely, and when they are held, participating parties are often bound by all kinds of limiting provisions. Nevertheless, in many cases (Indonesia, Iran, Pakistan, Turkey) such elections demonstrate a preference for moderate Islamic parties and/or illustrate an aversion to mismanagement, lack of security, corruption, and so on. Findings by the World Values Survey indicate that in a number of Muslim countries democracy is valued highly and there is a rejection of autocratic government (Inglehart and Norris 2004). These findings were confirmed by The Pew Global Attitudes Project, whose research revealed a wish for more political freedom and openness but also for Islam to play a major role in politics. At the same time, there was a general preference for the separation of mosque and state (Pew Global Attitudes Project 2003). Recent actions by the populations of countries such as Lebanon, Uzbekistan, Egypt, Kuwait, and Saudi Arabia also point in the direction of a desire for more democracy. This could mean that the ideological grip of radical Islamic movements on the populations is limited or is becoming more limited, or that these movements themselves have given up their anti-democratic inclinations in order to attain political power. It is likely, however, that, in the current state of Islamic awareness, the rapprochement with concepts of democracy and human rights is more likely to take place in an Islamic rather than a humanitarian framework.

The next chapter will take a more in-depth look at the question of whether a dynamism in this direction is actually operating in Islamic movements and which factors play a role in this development. In anticipation of this discussion, we have indicated here that the schools of thought discussed in sections 2.2 and 2.3 do indeed differ greatly but also share significant similarities. Both are part of Islamic activism: schools of thought and movements directed towards raising the political and social consciousness of Muslims using Islam as a common vehicle (see Chapter 1). The schools of thought distinguished here are both directed towards activism and thus against religiously motivated traditionalism and an inwardly directed experiencing of the faith. They also set themselves in opposition to the self-evident authority of the state: the one strand of thought by restricting the role of the state by using Islamic norms, the other by arguing for democracy and human rights. What is held in common, then, is the pursuit of change and breaking out of the stagnation in the Muslim world. All the authors discussed also seek this revitalization in a rehabilitation of Islamic culture. This holds true for authors like Arkoun, Soroush, and Abu Zayd, as well, who are interested in the openness of cultures and seek the revitalization of Islam through modernization of the faith. The call for restoring the relationship with the 'authentic' culture should be placed against the backdrop of the long periods – both in the colonial and postcolonial eras – in which Islam was banished to the private sphere and seen as an obstacle to progress. This marginalization gave many groups the feeling that they stood 'outside history' (Göle 1996). By emphasizing the importance of the expressive power of Islam for society, and by showing that one can be proud of an authentic Islamic culture, those who were previously marginalized are once again placed 'within history'.

In this view, Islamic activism is comparable to some other emancipation movements, both in terms of internal variation and composition and violent outgrowths of its radical wings. That the need for recognition is sometimes expressed in radical phrases, is not unfamiliar to emancipation movements; the accompanying use of violence, however, is less common. In the black movement one heard the phrase 'black is beautiful, and white is pig'. Scott points out that subordinate parties protesting their position often make use of a symbolic reversal of their qualities and those of the dominant group (Scott 1990). Such a rhetorical reversal of values is also a functional tool for mobilizing followers. It has been used in the communist revolution, for instance, as seen in the aiming for a 'dictatorship of the proletariat'. That the ends justify the means for these movements is well known. The fervor of the 'front mentality' in the mobilizing phase and the accompanying use of violence, however, are not immanent or permanent qualities. They are a function of the indignity experienced and of the obstacles that are seen to stand in the way of recognition.

Radical rhetoric and means in the battle for recognition need not rule out a later democratic inclination. The liberal Muslim thinker Muqtedar Khan sees a marked connection between the call for Islam as a resistance ideology by the radical thinker Qutb, discussed in section 2.2, and the pursuit of a government that respects freedom. Qutb's views represented a revolutionary message for the Muslim world because they included an attack on the legitimacy of tyrannical regimes. Khan sees Qutb's call for armed rebellion, if necessary, against these regimes, as similar – even in terminology – to the rhetoric of John Locke in the seventeenth century. According to Khan, Qutb's wish to make God's sovereignty absolute should also be seen as primarily turned against the absolute power of the ruler. As one of God's creations, the individual human is free and owes obedience to only one authority: God. Based on this thought, the individual can position him- or herself against the ruler. In Khan's opinion, this vision of human freedom is comparable to Locke's inalienable natural freedom. Thus, in the end, authority is only legitimate if it is built on the values of the governed (Khan 2003).

If the element that links the authors discussed in this chapter is that the 'own' values of the governed need also be given their due in the political sphere and that the power of the ruled must be a limited power, it is not inconceivable that in the course of time even more radical movements might recognize that this is precisely what democracy and human rights are about. Other movements have shown us that the radical, *maximizing* first phases may be followed by less radical ones concerned with *optimizing*. We can point to an example from the Netherlands: the pre-war SDAP (Social Democratic Workers' Party) slogan 'the state is a lie' evolved into the strongly pro-state stance of the post-war PVDA (Labor Party); the experience that the state may be influenced in favor of the party's own desiderata formed the basis of this transformation. Muslims' experience with democracy is still very limited, but it has been hopeful. The Indian Muslim party Jamaat-i-Islami, for example, evolved from an originally anti-democratic party directed towards the establishment of an Islamic state, to a fully democratically-oriented party. After experiencing the advantages of participating in the Indian democracy, the party gradually renounced all its originally radical Islamic doctrines (Ahmad 2005).

55

2.5 CONCLUSION

This chapter shows that Islamic political thought exhibits great diversity. On the intellectual level, rapprochement with concepts of democracy and human rights can certainly be observed. The thinkers discussed in section 2.3 have gradually demolished the dogmatic obstacles, making acceptance of these concepts possible. The actual political effect of these concepts in Muslim countries is unclear and often takes place underground. Nevertheless, representatives of this way of thinking, such as Seyyed Muhammed Khatami in Iran and Abdurrahman Wahid in Indonesia, have held high positions in their countries. This plurality makes it clear that the sacred sources of Islam can be read and interpreted in many different ways. The battle for the proper interpretation has strongly intensified with the emergence of Islamic activism in the Muslim world. The influence of views which allow no deviation from the literal text of the sources is probably considerable, in part because in many Muslim countries militant means are employed to enforce these views.

This diversity in itself forms a reference point for a policy that pursues processes of democratization and the strengthening of human rights in the Muslim world. The argument that Islam is principally incompatible with these ideas is simply untrue. This does not necessarily mean, however, that such a policy will achieve great success in the short term. Not only are power relations stubborn, but views do not change overnight. All kinds of developments may be of influence, such as higher education, women participating in the workforce, migration, and media consumption. For this reason, the present limited influence of positive views of democracy and human rights does not mean that their potential influence will be as limited. Changes in individual behavior as well as changes in the political make-up can increase the need for interpretations of Islam which support democracy and human rights.

3 THE DEVELOPMENT OF ISLAMIC POLITICAL MOVEMENTS

3.1 INTRODUCTION

Islamic political movements have been in the spotlight for some time. Far-reaching political events such as the Iranian revolution (1979), the struggle of the Taliban in Afghanistan since the 1980s, the assassination of President Sadat (1981), and the bloody civil war in Algeria after the election victory of the Islamic FIS party and the cancellation of the election results (1992) focused worldwide attention on militant Islamic groups. They gave violent expression to the Islamization effort: the establishment of politics, the state, society, and law on Islamic principles (Piscatori 1984: 1). That these are not isolated events is evident from the armed struggle of Islamic groups elsewhere since the 1980s, from Chechnya, Indonesia, Thailand, Pakistan, to Yemen and Sudan. Since the terrorist attacks in, among other places, the US, Indonesia, Turkey, Morocco, Spain, and England, these Islamic political movements have been followed with more than passing interest also by non-experts in the West. Even if they are not reputed to be violent, they are at least considered radical, in the sense that they aim to bring about a thorough change in the political and social order. They are also usually considered to be fundamentalist, ultraconservative, and anti-democratic, given that many call for the Islamization of society based on the example of the founding era of Islam (Noyon 2003: 47).

This chapter analyzes the development of Islamic activism by examining the influence of concrete Islamic political movements on the political arena in Muslim countries. The central questions are: What insights can be gained from the development of these movements since the 1970s? What reference points does this offer for rapprochement with the concepts of democracy and human rights?

The chapter first looks at the most important features and ideas about the state and politics that arose in Islamic activism in the 1970s (sec. 3.2). Then it examines the interaction between Islamic activists and the state in the subsequent decades, and the influence of this activism on the political order in Muslim countries. First we will look at the countries where Islamic political movements have (temporarily) assumed state power since the 1970s: Iran, Sudan, and Afghanistan (sec 3.3). In these cases they were able to realize their ambition to oust the secular state and to create an Islamic state. We will also briefly examine developments in Pakistan, the most important Muslim country in the South-Asian region. There the government to a great extent adopted the Islamization agenda of the Pakistani Islamic political movements. Revolutionary movements have not come to power in other Muslim countries. But also in those countries the political order does not seem to have been immune to the pressure from Islamic political activists. Everywhere in the 1980s and 1990s the state engaged in its own national Islamization politics in areas such as education, banking, family law, public morality, and the media. In many Muslim countries the state had to allow, if not national, then regional or local space for Islamic movements or grant them some concessions (sec 3.4). As a result, these movements also shifted their own strategies and ambitions. To conclude, section 3.5 will analyze the most significant changes within the broad spectrum of Islamic political movements and the current regimes in the Muslim world, and evaluate the factors that favor and hinder these countries' (further) rapprochement with the concepts of democracy and human rights.

3.2 ISLAMIC POLITICAL MOVEMENTS IN THE 1970S: BACKGROUND AND CHARACTERISTICS

3.2.1 STATE-FORMATION, SECULARIZATION, AND ECONOMIC MODERNIZATION

Throughout the long history of the Muslim world there have been numerous episodes in which rebellious groups have opposed their rulers in the name of Islam. Often it was individual spiritual leaders who mobilized the believers around specific grievances. From the end of the nineteenth century Islamic movements arose that joined the struggle against colonial rulers. What then are the characteristics of the Islamic political movements of the 1970s? How do they differ from earlier (religiously-inspired) protest movements? Recent research provides no single, simple answer to this question (Piscatori 1984: Wiktorowicz 2004b; Tibi 2001; Esposito and Burgat 2003). It is certain that they were fueled by the discontent in many Muslim countries over the post-colonial phase of forced national state-formation, especially over the secularization imposed from above and the economic modernization forced upon them.

After independence many political leaders in the Muslim world continued to work, first and foremost, to consolidate a national state with a strongly centralized, powerful, executive. Usually the leadership fell into the hands of Western-oriented political or military elites who legitimized the state in secular terms with the help of nationalist, liberal, or socialist ideologies and symbols (Lapidus 2002: 818). At that same time these elites did not shy away from using religion as a social agent to strengthen the national state. Some movements within Islam were associated with the national political agenda, while others, usually the more folkish or mystical movements, were excluded from it.

Except in Saudi Arabia and Morocco, all the countries put the religious institutions under official government control. Giles Kepel makes a broad distinction between monarchies where the traditional, rural social classes (the tribal aristocracy, landlords, and bazaar merchants) were in control and states were governed by a new urban elite who had pushed the previous leaders aside. In the first group of countries (with Saudi Arabia as the extreme example) religious leaders (ulama) and institutions maintained their prominent but usually dependent positions in society. They were not displaced but embedded in the regime. In the second group the land and other property of religious groups was seized and the ulama were paid salaries as government employees (Kepel 2002: 47).

Thus the process of secularization mostly had the character of a subordination of an official version of Islam to the state and an enforced banning of religious affairs from public life. However, other versions of Islam continued to play an important role in local social and cultural life everywhere. This 'folkish', usually non-urban Islam was characterized by attention to individual piety, the mediating role of local spiritual leaders and mystical brotherhoods (Kepel 2002: 46-54; Yavuz 2003: ix). It was tolerated by most regimes for the sake of social stability or, as in Turkey (after initially being forbidden), Algeria, and Saudi Arabia, restricted in its freedom of movement. Some regimes manipulated the traditional Sufi-brotherhoods into the position of a buffer against socialist, communist, and later also radical Islamic factions.

The post-colonial elites gave the state supremacy over society and the individual. The nationalism that they employed, claimed to be acting in the name of popular sovereignty, but in practice only a limited, selective participation by the masses in political power was allowed (Utvik 2003: 43; Fuller 2003: 14). Sheri Berman describes how the new regimes succeeded in mobilizing the masses through a large bureaucracy and an official state culture and ideology and at the same time managed to keep them at a great distance. She speaks of a silent contract between the state and society: in exchange for self-respect, self-reliance, and broad participation in education, health care, employment, and subsidies, citizens were expected (temporarily) to defer their claims to individual political and civil rights (Berman 2003: 259). From an economic perspective this meant a very activist role for the state, which in some countries (including Libya, Egypt, Indonesia, Yemen, Algeria, and Iraq) embraced an explicitly socialist and/or communist program. The best-known example of this is undoubtedly the Arab nationalism of Gamal Abdel Nasser. Nasser's program encompassed an unprecedented, ambitious socialist-tinged development program that, among other things, included the nationalization of key industries, fundamental reforms, and prestige projects like the construction of the Aswan Dam.

From the implicit contract with the central state that was geared toward economic achievements there initially flowed a great measure of tolerance towards state interference in daily social, cultural, and religious life. Civil society organizations were compelled to show loyalty above all to the regime in power without actually being able to get involved in the political arena. Cultural pluralism was suppressed in favor of the project of building the nation-state. However, groups and layers of the population that were more or less excluded from this project sought refuge in their own religion and/or ethnicity. Kurds in Iraq and Turkey, for example, were more or less forced to seek refuge in the local arenas where the state had little control. Paradoxically, this process of political and social marginalization in the long term reinforced the significance of informal neighborhood, clan, and religious loyalties and identities (Yavuz 2003: 52).

In many places in the Muslim world in the 1970s and '80s, the high hopes crashed into the reality of the disappointing achievements of the state. The social contract was, as it were, unilaterally terminated by all those groups in the population that were disappointed by the economic failures and the lack of individual and political rights (Berman 2003: 259-260). This applied in particular to the younger generation that reached adulthood in the 1970s during the mass migration from the countryside to the cities and their outskirts. This was the first generation to be educated in their own language. They could read and write and cherished no memories of the colonial era. The knowledge, ideas, and culture of their (mostly illiterate) parents from the countryside offered these youth too few reference points for the new urban living conditions. They wanted the political leaders to account for their large promises, and they sought ways to make themselves heard in the political and social spheres (Kepel 2002). The ideas of thinkers such as Mawdudi, Qutb, al-Banna, Shariati, and Khomeini, which were sketched in Chapter 2, even though diverse, fulfilled this need. Their ideas also gave the new generation reference points to identify and interpret this new, modern society and to provide their own critical (Islamic) alternative.

3.2.2   FACTORS OF MOBILIZATION

Research into (revolutionary) activism and social movements reveals that a breeding ground of malaise and grievances is a necessary but not a sufficient condition for activist political protest (Berman 2003: 258; Hafez 2003: 17; Baylouny 2004). Not all the societies that have been exposed to economic, social, cultural, and demographic pressures since the 1970s have produced political revolutions or influential (Islamic-)political movements. Apparently, there are other mechanisms and conditions that determine when and how social discontent translates into social and political mobi-

lization and in what direction these forces develop. We will examine these mobilization factors by looking at three components:
1 the availability of means and mobilization structures;
2 the opportunities and obstacles in the internal and external political environment;
3 culture and processes of giving meaning (Wiktorowicz 2004b).

Addendum 1   Means and mobilization structures

Material, organizational, and institutional resources are crucial for the effective mobilization of population groups and the coordination of collective action. Islamic political activists generally manage to make productive use of existing, many-branched networks of mosques and religious schools, volunteer organizations, and informal contacts for the dissemination of their ideas, the recruitment and mobilization of (potential) followers, and the raising of funds from ordinary believers as well as from rich donors and migrants from the Gulf States. In most Muslim countries state oversight of mosques and NGOs has been intensified since the 1980s. Nevertheless, medical clinics, hospitals, and educational and cultural institutions remain relatively effective platforms for strengthening ties with local communities and population groups and for spreading the religious and political message without having to fear immediate state repression (Bayat 1997; Wiktorowicz 2004a and 2004b; Berman 2003). After all, open attacks on religion or religious institutions often lead to a further loss of legitimacy for the state.

61

The leadership and the shura were important organizational concepts in many early activist political movements. However, there were considerable differences regarding how to interpret these concepts. According to the influential model of the Egyptian Muslim Brotherhood, the leader should be chosen by the shura. Once installed, the leader's position was nearly sacrosanct because the shura could play only an advisory role. The leader would have at his disposal a supporting general executive committee, special committees (including among others for missionary work – da'wa, and for specific target groups like students, farmers, workers, and women) and eventually also a military, whether or not underground, branch. Radical armed movements put more emphasis on leadership than do non-military variants.[1] Opinions regarding the most desirable make-up of the shura were equally divided, and three models served as inspiration: a shura of only clerics, only intellectuals, and of the whole community (Roy 1994: 44-45). The first model we find only in Central Asia, namely in the Afghan Jamaat-i Islami and the Soviet Islamic Renaissance Party. Most other movements rejected the authority of the traditional ulama. Most common (especially among Sunni movements) was a shura made up of a modern, often militant, advance guard of urban professionals, students, and intellectuals.

The third ('Iranian') variant most resembled Western parliamentary democracies and for this reason met with much criticism from fundamentalists (Roy 1994: 45).

Particularly since the Iranian revolution there has been extensive attention to movements aimed at taking over the state and installing an Islamic order by revolutionary means. Some factions, inspired by Sayyid Qutb, indeed wanted a revolution – violent if necessary – from above (see section 2.2). Others regarded the overthrow of the incumbent regime as permissible only if the state had taken on the role of extreme enemy of Islam and all the other peaceful means had been exhausted (Roy 1994: 41-42). Their more gradual path within the existing political order took the form of political movements and parties, and the infiltration of parts of the public sector and the state apparatus (like the bureaucracy, the army, the police, education, the judiciary, and specific ministries). Research shows, however, that much of the underlying conflict between and within Islamic movements did not concern the use of violence or large blueprints for an Islamic state, but issues of identity and culture. In everyday practice this meant convincingly describing the problems and concerns of potential supporters, and that worked best by using authentic symbols and language (Wiktorowicz 2004b: 16; Yavuz 2003; White 2002; Esposito 2003). Sharia, as a symbol of an authentic Islamic system of values based on social justice and good governance, quickly became the focus of the moral struggle (Hourani 1984: 228). Thus taking over or transforming the state was for many movements not an end in itself but only one of the many possible ways to bring about changes.

With the rise of Islamic political activism organizations for proselytizing (da'wa) among (apostate) Muslims also became more popular in the Muslim world. Da'wa calls on ordinary Muslims to reform their personal lives. If the 'struggle for hearts and minds' receives sufficient support among the broad public, so goes the thinking, it will be possible in the long run to compel the Islamization of government and law-making from the bottom up, without having to have a direct confrontation with the state. Modern da'wa-movements manage to mobilize citizens chiefly thanks to their subtle moral critique of the prevailing political regime.[2]

Addendum 2   Opportunities and obstacles in the internal and external political environment

The nature of the political and social system (such as the degree of openness or lack thereof in the political arena and institutions, the presence of political allies and competitors, the stability and legitimacy of the incumbent regime, and the degree of violent repression by the state apparatus) determines to a large extent whether and how activists succeed in translating protest into collective action. We see the dominant position of the state and the limited space for political opposition and activism again in the classification of political systems in the Muslim world. On the eve of the rise of Islamic activism in the 1970s most of the governments by far were considered to be autocratic and 'not-free' (see box 3.1 and appendix 1). Since that time they have developed ever more sophisticated techniques to deal with internal and external pressure from Islamic activists. Instead of banning every form of political opposition and debate, for example, they switch to banning political parties of a religious nature, manipulating elections by the redrawing of electoral districts, election commissions etc., restricting press freedom and access to the media, adopting the rhetoric and some of the agenda items of Islamic activists, and harassing and arresting political opponents.

Box 3.1   The political system of Muslim countries at the beginning of the 1970s

The so-called Polity IV score is a frequently used, compiled index for indicating regime characteristics and types. The Polity IV score measures the democratic quality of political systems on a scale ranging from -10 (high autocracy) to 10 (high democracy) (see also the notes in appendix 1). This index reveals that in the Middle East and North Africa only Lebanon had the status of a democratic country (a Polity score of 4 or higher) at the beginning of the 1970s. North Yemen, Kuwait, and Morocco received the classification 'partly free' from the better-known but more controversial Freedom House index; however, these countries had low Polity scores. The cautious political liberalization during the 1970s and '80s in countries such as Egypt, Algeria, and Jordan meant that Islamic movements and parties were recognized formally or informally and got access to a political platform. For the most part there was no direct, substantial influence on political decision-making but there was indirect influence, on account of the fact that they received massive support from the grassroots during elections or demonstrations. In sub-Saharan Africa the political climate of the early 1970s was freer, although only Gambia was considered free and democratic by both measures. Burkina Faso, Nigeria, and Sierra Leone received the designation 'partly free' from Freedom House, but scored poorly on the Polity IV index. According to the Polity IV index, Malaysia and Bangladesh, out of a small group of independent Asian countries, were deemed to be relatively democratic in the early 1970s. It is notable that the average scores for political and civil rights of this group of countries were higher than in the other two regions.

In addition to domestic political factors there are, of course, also factors from the international environment that influence the development opportunities of Islamic activism. As Chapter 2 revealed, the Iranian revolution of 1979 had an important catalyzing function. For the first time in recent history could a country in the name of Islam claim complete authority over all aspects of the state system. The revolution unleashed a process of Islamic consciousness-raising for which political thinkers like Mawdudi, al-Banna, and Qutb had earlier paved the way. The awareness of the underlying connection of Muslims all over the world was reinforced, as was the fervor of Islamic intellectuals, activist factions, and parties who opposed authoritarian regimes (Kepel 2002: 130-132). The new Iranian Islamic Republic also tried to export the Islamic revolution (the 'people's Islam'), in part as a means to be able to claim the leadership of the *Ummah*. The conservative regime of Saudi Arabia became the main target in the propaganda war but also other Sunni Muslim states (including the Gulf States) and Iraq were involved. After the Iranian revolution quickly assumed an expressly Shiite character, the Saudi regime in turn, using enormous quantities of petrodollars, stimulated further mobilization of Sunni political movements.

Addendum 3   *Culture and processes of giving meaning*
Like most social groups and movements, Islamic social movements have developed their own ideological frames of meaning and thought. These frames involve conscious strategies to enable them to interpret the world around them and their place in it in order to legitimize and incite collective action (Hafez 2004: 156). Every frame of meaning consists of three parts: a clear diagnosis of the social problem and those chiefly responsible; unambiguous solutions, tactics, and strategies; and clear motives to shift to support or collective action. The more successfully social movements manage to match their frame of meaning with those of their potential followers, the greater their mobilization power (Wiktorowicz 2004b: 16; Hafez 2004).

As Chapter 2 revealed, many leading Islamic movements saw the spreading of Western influence and values as the most important cause of widespread corruption, inefficiency of the state, mass unemployment, and great social inequalities. The West had undermined Islamic institutions, customs, and values, diverted Muslims from the correct path, and brought the entire Muslim world into a state of crisis and moral decay. Many found the solution to these problems in a return by the individual Muslim and the state to the pure sources and practices of Islam, the rejection of Western influence and values, and the creation of an Islamic state.

'*Ummah* threatened by the West' had a prominent mobilizing function in the ideology and rhetoric of Islamic political movements, but their concrete tactics and strategies were directed chiefly to the arena of their own national state. Supporters of a theocracy along the Iranian model usually endorsed the vision that only God and not man is able to do good. Therefore only God – or his representatives on earth – should have control of rights, and people must subject themselves to the interests of the *Ummah* and the leadership of the state. Other activists rejected the notion of an unimpeachable, all-encompassing God-given order that encourages a theocracy. They saw in the concepts of the shura, consensus, and assent by the public (*baya*) reference points for an Islamic democratic government. Again others endorsed the importance of the separation of powers, but appeared extremely fearful of political party formation and multi-party systems, since parties would undermine the unity and consensus of the Muslim community which they considered so crucial (Berger 2006). And a small minority concluded that a democratic system offered Muslims the best guarantee by far that they could follow their religion. Democracy would after all guard against the misuse of religion by those in power and, through the freedom of worship, would create an important condition for a truly religious society (Abu Zayd 2006).

3.2.3 CONCLUSION

After 1970 many countries in the Muslim world became breeding grounds for political unrest and activism. Large groups of well-educated youth who had reached adulthood wanted to hold their political leaders to account and looked for ways to exercise political and social influence (Kepel 2002). The Islamically inspired ideas of thinkers such as Mawdudi, Qutb, al-Banna, Shariati, and Khomeini fulfilled this need. Whether discontent leads to mass support for activism and influential political movements, however, depends to a major extent on the degree to which these movements have at their disposition institutions, financial resources, and local networks to disseminate their political message, maintain their links with their potential supporters, and succeed in gaining access to the domestic or international political arena. Furthermore, it is of great importance whether movements can offer a mobilizing perspective with a clear diagnosis of and solution to existing social problems. Measured by these indicators, *Islamic* activist movements turned out to be pre-eminently in a position in many Muslim countries to possess a relatively large mobilization-potential.

65

3.3 ISLAMITIC POLITICAL ACTIVISTS IN POWER

3.3.1 INTRODUCTION

To date Iran, Afghanistan, and Sudan are the only countries that since the 1970s have been transformed into Islamic states by a takeover of power by Islamic activist movements. (Saudi Arabia has for a much longer time been an absolute theocracy. See box 3.2). Pakistan is a borderline case. Since its partition and separation from India in 1947, the country has been the scene of struggle between Islamic movements and political leaders who continually manipulate eachother and Islam to reinforce their political power base (Shah 2003). But it was above all thanks to the pressure of Islamic political parties that in 1973 Pakistan got a new constitution which declared Islam to be the official state religion, and the state took on an active Islamization role (Fair 2005: 272). In Iran the transformation occurred through an unexpectedly fast revolution in 1979 under the leadership of the Shiite clerics and with mass support from Islamic political youth, followed by a period of Islamization from the top down by the state. In Afghanistan the transformation occurred by means of a civil war between combatants of the war against the Soviet Union, that was ultimately won by the Taliban, one of the many Islamic movements in the region. In Sudan it took place via the gradual expansion of the power base of an Islamic political movement that seized power in a military coup in 1989. In the cases of Afghanistan and Sudan the take-over of power occurred against the background of deep ethnic, tribal, and religious divisions, regional conflicts, and external interference. They resulted in the collapse of the state, civil war, and political chaos, and in the case of the Darfur region of Sudan also in mass death and destruction. Below we will examine in greater detail the concrete experiences of recent 'Islamic activism in power' in Iran, Sudan, and Afghanistan. After that we will look briefly at developments in Pakistan.

Box 3.2   The political order in Saudi Arabia

Saudi Arabia is an absolute monarchy that since the unification of this country in 1932 has been ruled by the royal family al-Saud. They derived their hegemony over competing tribes by linking the legitimacy of the political order and the state to a traditional Wahhabist interpretation of Islam. The current king is also prime minister and his successor is chosen by the royal family itself from among their own members. He occupies the position of vice-minister in the cabinet. The three key positions in the cabinet (Minister of Foreign Affairs, Minister of Internal Affairs, and Minister of Defense) are all held by members of the royal family. Article I of the 1993 constitution states that 'God's book and the Sunna' shape the constitutional conditions of this country. The monarchy has an official duty to protect Islam, the sacred sites, and the pilgrimage to Mecca (*hadj*) and to implement Sharia. Therefore the state charges the people to 'to do good and to avoid evil' (art. 23). The state helps them in this regard by disseminating the traditional Islamic discourse via the texts of the Friday sermons, by strongly controlling state media, and by banning as much as possible other interpretations and discourses. All citizens are assumed by law to be (Sunni) Muslims, although also some Shiites live in the eastern region of the country. In 1993, under external and internal pressure after the first Gulf War, the king established a 120-member consultative body (conforming to the Quranic principle of shura) with extremely limited authority. In February 2005 men could vote for the first time in the history of this country for half of the members of the municipal council. (The other half are appointed.) What powers this council will receive is still unclear. The forming of political parties and the freedom of assembly and association are still outlawed, and criticism of the closed, corrupt regime is mercilessly punished. In the 1970s it looked as though rising prosperity and modernization would gradually displace traditional Wahhabism, but religious conservatives successfully mounted a counteroffensive. Inspired by Khomeini's actions against the Shah of Iran, 500 dissidents stormed the sacred mosque in Mecca at the end of 1979. They demanded an end to the reign of the al-Saud family, whom they accused of corruption, Western decadence, and a lack of legitimacy. They also reproached the ulama for letting themselves be misused to further the political agenda of the royal family. After the regime, with help from France, had put down this revolt, the rulers implemented a new Islamization offensive to reinforce their legitimacy.

Source: Barends and Van Eijk in Otto et al. 2006; Raphaeli 2003.

3.3.2 IRAN

The authoritarian regime of the Shah of Iran had outlawed all competing political parties and movements as well as all alternative protest channels. Thanks to the unambiguous leadership and institutional resources of the hierarchical Shiite clergy, the widespread unrest among students could, in a short time, be mobilized into a mass revolt under the banner of Islam. What emerged was a classic protest movement: directed *against* the existing order and in favor of the take-over of the state, but without a coherent ideological program like the ones available to activist movements in Egypt and Algeria. This made it possible for the religious leaders to create an Islamic state that would carry out a process of Islamization from the top down (Bayat 1997: 168).

Thus Iran became the first Islamic theocracy in the modern history of the Middle East, with a constitution and political system based in part on a Western model and direct general elections for the parliament and president. Although the Iranian political process is more open and livelier than those elsewhere in the region, it is still subject to the *vilaya-i-faqih*, the supreme spiritual leader and his Council of Guardians (Fuller 2003: 103-104; Dekker and Barends in Otto et al., 2006).[3] The Supreme Leader is considered to be above political parties and to 'protect' the religious state in moral respects, as it were, against the democratic role of the elected parliament. Unlike the president, he is not elected but chosen by a circle of prominent clergy. He can reverse the democratically made decisions of the parliament and is not accountable to the public. Moreover, he holds the function of commander of the armed forces (with even the right to declare war and mobilize the troops), head of state radio and television, commander-in-chief of the revolutionary guard, the ordinary army, and the security services. These positions made it possible over the past years to thoroughly Islamize the state apparatus with respect to personnel. Religious conservatives occupy nearly all the posts. The Supreme Leader has a personal staff of around 600 persons, including advisors on military, economic, cultural, and media matters. Around these there is a circle of about 2,000 personally appointed or approved religious 'representatives' in all the important posts in ministries, other government bodies, courts, 'councils', and leading revolutionary, religious, and cultural organizations in Iran and abroad. Together with the many security services and conservative foundations (*bonyads*) these civil servants provide spiritual leader Khamenei a firm grip on executive and legislative power. They also fervently pay attention to the maintenance of the many codes of behavior and social-cultural prescriptions that guard the Islamic morals of the country.

3.3.3   SUDAN

The Islamization of the state in Sudan, in many respects, followed the opposite course. While Iran had a revolution followed by a state-led Islamization, the Sudanese state, since it gained independence in 1956, has been continually exposed to pressure from within and outside the ruling coalition for a progressive Islamization and 'Arabization' of the political and juridical establishments (Bayat 1997; Köndgen in Otto et al. 2006). In addition, there raged a persistent struggle over the question of whether this Islamization should be restricted to the Islamic north or should also encompass the Christian south, as well as whether an orthodox or rather more liberal interpretation of Islam should determine the polity of the state. All these factors formed the ingredients for successive civil wars and military coups, alternating with short periods of democratic rule. It was only in the 1980s that an Islamic movement would take control of the state, after having first, it should be noted, gone through a learning period in opposition to the communist regime of Jafaar Muhammed Numeiri, who would later become an Islamic activist and coalition partner. The Muslim Brotherhood and subsequently the National Islamic Front (a broad coalition of Muslim Brothers, Sufis, tribal leaders, ulama, and army officers) under the leadership of Hasan al-Turabi pursued a policy directed toward the elimination of the more moderate Islamic political movements, the gradual broadening of the economic power basis (including through Islamic banking and take-over of the oil fields), the expansion of support within education and the judiciary, and the building-up of a parallel military structure and security service.

Once in power, the president renamed himself 'leader of the believers' and transformed parliament into a consultative council (in conformity with the Quranic principle of shura) that owed allegiance only to him. Also all the important government institutions including the judiciary were staffed by

Turabi loyalists. The new regime could introduce Sharia legislation (with the punishments for the five *hadd* crimes named in the Quran) and deploy the army and financial reserves in the long, drawn-out civil war against the south. More top-down Islamization was compelled by the implementation in 1996 of the so-called Khartoum Public Order Law, designed to control 'immoral behavior' in public, but at the same time it further restricted freedoms, and lawlessness and arbitrariness increased. The existing morality legislation and the bans on alcohol consumption, prostitution, and immorality were further supplemented with Islamic clothing prescriptions for government buildings, schools, and universities, and all sorts of prohibitions and commandments.

The 1998 constitution seems chiefly to be an attempt by the regime of Omar Hassan Bashir to gain international legitimacy after the illegal military takeover and the disruption of the democratic process. The current text designates Sudan not as an Islamic state but as a country 'where the religions accommodate eachother' and Islam 'is the religion of the majority' (Köndgen in Otto et al. 2006). Article 24 guarantees the freedom of religion provided that its exercise 'does not offend the feelings of others' and that no damage is caused to the public order. Similarly vague passages deal with the freedom of conscience and expression and the right to privacy. The Law on Political Association ended the ten-year ban on the formation of political parties, as a result of which many new parties were founded. However, this same law requires that all the new parties endorse the ideology of the ruling party. The registration of parties, moreover, is in the hands of a member of the governing party while the room for maneuvre is restricted by emergency decrees and intimidation by the security forces (UK Home Office 2005; IFES Sudan, undated). For example, a week before the election in 2000 seven leaders of the National Democratic Alliance, a broad opposition coalition of northerners and southerners, were arrested and accused of conspiring with an American diplomat. Ultimately only Bashir's National Congress and a few small minority parties that were largely unknown to the voters participated in the presidential and parliamentary elections at the end of 2000; the leading opposition parties boycotted the elections, and as a result, the National Congress won 355 of the 360 seats.

3.3.4 AFGHANISTAN

The takeover of the government in Afghanistan by the Taliban movement, a movement dominated by the Pashtun ethnic group, was the result of an ad hoc coalition of domestic and international forces. In the ten-year-long civil war that followed the war against the Soviet Union, various ethnic groupings, clans, and tribes struggled over power under the leadership of local warlords. This struggle left the country and its people destitute; the infrastructure and the economy were devastated, and the central authority, the government institutions, and the constitutional state were fragmented. In the meantime the 'holy war' of the local warlords against the 'godless' Soviet Union promoted the dissemination of radical Islamic thought among the Pashtun community and strengthened the role of local spiritual leaders of religious schools (*madrasas*), in part thanks to the support of Pakistan, the US, and Saudi Arabia (ICG 2003b).[4] When the Taliban fighters began their offensive in 1992, they could use their ethnic ties with the southern Pashtun communities to achieve quick victories. Four years later they succeeded, thanks in part to financial and military help from al-Qaeda, in conquering the capital Kabul. Troops under the leadership of ousted President Rabbani ultimately controlled in the north only ten per cent of the total territory (ICG 2003b; Yassari and Saboory in Otto et al. 2006).

The top-down Islamization carried out by the Taliban regime began with the proclamation of the Islamic Emirate of Afghanistan and the implementation of *hadd* punishments. There followed the draconian social and cultural regulations of the Ministry of the Promotion of Virtue and the Prevention of Vice, which seemed to have been borrowed from the strict Islamic interpretations of the ideas of traditional Deobandi and Afghan-Islamic tribal traditions. The regulations affected city-dwellers the most, as they concerned the exclusion of women from public life, schools, universities, and government functions and the banning of television, music, sports, games, and photography. Minorities such as the Shiite Hazara and the one-and-a-half million Afghan refugees in neighboring Pakistan were also particularly hard hit; the Taliban and their local sympathizers tried to force these groups by intimidation and violence to submit to the Taliban's Islamic norms and regulations (Yassari and Saboory in Otto et al. 2006: 188; Fuller 2003: 114-117).

After the military intervention by the US and the victory of the Northern Alliance in 2001, the Taliban government had to step down. The new constitution of 2004, which was adopted by the Loya Jirga (consultative assembly), describes Afghanistan as an Islamic republican state where the president, elected directly by the people, fulfills the role of protector of Islam, the constitution and the other laws.[5] It is the duty of the state "to create a prosperous and progressive society based on social justice, protection of human dignity, protection of human rights, realization of democracy, and to ensure national unity and equality among all ethnic groups and tribes" (art. 6). Law-making rests with a parliament consisting of a directly elected house of representatives and a composite senate that is partly indirectly elected and partly directly appointed. The right to form political parties is also anchored in the constitution (art. 35), but is linked to the clause that the program and charter of parties may not violate the principles of the sacred religion of Islam and the conditions and values of the constitution. In addition, the article forbids the formation of parties on the basis of ethnicity, language, region, Islamic school of thought or doctrine.[6] At the same time article 83 includes measures that the election system provide "general and just representation for all the people." Article 2 recognizes the freedom of religion (within the limits of the law), but article 3 adds the phrase: "In Afghanistan, no law can be contrary to the beliefs and provisions of the sacred religion of Islam" (International Constitutional Law: Afghanistan, undated). Although Sharia is not explicitly mentioned, moderate and secular forces fear that conservative religious leaders will employ this article to maintain the stifling social and cultural climate of the Taliban era.[7] Given the long history in Afghanistan of conservative forces' manipulation of progressive constitutions, that fear is not without foundation. This is all the more so because the central political authority still does not have complete military control over its own territory and the Afghan economy is largely dependent on the illegal production of opium. The establishment of a democratic system and the maintenance of political and civil rights are therefore encountering major obstacles (Freedom House 2004).

71

3.3.5 PAKISTAN

After his election victory and the separation of Bangladesh in 1971, President Zulfikar Ali Bhutto tried to strengthen his legitimacy by a policy of Islamization: the banning of alcohol, the adoption of the Islamic Friday, and the closing of night clubs. In part under pressure from clerics in the political opposition, he also orientated himself more emphatically towards the Arab world. In spite of the defeat of the Islamic parties in the elections, he gave them a role in framing a new constitution, which declared Islam to be the state religion and charged a Council for Islamic Ideology with the further Islamization of the country (Fair 2005: 272). After a military coup led by General Zia Ul-Haq in 1977, Sunni movements such as the Deobandi and the Jamaat-i-Islami saw a chance to expand the Islamization offensive with the support of the army. Among other measures, Zia introduced by decree classic Islamic corporal punishments, instituted one federal Sharia court with a Sharia chamber as an appeal body, and promulgated laws against blasphemy, especially directed at non-Muslims and Ahmadis. He promoted Islamic banking and Islamized sectors such as the media, education, and the civil service (Barends and Otto in Otto et al. 2006: 242-246; IGC 2005d).

Zia's opportunistic Islamization offensive has left a dangerous legacy of institutional intertwining between religious schools (madrasas), militant

Islamic activism, and the army. The current president and commander of
the armed forces, Pervez Musharraf, also sees himself forced by a lack of
political legitimacy to lean on coalitions between the army and religious-
extremist forces (ICG 2005d). The result is that Pakistan continues to be
afflicted by instability, sectarian violence, and lawlessness, and offers a
home base to diverse nationally and transnationally active terrorists
groups (Shah 2003; Kurpershoek 2004; ICG 2005d). For these reasons and
also because of the repeated manipulation of the elections, moderate
Islamic, liberal, and secular political parties have little chance to make an
impact, in spite of their potential support among a broad layer of the
population (Kurpershoek 2004: 33).

3.3.6 CONCLUSION

What tentative conclusions can be drawn from the experiences of the
exercise of power by Islamic activists and their sympathizers? The
expressly Islamic-labeled regimes in Pakistan, Sudan, and Afghanistan
remained caught in the 'classic weaknesses' of their own political culture,
such as the authoritarian, unlimited exercise of power, corruption, and
gross human rights violations (ICG 2005d; Fuller 2003: 117-118). They
have not succeeded in developing an Islamic model for state and society
that is broadly supported and legitimized by the population (see also
Chapter 2). Instead they remained stuck in what Bayat accurately terms
'cheap Islamization': a heavy-handed imposition of strict, conservative
Islamic codes of behavior and regulations (Bayat 1997). This applies most
clearly to Afghanistan under the Taliban, where the regime under Mullah
Omar linked literal interpretations of the Quran to traditional Pashtun
tribal codes and thereby seriously reduced the role of many other ethnic
groups as well as the position of women. This also applies to Pakistan,
where the cooptation by the state of militant, Islamic groups bent on
political influence has put a stranglehold on more liberal and democratic
groups and parties. In short, the Islamic regimes of former Islamic
activists have established little credit among Muslims themselves. They
have alienated themselves from the ordinary citizens who are hoping for
a better existence and a more just society, and they function almost exclusively as evidence that with their presence they can amply defy 'the West'
(or the US).

Iran is an exception because, unlike the other countries, it has experimented with modern forms of politics, government, and law on an
Islamic basis. At the same time it has not avoided a strongly nationalist,
anti-American, and pro-Shiite course that has resulted in support for
violent Islamic movements elsewhere and a curtailing of political freedoms and human rights in the name of Islam. Iranian intellectuals and

democratically minded politicians from the opposition try on the basis of these experiences to link Islamic principles with new, more inclusive, pluralist and democratic policies and governing institutions (Fuller 2003: 118). They are convinced that democracy and human rights are in themselves valuable products of human reason that relate positively to the intentions of the Quran. This tendency is also known as post-Islamism (Bayat forthcoming). They have, however, so far come up short in the struggle for power with conservative clerics, who occupy the most important positions.

3.4   ISLAMITIC POLITICAL MOVEMENTS IN THE POLITICAL AND SOCIAL ARENA

In the great majority of Muslim states Islamic movements have not yet succeeded in taking over state power by revolution or gradual infiltration of the state system. But Islamic political movements there have shown themselves within or on the margins of the national political area, in state institutions, and in society. The movements blossomed at first in universities in large cities in Egypt, Iran, Pakistan, and Afghanistan and then spread to students in the Palestinian territories, Algeria, Morocco, Tunisia, Malaysia, and Indonesia, among other countries. Additionally, various groups developed transnational activities, in part because Muslim groups everywhere in the world have increasingly easier contact with eachother thanks to the advances in media, information, and communication technology. At the same time foreign governments and international organizations have pressed the ruling political elites to bring about democratization and the improvement of human rights.

What is the influence of these groups on the political and social arena? To what extent and in what ways have activist movements succeeded in Islamizing the political and social order and discourse? What consequences does this have for the nature of the regimes and perspectives for democratizing and the advancement of human rights? To answer these questions this section will discuss the interaction between contemporary Islamic activists and the state, partially in light of the mobilization factors listed in section 3.2.2. Of course, it is not possible to sketch a complete pattern of the development of activist movements. Therefore this analysis will discuss a limited number of Islamic countries and movements. The developments in Egypt, cradle of Islamic legal rules and philosophy and home base of the influential Muslim Brotherhood, are in many respects exemplary for what is happening in much of the Arab world. The Egyptian developments, moreover, have a radiating effect on other regions and movements. Therefore we will first treat extensively the case of Egypt.

3.4.1   EGYPT

In the 1970s a new generation of youth were directly confronted with the tangible results of the ideological, economic, and foreign policy failures of the authoritarian Egyptian state: overcrowded universities, deteriorating education, and – in spite of the false hope of the 'right to work' promised by the state – after graduation almost no prospect of a job and a marriage.[8] The policy of economic liberalization and government cutbacks of the successive governments of Sadat and Mubarak made the path to positions in the state bureaucracy more difficult, and the few jobs that were available did not pay enough to make ends meet. The economic recession of the end of the 1980s in the Gulf States and the first Gulf War of the early 1990s also meant that Egyptian migrant laborers were forced from those countries and back onto the domestic labor market. Thus there arose an intelligentsia of university-educated youth who, after nine years of study, could begin their career as a street sweeper and end it as a poorly paid civil servant (Rosefsky Wickham 2002: 62; Roy 1994: 51). Their fate stood in stark contrast to that of a select group of foreigners, less-educated Egyptians, and (corrupt) civil servants who could profit from selective economic liberalization. These 'new rich' paid their housekeeper and nanny many times the salary of a recent graduate. Most university-educated youth thus concluded that Western consumption goods, social mobility, and economic status were visibly present but lying far out of their reach, and that connections and a bit of luck provided more social success than intellectual achievements and hard work (Rosefsky Wickham 2002: 62). These youth ranked high as potential followers of activist movements.

Discontent and deep frustration do not on their own, however, lead to political mobilization. Apathy and aloofness are even more obvious reactions, certainly in authoritarian societies where taking part in political opposition involves high personal costs. The step toward mobilization was initially made easier because successive governments between the mid-1970s and the early 1980s introduced selective political liberalization. The government propaganda of the state media and the education system were reduced, and a few political parties representing the opposition could for the first time take part in the elections for parliament along with the ruling National Democratic Party (NDP). Unlike his secular nationalist predecessor Nasser, Anwar Sadat presented himself publicly as a believer, in the hope of getting the support of Islamic movements as a political balance against the leftist opposition (al-Sayyid 2004: 6). He released from prison members of the Muslim Brotherhood and allowed others to return from exile. He promoted the establishment of Islamic student associations as competitors to the formerly popular leftist associations and also gave support to Islamic programs in schools, universities, and in the media.

74

A small minority of radical Muslim groups around university cities and the poorest neighborhoods of the major cities emphatically refused to cooperate with the state, however. When Sadat not only offered hospitality to the deposed Shah of Iran but in March 1979 also signed the Camp David Accords, the result was massive street demonstrations of both Islamic activists and secularists. Although the Islamic establishment of al-Azhar University supported him and even declared the Camp David Accords in agreement with Islamic law, some small, radical groups were stirred up. Sadat was assassinated in October 1981.

Sadat's successor, Hosni Mubarak, maintained the state of emergency, which had been instituted earlier and which is still in effect. The president remained the dominant executive power and retained his position as commander-in-chief of the army and the intelligence services, head of government and the ruling party. Furthermore, he retained the authority to appoint ministers, to dismiss parliament, and to rule by decree when parliament is not in session. The freedoms of expression and assembly were also not expanded. Neither was the Brotherhood formally recognized as a political party, even though it had by far the largest number of supporters and the most resources to mobilize politically.

The long-term consequences of this selective liberalization were paradoxical. On the one hand, a far-flung network of flourishing private mosques, Islamic voluntary organizations (in areas such as education, culture, and health), Islamic businesses, and (investment) banks quickly developed. They took advantage of the influx of private capital from the oil-rich Gulf States and the voluntary religious contributions (the *zakat*). And although voluntary organizations are formally under the supervision of the Ministry of Social Affairs, many managed to get around these controls thanks to their close ties with mosques and religious foundations. With respect to organization and finances, they therefore had it easier than their secular counterparts. Moreover, initially Mubarak needed these institutions to consolidate his regime. On the other hand, the selective opening of the political system ultimately led to a multi-party system in which exclusively political parties were active that had no real connection with the population and that could easily be co-opted by the regime.[9] The result was that the adjusted political order maintained the old client-based power structure and the formal political parties became further isolated, in terms of ideology, from the ordinary people.

The growing group of university-educated youth in the cities, who were originally active in student associations, turned away en masse from regular politics and directed their hopes to the available parallel sector of voluntary (religious) organizations (see box 3.3). Although they did not them-

selves explicitly engage in politics, they could give, initially covert, financial, logistical, and ideological support to the banned Islamic political
groups (Rosefsky Wickham 2002: 97-102). In addition, they got secret help
from sympathizers within the bureaucracy, the municipal governments,
the official ulama, and the education system (Clark 2004). In short, while
the Mubarak regime forcefully combated open opposition within the
formal political system, new opportunities for mobilization sprung up on
the margins, in religious social organizations and networks, precisely
where banned Islamic movements such as the Muslim Brotherhood could
count on a growing number of supporters.

Box 3.3   Voluntary organizations as mobilization channels for Islamic activism

How were the politically aloof, skeptical youth aroused to activism in spite of the repression from the secret services, the army, and the police? The religiously inspired networks
of volunteers form crucial links for transmitting religious and political ideas and practices
to individual Muslims. They offer selective incentives (such as services, jobs, common
identity and ideals, moral and emotional support and status with the group) that often
seamlessly fit the needs and convictions of these youth. Empirical research shows that
many Islamic networks and political parties employ modern interpretations of proselytizing (da'wa) for the ideological underpinning of religious activism. It is a religious duty to
spread the faith among ordinary Muslims in one's neighborhood, under the slogan: first
Islamize the individual, the neighborhood, and society and after that also the state. The
da'wa of the Muslim Brotherhood, for example, propagates the idea that every true Muslim
has the obligation to help bring about social and political reform (Rosefsky Wickham
2004: 239-244). Youth, who usually have little theological knowledge but are receptive to
concrete material and social support or are spiritual 'seekers', often derive their identity
and social status from their role within Islamic voluntary organizations and religious study
and discussion groups.

Such Islamic networks play an important role in helping the youth deal with the psycholo-
gical and social stress that results from poor social perspectives. They contribute to a
process of 'religious reassessment': the embracing and upgrading of codes and norms labeled Islamic. This reassessment happens in all fields, ranging from education, gender relations, and clothing to politics. Young men without enough money to marry are advised to
pray and fast to suppress their sexual desires. Recent female graduates don the niqaab.
They marry a classmate who cannot pay a dowry and settle into a ramshackle apartment.
Goals which more than ever lie out of reach – a job with rewards based on one's achievements, a good house, consumption goods, and a marriage according to the traditional
norms of their parents – will, among believers, become explicitly devalued as the un-Islamic
attainments of the parents, apostates, or 'the West'. Thus they gain authority and status
and can thereby also more easily reject the social conventions and control of their parents.
Especially for young female graduates from the lower-middle class this can often have

surprising consequences that in part are determined by specific local circumstances. Some can move more freely in the public space precisely because they appeal to their rights within 'Islam'. Participating in religious discussion and study groups brings them into contact with (Islamic) feminist ideas that liberate them from the claims of men (Göle 1996; Rosefsky Wickham 2004: 244; White 2002; Yavuz 2003). Others are weighed down by the increasing social control and isolation of small, inwardly focused groups, and even become receptive for religious radicalization (Singerman 2004: 157).

In Egypt the openings in the political system caused Islamic groups like the Muslim Brotherhood to shift more to the political center, in spite of their illegal status. Since the 1980s political leaders within the Brotherhood have been able to run as independent candidates in parliamentary elections and form alliances with approved opposition parties in exchange for support for the principles of non-violence, pluralism, and gradualness. After the 1987 elections the Muslim Brothers were the largest opposition group in the parliament. They hammered on the issue of greater parliamentary authority to control executive power, election reforms, introduction of Sharia, more democracy and respect for human rights. Muslim Brothers and other Islamic activists also became increasingly dominant in the professional associations and voluntary organizations of engineers, doctors, lawyers, teachers, and journalists (Esposito 2003: 84).

77

However, the Brotherhood was criticized by radical Islamic groups such as the Jamaa al-Islamiyya and Islamic Jihad for participating in politics. They reproached the Brothers for legitimizing the oppressive regime and dividing the Islamic movement. The Jihad chose to work underground on its own to prepare a military coup. The Jamaa followed a strategy of military actions aimed at 'soft targets' ('immoral' locations such as discotheques, bars, and video clubs) along with a social reform strategy of assistance to the poor. Both paths were designed to lead to a broad revolutionary mass movement that will take over the state in the future. In spite of its anti-state rhetoric, the movement organized almost no militant actions against the state itself (Hafez 2003: 52).

Other political parties such as the Labor Party and the Liberal Party have combined their election lists under the name of Islamic Alliance and have even adopted some of the agenda and criticism of the Muslim Brothers. This initially confirmed for many Islamic activists the idea that the parliamentary route, however gradual, was better than the route of open struggle against the state (Hafez 2003: 48-52). Their position changed in the early 1990s, when the process of political liberalization appeared to stagnate and the state apparatus resorted to large-scale repression after an uprising of Islamic rebels in Upper Egypt. The number of formal political parties had grown to thirteen, but the role of the Brotherhood, which had become in the meantime the largest opposition force, was further restricted, in part by a redrawing of electoral districts. The Brothers thereupon boycotted the elections, and in 1990 a new parliament convened in which the opposition (with only two per cent of the seats) was even more poorly represented than in 1979. The 1995 elections were interfered with by the regime, which had hundreds of political representatives and officials of the Muslim Brotherhood arrested beforehand and later sentenced 54 leaders to prison for terms of from three to five years. Only one of the 150 candidates of the Muslim Brothers was elected to parliament. A year later, however, he was forced out of office on the grounds of belonging to a banned organization. The parliamentary political opposition in the 1990s seemed to be ultimately less representative than in the 1980s (Hafez 2004: 53).

Except for 'cheap' concessions (such as more religion in the schools and in the state-controlled media, stricter supervision of morals, etc.) neither the Muslim Brothers nor other Islamic parties and candidates had much political success in the 1990s. Attempts to assert themselves politically again through the free elections to the national professional associations were initially successful but meant that the regime then imposed strong controls on the remaining political space (Rosefsky Wickham 2002). Unlike in the 1980s Mubarak felt sufficiently confident of his power to abandon his tolerant stance and to silence his critics. That gave radical Islamic groups like Islamic Jihad and the Jamaa al-Islamiyya, that up until then had been relatively quiet for fear of losing legitimacy, arguments to denounce the Brothers even more strongly and to mobilize grassroots support for armed revolt. The political leader of the Jihad, Aboud Zumur, pointed out that even secular states like France, Germany, and Italy allowed religious political parties, but that Egypt stood out for the fact that it banned such parties (Hafez and Wiktorowicz 2004: 75).[10] He called upon the youth to abandon 'fake democracy' and to join the ranks of the holy fighters for the sake of uprooting the unjust and tyrannical state (Hafez 2003: 55).

The political leaders of the Muslim Brotherhood tried to rebut systematically these radical ideas (see table 3.1). While Jamaa defended armed resistance against the incumbent regime by referring to the sovereignty of God and the superiority of Sharia, the Brothers developed a moderate and conciliatory discourse. In their view the state in an Islamic society must stay true to the principles of Sharia, but the same state must also be accountable for its actions. They also emphasized that Sharia had very few fixed tenets: some basic principles intended to achieve justice and social and economic equality and to protect human rights such as the right to human dignity and the right to property. Moreover, juridical innovations and ijtihad were available to adapt interpretations to changing circumstances (Hafez 2003: 175). In these views we can recognize the ideas of modern reformers, such as the pupils of Mohammed Abdu (see sec. 2.3).

In a similar manner the Brothers tried to rebut the radical ideas surrounding such subjects as the place of Islam, the position of the Muslim world, jihad, and the role of democracy. They interpreted democracy and pluralism as components of the Islamic shura. On this basis they advocated democratic elections, regular alternations of power based on the electoral results achieved by political parties, and respect by the political majority for the position of minorities (see table 3.1).

Hafez shows that the taking away of political freedoms at the beginning of the 1990s does not in itself explain why Egypt was plagued by successive cycles of violent mobilization and repression in the period 1990-1997. He reveals that it was chiefly the *reactive and undifferentiated character* of the violence on the part of the government that contributed to the ability of

Table 3.1   Discourse of Jamaa al-Islamiyya (up until 1996) and Islamic Jihad versus the discourse of the Muslim Brotherhood

Theme	Jamaa and Jihad Movements	Muslim Brotherhood
The Primacy of God's Sovereignty	Only God is sovereign and can make laws. The state needs to obey His laws and rules. The interest of Islam must be above all other loyalties. Regimes and institutions that do not recognize God's sovereignty, or want to replace it, must be brought down.	God is sovereign. Islamic law has given Muslims the freedom to bring about juridical innovation and independent judgments (ijtihad). The legitimacy of the regime in an Islamic society depends on the ability of the government to earn the approval of the people.
Permissibility of Democracy	Democracy is comparable to polytheism because the system places the will of the people above that of God. Democracy is based on the concept of absolute freedom and equality. The first is impermissible as that would give Muslims free religious choice. The second is objectionable because it would imply that Muslims, Jews, and Christians, and also men and women are equal.	Democracy and pluralism are both permissible and desirable because they are part of the Islamic concept of consultation (shura). This corresponds to the democratic order that puts the power in the hands of the majority without injuring the rights of minorities who disagree or hold another position. Shura is also an extension of the authority of the nation, which designates, judges and corrects its leaders. In an Islamic society party pluralism means that executive power alternates between political parties through regular election cycles.

Source: Hafez 2003: 174-182

the Islamic activists to legitimize violence (Hafez 2003). In the 1980s the regime had more or less turned a blind eye to the fact that Islamic movements had created their own Islamic free-zones with their own paramilitary forces in Upper Egypt and Cairo. The Jamaa al-Islamiyya not only provided assistance and services to the poor, but also formed its own militias for 'supervising morals', including the enforcement of the segregation of men and women and the banning of gymnastics for girls. Jamaa's taking justice into its own hands, which was coupled with intimidation of those who did not agree with it and sectarian violence against Copts, was initially not punished by the regime as long as its actions did not draw the attention of the national or international press (Hafez and Wiktorowicz 2004: 77).

After a number of provocations the state took action at the beginning of the 1990s and assassinated the official spokesman of the Jamaa. In retaliation the movement created out of the existing militias an armed wing that attempted to murder the former chairman of the Egyptian parliament. In the course of the 1990s the military wing would generate ever more radical, militant splinter groups and underground cells that would operate independently of eachother and of the central leadership. This development also made more difficult the attempts to reach a ceasefire by secret means (Hafez 2003: 131-137). The result was successive cycles of mobilization, violence, unbridled repression, and even more violence, which reached a temporary nadir with the 1997 Luxor attack by a unit of the Jamaa, which killed 66 victims (57 of whom were tourists). In the entire period between 1992 and 1997 there were 1,200 deaths, and 47,000, mostly militant activists, were arrested.

During the first years of the struggle, the Egyptian security apparatus had no clear strategy to deal with the violence of the Jamaa; it reacted as if it were exclusively a matter of isolated incidents. Later it employed massive repression, rounding up not only the hard-core elements of the militant Jamaa and Islamic Jihad, but also the grassroots, sympathizers, family members, and anyone who (especially by appearance, such as having a beard or moustache) could be considered as an Islamic activist. There was indiscriminate torture and abuse. Wives of suspected militants were seized and held hostage and abused until their husbands finally surrendered. The activists were sentenced without trial by military courts (Hafez and Wiktorowicz 2004: 78-80).

The heavy-handed and arbitrary acts of the regime created ever more sympathizers who joined the underground militant activists in order to avoid long prison sentences or to take revenge on the state. Given that peaceful protest in favor of Islamic activism no longer meant protection from state violence, violent acts against the state, including also attacks on civilian targets, came to be seen as a logical and acceptable part of the political repertoire. The ideological frames and discourse of Jihad and Jamaa, the leading violent Islamic groups, became increasingly polarized and directed against the state. This polarized discourse referred to a struggle between Islam and heathenism (jahiliyya), between the sovereignty of God and the sovereignty of the people, and between the party of God (hizb Allah) and that of Satan (hizb al-shaytaan). Moreover, the ever-more-radicalized splinter groups of both organizations became continually more isolated from the mainstream and therefore outside of the control of the original central leadership. This was especially apparent from the initiatives by the Jamaa leadership for a unilateral ceasefire and pleas for the renunciation of violence in 1996. These efforts would have success only after the Luxor attack in 1997, when the militant resources of the splinter groups were exhausted and their leaders were imprisoned or had fled abroad (Hafez 2003: 137).

The decision to renounce violence led, remarkably enough, to a secret accord with the government in 2002 and a historic public explanation from the imprisoned Jamaa leaders about their change of course. The Egyptian authorities even allowed them to travel around the various prisons to give an account to their followers. The leaders also published four books in which they gave an underpinning, on the basis of the Quran, the Sunna, and the interpretations of legal scholars, for the thesis that armed Islamic struggle is not legitimate. Furthermore, they distanced themselves from the Jamaa doctrine and practices of the 1970s and '80s, including the strict interpretation of the sovereignty of God by Mawdudi and Qutb. In order to avoid any misunderstanding that they indeed represented a new, official position of the Jamaa, they included the names of all the authors and their sympathizers as well as all its founders and historic leaders. Some of them revealed in interviews that their process of reconsideration had begun in 1982 but had been eclipsed by the escalation of violence and radical splintering during the confrontations with the regime. In the meantime their books were widely distributed in the Arab world. According to al-Sayyid, the fact that these books based the argument for non-violence expressly on *Islamic* grounds is reason to assume that they are influential (al-Sayyid 2003: 16-19).

In the first book the authors explain that the call for a cessation of violence is based on the self-interest of the Jamaa and the *Ummah* in preventing internal strife. Continuing the armed struggle would only play into the hands of the enemies of Islam, including Israel, the US, and the secularists in the Muslim world. Moreover, Sharia forbids violence against Muslims and non-Muslims, even in the name of jihad. The second book continues with this theme. It explains that the Jamaa had erred by seeking armed confrontation with the Egyptian regime. Furthermore, it implicitly distanced itself from the jihad ideology of Muslim scholars such as Ibn Taymiyya (who lived in the thirteenth century); it is precisely the obligation of Muslims to protect tourists and guests. Books three and four, to conclude, take positions against the practice of *takfir* (pronouncing someone an apostate), which some groups within Islamic movements use against politicians, intellectuals, and others who, in their view, do not give the 'correct' interpretation of Islam or who cooperate with non-Muslims. The authors confirm that this practice is based on an extremely strict interpretation of Islamic scholarship that stems from a misunderstanding of the true nature of the religion and the meaning of the scriptures. They also distance themselves from earlier practices of the Jamaa militias and other fanatic followers, such as acts against 'decadent behavior' or using intimidation and violence to enforce their own rules and religious interpretations.

In spite of the moderation of the Brotherhood and the Jamaa, the regime continued its predominantly repressive approach. It even appears that Mubarak found the more moderate tone and the electoral successes of the Brothers more threatening than the violence of the terrorists (Rosefsky Wickham 2002: 215). In the full glare of the state-controlled media, he had prominent leaders charged with membership of a banned organization and the undermining of state security. Through the imposition of prison sentences they were removed from the political arena and many other political activists were frightened off. Therefore, the Brotherhood ended up initially further on the political sideline and experienced a crisis. The older leaders encountered increasing criticism from the younger generations, who reproached them for being ideologically rigid and autocratic, and insufficiently open to constructive debate and coalitions with other parties. In 1996 several prominent critics decided to form a new party called *al-Wasat* (the Center). This party, whose founders included women and Copts, was initially considered by the regime as a clone of and front for the Brotherhood. One of the principal founders, the now 47-year-old engineer Abu-l-Ila Madi, two party sponsors, and thirteen leaders of the Brotherhood were arrested and accused of membership of an illegal organization and of conducting political activities without authorization. Ultimately eight Muslim Brothers were sentenced to prison terms. The Wasat founders were released after the Egyptian authorities had assured themselves that the relations between Wasat and the Brotherhood were anything but amicable.

Unlike the Brotherhood, which remains vulnerable to being officially accused of being a religious – and therefore banned – movement, Wasat emphatically labels itself a political party that is not linked to the Islamic faith but to 'Islamic culture' on the basis of *citizenship*. With this concept

the party stresses the striving for a society in which Muslims and Christians would have an equal place as Egyptian citizens (ICG 2004b: 17).
They expressively distance themselves from the da'wa and Islamization
policy of the Brotherhood and following the example of modern, formally
recognized, Islamically oriented parties in Turkey, Jordan, Yemen, and
Malaysia are trying to become a broad party with a moderate, democratic,
and reform-minded direction and a willingness to form alliances. Because
of this stance, they have also received support from a number of prominent
secular opposition leaders (Rosefsky Wickham 2002: 211-220). The party
(now officially called Hizb al-Wasat al-Gedid, the New Center Party)
seems close to winning official recognition.

The Brotherhood in the meantime seems to have learned from this political
competitor and is making an unexpected political comeback. It seems clear
by now that a moderate, more inclusive and democratic position appeals to
voters. During the November 2005 parliamentary elections no fewer than
88 of the 444 seats were won by politicians from the Brotherhood, who
presented themselves as 'independent' candidates. They were allowed
to stand for elections in a mere 150 of these 444 districts. Although still
formally banned, the Brotherhood is now the largest opposition group in
the parliament (*Economist* 2006).

What tentative conclusions can we draw from the emergence of Egyptian
Islamic political movements? It is clear that the actions of the state had a great
influence on the movements' development (al-Sayyid 2004: 6; ICG 2004b:
2). Under Sadat the state initially tried to strengthen its political legitimacy
by giving a clear field for Islamic activists of the Brotherhood and by consciously playing the religious card. For example, in 1971 and in 1980 he had
Sharia introduced into the constitution as respectively 'a' and then 'the main'
source of legislation (see Chapter 4). His successor Mubarak, who had to
maneuver extremely carefully after the Camp David Accords, initially
offered more political and social space to Islamic activists. At the same time
he adopted parts of the Islamization agenda, especially in sectors and
institutions such as religious education, the state-controlled media, and universities. In addition to reinforcing his legitimacy this effort was expressly
intended to maintain his grip on the official interpretation of Islam and to
give alternative tendencies as little opportunity as possible. For these reasons for the past two decades he has also strengthened the position of the
traditional, orthodox-oriented ulama at al-Azhar University, a policy that is
at the expense of free-thinking and enlightened as well as radical and fundamentalist interpretations of Islam (Wessels 2001: 70; Kodmani 2005: 9-14).
What Mubarak initially underestimated was the speed and effectiveness
by which Islamic activists could use resources and mobilization channels
to mobilize their grassroots (Hafez 2003). With their own, more effective

social services and institutions they merciless exposed the shortcomings of the government bureaucracy. The Brotherhood, in particular, thanks to a strong, well-organized network of volunteer organizations and ample financial resources, became in a short time a dominant factor in social life. This has become clearly visible in the public discourse and the public space, where more and more religious schools, clinics, and banks have sprung up, where Islamic symbols have appeared, and where religious literature in great quantities is sold. There is also an increasingly more massive following of the religious prescriptions regarding clothing and behavior (such as the head scarf, the ban on alcohol, attendance at Friday prayer, and fasting during Ramadan) (Esposito 2003; al-Sayyid 2004). This increases the dilemma facing the regime and the secular elite; through the ban on Islamic parties, they preserve the predominance of Islamic movements in social welfare.

The decision to finally dismantle individual radical groups with massive violence after a phase of tolerating them led to a predictable pattern of escalation: exclusion and further radicalization was answered by violent repression by the security apparatus and that led again to resistance, further marginalization, radicalization, and violence (Hafez 2003: 201). The state in these actions struck not only at violent terrorist groups but also at groups that were prepared to follow the rules of the political and legal order. Thus the borders between protecting the constitutional state against terrorism and violating human rights became blurred (Esposito 2003: 85).

Since breaking out of the spiral of violence in 1997 the overwhelming majority of Islamic activists have renounced violence. Nevertheless the position of Islamic parties and movements remains uncertain. Their leaders are sometimes tolerated or co-opted into the political and social order, and at other times they are rounded up and declared an enemy of the state. They are not given formal recognition out of fear that the ruling NDP and other, marginal, secular parties would lose still more ground (ICG 2004b: 2). As long as other credible (Islamic) social and political counter-forces are still lacking, this same political elite is, however, not prepared to abandon the status quo (Perthes 2004a: 304, 2004d: 34). On the other hand, the voters seem to have rewarded the candidates of the Islamic parties for their responsible attitude during the election campaign at the end of 2005 and their readiness to reach compromises with other democratic opposition forces (Kodmani 2005: 20).

3.4.2 ELSEWHERE IN THE MUSLIM WORLD

In the 1970s and '80s the Algerian regime was considered as the typical model in the Middle East: an authoritarian government that after independence, under pressure from the precarious geopolitical situation in the

region, became increasingly dependent on the army and the security apparatus (Singerman 2004: 146). Like Sadat in Egypt, President Boumediene
undertook a charm offensive just after the rise of Islamic groups. He gave
the traditional religious elite more influence within the Ministries of
Education, Religious Affairs, and Justice. His successor Bendjedid introduced new family legislation that reflected conservative interpretations of
Islam. But at the same time he also tried to channel via political institutions
the discontent among the population about the state's economic mismanagement. After more than thirty years of rule by a single party, he amended
the constitution to end the dominant position of the National Liberation
Front (NFL). He allowed formal recognition of political parties, which
brought about a multi-party system. Fourteen parties were founded,
including the Islamic Social Movement (Hamas), the Islamic Renaissance
Movement (MNI), and the Islamic Salvation Front (FIS), an umbrella organization of Islamic opposition parties that could count on broad support
among the population. In addition to a moderate, liberal wing, the FIS also
revealed a militant side; for example, during political protest marches and
mass demonstrations there were calls to have the Islamic shura as an alternative to democracy. Nevertheless, the leadership of the party was not
ready to introduce an Islamic state by revolutionary means because in a
short time the new parliamentary path had already produced too many
direct benefits and had won respect among the population. The result was
that the radical groups still occupied a marginal position in 1991 (Hafez
2003: 42-43).

Bendjedid hoped to be able to use the FIS strategically to counter the old
leftist guard of the FLN and the army that remained strongly opposed to
far-reaching economic liberalization. He declared himself ready to cooperate with a FIS-dominated parliamentary majority, even when this party at
the end of 1991 after earlier mass demonstrations and a victory in local elections, was on the point of winning an overwhelming victory during the
national elections (Noyon 2003: 121).[11] Soon after that the army intervened,
however. It announced a state of emergency, forced the president to resign,
invalidated the election results, and banned the FIS. Nevertheless the leaders of the party still tried to find a political solution by taking a common
position with the FLN and the socialist party against the military coup.
They also appealed to the Supreme Court for a lifting of the ban on the
party and called for the release of political prisoners and the resumption of
the election process.

These interventions, however, were of no avail because the radical groups
within and outside the FIS were stirred up due to the military coup. They
managed to convince many disappointed FIS supporters that the democratic process ultimately served only the interests of the secular regime. If

the outcome did not suit the regime, the process would be scrapped (Hafez 2003: 43). Neither could the FIS count on international support because the official reading of the events, and one that was also accepted by the West, was that the Algerian army had intervened to protect democracy from the FIS strategy of one man, one vote, one time (Esposito 2003: 80). In reality, the army acted mercilessly against all Islamic activists, regardless of the nature of their activities. In early February 1992 between 6,000 and 30,000 FIS activists, including 500 mayors and municipal councilors, were thrown into jails in the Sahara and tried as terrorists before special military courts. Persecuted by the army and the security forces that more and more often perpetrated mass killings and 'disappearances', the FIS broke into compet- ing radical splinter groups. In 1993 a number of them came together to form the Gamaa al-Islamiyya al-Musalaha (that is, the GIA), a movement that underwent radicalization, as had the Jamaa al-Islamiyya and the Islamic Jihad in Egypt. Here, as well, undifferentiated repression resulted in a radicalization and further escalation of violence against military and civilian targets.

In Syria (secular) students, trade unions, and Muslim Brothers pursued simultaneous and sometimes joint opposition by means of strikes and protest marches. By co-opting some of the secular political leaders (partic- ularly those from the middle class) and by heavy repression of other forces of the secular opposition, the socialist regime of al-Assad succeeded in driving a wedge between them. Just as in Egypt, there arose among the Syrian Muslim Brothers a division between the activists who wanted to reach their goal through peaceful means and those who chose violence. However, the regime shifted to persecuting both groups. This again led to a spiral of violence and repression, in which the violent wings of the Muslim Brothers carried out guerilla actions and terrorist attacks, and the regime acted across the board with increasing repression against its own popula- tion.[12] A direct result was that the majority of the population, certainly including the secular opposition, became just as averse to its own repres- sive state as to violent Islamic activism.

The manner by which the regimes in the Middle East attempted to control Islamic activist movements was certainly not unique. We see that regimes everywhere aimed at the granting of concessions to religious activists, the use of Islam to legitimate their power, and the reinforcing of control over (official) religion. The degree to which this occurred, however, was deter- mined in part by the internal and external room for maneuver of these regimes. In countries where the process of nation-building was already under severe pressure (such as in Pakistan after Bangladesh split off in 1971 and in Afghanistan) it turned out that the concessions could not be with- drawn or reversed. In Pakistan, for example, General Zia continued his

destructive Islamization policy. Moreover, he employed, under the supervising eye of the Arab world and the US, the Jamaat-i-Islami as a foreign
policy instrument in the struggle against Soviet troops in Afghanistan
(Fair 2005: 273; Roy 2004: 291).

It is notable that regimes outside the Middle East offered openings for political participation well before the revival of Islamic activism in the 1970s.
Thus countries such as Malaysia, Bangladesh, and Indonesia appeared to be
better able to take the wind out of the sails of radical Islamic movements and
parties. In Malaysia the ruling coalition under the leadership of the UMNO
managed to introduce, with the support of the Malaysian Islamic Party
(PAS) and the large Muslim youth movement (ABIM), a policy balancing
secularism, economic modernization, and a restricted Islamization of the
state and the law for the benefit of the Muslim population (55 % of the total
population). Non-Muslim minorities (Chinese, Indians) remained largely
protected from the effects of Islamization (Harding in Otto et al. 2006).
At the same time the government of Prime Minister Mahathir took strong
action against violent Islamic groups. In Bangladesh the government initially
embraced the secular state and repressed the Islamic forces. The 1975 military
takeover led, however, to a fifteen-year period of military rule (including
subsequent military coups) during which Islamic political forces gradually
were granted a place in the political arena. Just as in Pakistan, this was
coupled with a policy of social and cultural Islamization, but unlike in
Pakistan, the path to further political liberalization in the early 1990s was
not blocked. Islamic parties were further integrated into the – otherwise
extremely turbulent – political climate. Indonesia, whose 1945 constitution
mentioned not Islam explicitly but "the belief in the one and all-powerful
God", nonetheless excluded Islamic movements completely from the political arena. After his military coup Suharto legalized three political parties
(Golkar, PPP, PDI) which came under the control of the government. The
Islamic PPP and the democratic-nationalist PDI could carry out a mild sort
of opposition within the margins of his stable police-state. Since his departure in 1998 Islamic parties have had a freer rein.

In other parts of the Muslim world as well political participation offered a
safety valve for Islamic activism which confined radical groups to the
margins. In African states like Mali, Mauritania, Senegal, Guinea, and
Niger, for example, Islamic opposition movements were less dominant and
the threat of radical Islamization was chiefly seen, in spite of the takeover
in Sudan, as a typically 'Arab' problem. At the same time these regimes
dealt in extremely pragmatic fashion with the Islamic opposition. In Mali,
for example, the new constitution of 1974 emphasized continuity with the
earlier secular constitution and the principles of universal human rights.
In practice, the government of President Traoré gave Muslim movements

preferential treatment with respect to Christians in certain areas (broadcasting time, for instance). This step was prompted by the political weight of prominent Muslim families with international business contacts in the Middle East (Schultz in Otto et al. 2006).

In Central Asia the role of Islamic activism is strongly tied to the legacy of Russian colonialism and the later, 'Sovietizing' of the region, that lasted around seventy years. In the 1920s the Bolsheviks carried out a merciless purification campaign against religion. In this way, Islam completely disappeared from public life in Soviet states such as Uzbekistan, Turkmenistan, Tajikistan, Kyrgyzstan, Kazakhstan, and Azerbaijan. The passing on of religious knowledge and rituals was restricted and Muslims in the Soviet Union were isolated from the modern political thought of people such as Qutb, al-Banna and Mawdudi. The result of this was that Islam remained to be sure a part of the local identity, but it was almost completely reduced to customs and traditions. Unlike in neighboring Pakistan and Afghanistan, where someone who called himself a Muslim also observed certain religious rituals, an Uzbek or a Turkmen, for example, could automatically consider himself a Muslim without regard for his personal religious convictions. After independence in the 1990s there arose in these new countries a search for a new national identity, in the course of which Islam was also 'rediscovered'. Religious education reappeared on the scene after seventy years, mosques were reopened, and Muslims came into contact with the ideologies and developments elsewhere in the Muslim world, in part thanks to the missionary work of diverse tendencies including Wahhabism, the Fetullah Gülen movement, Hizb ut-Tahrir etc. Moreover, the new interest in Islam extended to its political manifestations, including activism directed against the secular establishment.

The former communist regimes that without exception remained in power after the revolutions were all fearful of Islamic activism. In Uzbekistan the repression of Islam led to the flight of many Muslim activists to Tajikistan and then to Afghanistan, where they formed the Islamic Movement of Uzbekistan which was allied with the Taliban. In Tajikistan the political opposition of the Islamic Renaissance Party (IRP) culminated in a civil war against the former communist regime. A peace accord was finally reached in 1997 after the former communist leader Rakhmonov approved the legal recognition of the IRP. Since then he has further undermined the position of the party in the political system, however, and, as a result, more radical, in part transnational, groups such as Hizb ut-Tahrir have gained in strength. The latter group, which in the meantime has been banned in Russia, Pakistan, Germany, and parts of the Middle East, presents itself as a non-violent group that advocates strict adherence to

Islamic behavior codes and strives through personal and social changes to establish an Islamic caliphate (ICG 2003c; Wessels 2001: 136). At the same time the movement does not renounce violent jihad, and individual members continue to be involved in terrorist attacks and military coup attempts in the Middle East (Baran ed. 2004).

In Turkmenistan President Niyazov has even combined the suppression of every form of independent religious activity with a personality cult that also draws on so-called 'Islamic' elements; mosques and schools are compelled to teach the *Rukhnama*, Niyazov's own book of folk wisdom, Turkmen history, and pseudo-spirituality, as a text alongside the Quran. Although the authorities in the other Central Asian countries do not go so far, they also consider all forms of Islamic activism as a potential threat to the political order which demands harsh and repressive government action. At the same time they try to engage Islam as an ideological instrument for their own political objectives. Just as elsewhere both developments increase the risk that not only the extremists but also the enlightened religious voices and activist groups will become marginalized. And that can quickly lead to further radicalization. Given the dramatically deteriorated economic and social situation, the restricted political freedoms, and widespread corruption of the past ten years, it is not surprising that Islamic activism, including radical underground movements like Hizb ut-Tahrir, are winning support even in the strongly secular former Soviet republics. After all, they now belong to the very few movements that expose the social, economic, and political problems in the region (ICG 2003c).

3.4.3   **TRANSNATIONAL MOVEMENTS**

In the above discussion the attention was chiefly focused on the interaction between Islamic social movements and networks, on the one hand, and the state, on the other. We saw that movements like the Muslim Brotherhood and the Jamaat-i Islami initially oriented themselves toward the worldwide Muslim community (the *Ummah*). Just as Islam itself never respected political borders and spread by trade, missionaries, and conquests, their ideal of the Islamic project still remains universal and not tied to the national state. In the meantime both 'mother-movements' functioned as international organizations with autonomous national branches. Just as, for example, socialist and communist parties respectively have their own Socialist and Communist Internationals through which they maintain mutual contact, the Islamic parties and movements use their 'mother-movements' as a forum for exchanging ideas, experiences, and strategies (Fuller 2003: 42).

Thanks to the global spreading of new technologies, means of transportation and communication, increasingly intensive migration, and the extensive network of transnational NGOs, Islamic banks, businesses, and educational institutions, such contacts are also easier to maintain (Mandaville 2000). At the same time most of the movements and parties in the Muslim world, just as many socialist and communist parties before them, over time have developed a political agenda and strategy attuned to their own specific political context. Where they have gained access to the national political arena and have to keep up their position in the regular political competition, most Islamic parties have renounced violence and for pragmatic reasons have abandoned the striving for ideological purity and exclusivity (ICG 2005a: 7-8). These processes of de-radicalization, 'nationalization of Islamic activism', and Islamization of the discourse on democracy, pluralism, and human rights are clearly visible in many places in the Middle East, Asia, and in Turkey (Roy 2004: 62-63).

On the other hand, some extremist movements have been gradually transformed into fragmented, informal, and closed terrorist networks with a transnational orientation. The roots of this phenomenon lie in the 1980s, in the reactions to the aftermath of the Iranian revolution, the war in Afghanistan, and the struggle of radicalized activists against the incumbent regimes in Egypt and Algeria. The anti-Western and pro-Shiite position of Iran under Khomeini (that supported, among others, the radical Shiite Hezbollah in Lebanon) was the direct cause for Saudi Arabia to mobilize internationally active, anti-Shiite and anti-communist forces. Supported by its ally, the US, and by conservative Arab regimes, the country launched itself as the disseminator of conservative Wahhabism to Sudan, Pakistan, Afghanistan, Indonesia, Central Asia, and also Europe, among other places. Also the Salafiyya movement mentioned above became increasingly more imbued with Wahhabist influences (ICG 2005a: 10). In particular, some Pakistani madrasas became breeding grounds for jihadists, who later would also be involved in the wars in Afghanistan, Bosnia, and Chechnya (Hafez 2003: 61; Singerman 2004: 157-158). In the 1990s these conflicts provided violent groups like al-Qaeda and Hezbollah important ideological stimuli, financial resources, and manpower to organize themselves transnationally. [13] Other groups that could rely on Saudi support included the Arab Muslim Brothers, Hassan al-Turabi's NIF, the Mujahideen in Afghanistan, the Hizb-i Islami in Kashmir, the Moros in the Philippines, the Deobandi movement and other radical splinter groups in Turkey. In addition, increasingly greater sums of money went to radical groups among the migrant communities in Europe, including the young 'diaspora radicals' (Wessels 2001: 58; Roy 1994: 118; Rabassa et al. 2005: 445-446).

This radicalized transnational activism has been characterized since the 1990s by its explicitly anti-Western character. Followers and sympathizers of such organizations as al-Qaeda no longer direct their attacks and propaganda exclusively at the governments of Muslim countries that they deem to be insufficiently religious but also at the US, Israel, and their allies. Their field of operations has become global and their tactics suggest 'elite urban terrorism' more than the traditional guerilla war of volunteers in Afghanistan (ICG 2005a: 16-17). With relatively limited resources, they have succeeded in giving 'Islamic', jihadist, and especially anti-Western overtones to existing geopolitical conflicts and rivalries within and outside the Muslim world, like the Balkan wars, the struggles in Kashmir and Chechnya, the Palestinian conflict, and the war in Iraq. This effect is reinforced by the influence of the (visual) media, which mercilessly magnify the interconnectedness between what takes place inside and outside a country's borders. They allow the image of continuous religious conflict between Muslims and non-Muslims to make a deep impression, which also arouses worldwide solidarity among Muslims (and their opponents). As Graham Fuller notes:

"Today Muslims see themselves as under siege, particularly Muslim minorities, but it is not just that Bosnians are perhaps being killed because they are Muslims; Bosnians see Chechnyans being killed, and Chechnyans see Palestinians being killed, and Palestinians see Cashmirians being killed. And Cashmirians see Moro's in the Philippines being killed. (...) young men [in Southern Thailand] have been watching television, and they have been watching the war in Iraq, and they are saying 'that is us!' They see themselves. There is this echo effect across the Muslim world. It is possible to see on television what is happening to other Muslims. And this intensifies the feeling that would not be the case if it was simply Rwandans, because their ethnic or religious links to Rwanda are very weak." (Fuller 2005: 24)

Since September 11 this mechanism has worked almost equally well in the West. The shared feeling of humiliation and being under siege in the Muslim world that Osama bin Laden so flawlessly managed to play on is the mirror image of the growing fear of Islam and Islamic terrorism that has seized non-Muslims in the West (Coolsaet 2005: 19-20; ICG 2005a: 25). That equally great tensions are arising *within* the Muslim world fades into the background.

3.4.4 CONCLUSION

In Egypt as in other parts of the Muslim world, the most authoritarian regimes tried to rein in the upsurge of revolutionary Islamic activism in the 1970s and the formation of Islamic political movements and parties through repression or co-optation. Many have also made use of Islam itself to legitimate their power. Since that time the religious establishment has either been made almost completely subordinate to the authoritarian government or has been co-opted in exchange for further Islamization of public life or government institutions. Nevertheless it appears in many countries that the mainstream of the Islamic activist movements has become in the meantime more reform-minded and moderate than revolutionary and violent. But if after a phase of political liberalization the moderate mainstream is suddenly confronted with complete political exclusion or violent repression, the chances increase that splinter groups will become radicalized. Algeria has become a notorious example of this phenomenon. Just as the Iranian revolution became the specter for many authoritarian regimes in the 1980s, so 'Algerian-type troubles' were dreaded everywhere in the 1990s. In addition to these dramatic events, the direct experience with the carrying out of (underground and regular) political opposition within the national arena spurred the opposition's pragmatic strategies of moderation, coalition forming, and support for the path of gradual change. The unconditional institutional inclusion of Islamic political tendencies and movements into the regular political order is certainly not without risk, as can be seen from the examples of Sudan and Pakistan. But a gradual moving towards the political arena, as the examples of Egypt and Turkey show, can in time also contribute to further moderation of the mainstream, to marginalization of the violent, radical minority, and to gradual democratization. It is in any case certain that as long as Islamic political movements enjoy the support of broad levels of the population and there are no credible alternative political movements, genuine democratization in the Muslim world cannot occur without them.

3.5   INTERPRETATION OF THE POLITICAL DYNAMISM

3.5.1   ACCESS TO THE POLITICAL ARENA

The current and future dynamism of Islamic activist movements and parties is closely linked to the degree of openness of the political arena. We saw earlier that during the rise of Islamic activism in the 1970s an overwhelming majority of countries had authoritarian regimes (sec. 3.2). In the Middle East and North Africa only Lebanon had the status of a democratic country (a Polity score of 4 or higher). If we compare these indicators with the most recent scores, we can observe the following: of the 48 countries with a Muslim majority, ten have a Polity score of four or higher (see appendix 1). In 2002 only six countries of the 48 were labeled 'electoral democracy': Mali, Niger, Senegal, Bangladesh, Albania, and Turkey (appendix 2). On the other hand, increasingly more Muslims (within and outside countries with a Muslim majority) live in a context of political liberalization and democratization; according to estimates, some 700 million Muslims at present live in an electorally democratic or democratizing society, namely those living in Indonesia, Bangladesh, India, North America, and Europe (United States Institute of Peace 2003).

The regional differences within the Muslim world are very great, however. Among Muslim countries in sub-Saharan Africa there has been an improvement of Polity scores, political rights, and civil liberties (appendix 1). Seven countries in the region are labeled 'partly free,' and Mali and Senegal are considered to be free. In Asia, the situation in Indonesia, the largest Muslim country in the world, had sharply improved, although it was not yet deemed to be an electoral democracy by the compilers of the Polity score in 2003. On the other hand, the situation in Afghanistan, the Maldives, and Pakistan has considerably deteriorated compared to the beginning of the 1970s. The Middle East region and North Africa show remarkably little improvement in political freedoms. To be sure, five of the 21 countries in the region are considered 'partly free' (namely Bahrain, Yemen, Jordan, Kuwait, and Morocco), but a number of countries (Libya, Qatar, Saudi Arabia, and the United Arab Emirates [UAE]) have experienced no noticeable improvement in Polity scores between the early 1970s and 2003. In short, the Middle East is still much more authoritarian than other regions. Just as the successive *Arab Human Development Reports* indicate, the lack of political and civil freedoms in the Muslim world is to a great extent (but not exclusively) a problem of the Arab world (see table 3.2).

93

What overall conclusions can we draw on the direct participation of (Islamic) political parties and movements in the political arena? Saudi Arabia is the only Muslim country that does not allow the formation of any political parties. In 2003 thirteen of the 48 Muslim countries were labeled 'politically closed'. Another seventeen were designated as countries where elections were held where no real political competition could take place (this type of regime is called, 'electoral, non-competitive, authoritarian', see appendix 2). Since the beginning of the 1990s more and more citizens (some for the first time or for the first time in a long while) are able to exercise the right to vote for legislative parliaments, which, however, have very limited powers. At the same time in many Muslim countries citizens still have no direct influence on the representatives with executive power (president, reigning king). Here the authoritarian regimes in the Middle East win hands down: elections are regularly held, parliaments are chosen, and there is a great deal of lip service rendered to the Islamic bases of the state and the law, but the possibility of an (Islamic) opposition party defeating the incumbent regimes through a democratic mandate remains for the time being out of the question. Those holding political power are

Table 3.2   Polity scores of Arab and non-Arab Muslim countries

Polity IV score, 2003	Non-Arab Muslim country	Arab Muslim country
+10		
+9		
+8	Senegal	
+7	Albania, Indonesia, Turkey	
+6	Bangladesh, Mali	
+5	Sierra Leone	
+4	Comoros, Niger, Nigeria	
+3	Iran, Malaysia	
+2	Djibouti	
+1		
0	Burkina Faso	
–1	Guinea	
–2	Chad	Yemen, Jordan
–3	Kyrgyzstan, Tajikistan	Algeria
–4		Tunisia
–5	Gambia, Pakistan	
–6	Kazakhstan, Mauritania, Sudan	Egypt, Morocco
–7	Azerbaijan, Eritrea	Bahrain, Kuwait, Libya, Syria
–8		Oman, UAR
–9	Uzbekistan, Turkmenistan	Iraq
–10		Qatar, Saudi Arabia

There are no scores for Afghanistan, Iraq, Lebanon, and Somalia because of an interruption of regime or a temporary regime. There are no independent Polity IV scores available for Brunei, the Maldives, and the West Bank/Gaza.

Source: Polity IV score

able to retain that power through shifting alliances, by playing opponents off against each other and buying off the interested parties, by continual alteration of the electoral system, and the maintenance or the periodic introduction of emergency rule. They manage to estimate the strength of the opposition and to attune their own actions accordingly. They continue to deal with the opposition from a dominant position from which they keep control of the (new) rules of the political game and can limit the authority of parliament. Parties and political leaders who reject this game, however, run the risk of being forced further to the political margins. Islamic political parties are relatively often confronted with exclusion, repression, and manipulation (Jones-Luong and Lust-Okar 2002).

The political elites in the Middle East and their allies in the West face major dilemmas. Their first dilemma is that the experiences of the population with parliamentary systems and more or less democratic institutions are still relatively limited, while those with terrorism lie still fresh in their memory. Secular elites in particular raise many questions about continuous political liberalization that is accompanied with political and economic instability (Noyon 2003). They fear the scenario of one man, one vote, one time, in which democratically elected Islamic parties abolish the democratic system. On the other hand, to date there has been no precedent for a situation in which Islamic activists have achieved power in a democratic manner via the voting booth and then have abolished democracy. As Roy concludes:

"The evolution of Algeria's FIS, Turkey's Refah Partisi (Welfare Party), Tunisia's Nahda party and the liberals in Iran towards if not democratic, then at least parliamentarian movements – advocating elections, political coalitions, democracy and the defence of 'civil society' in the face of authoritarian secular states or conservative religious leaders – is evidence enough that many Islamic groups have become 'normal' national parties, and that the principal obstacle to democracy is not the Islamists *per se*, but the Muslim world's more or less secular authoritarian state, supported by the West."
(Roy 2005: 2)

95

The second dilemma concerns the great distance between the political process and the ordinary people in many Muslim countries, a distance that Western societies increasingly must also have to face today, for that matter. In 1992 Fatima Mernissi expressed aptly why certain groups of Moroccans, for example, still distrusted democracy. All of them, regardless of education or class, could see the advantages of a mobile telephone or owning a car but not of a relatively abstract concept such as democracy. Therefore some had the idea that democracy was mostly for university-educated, cosmopolitan youth with a knowledge of Western culture.[14]

3.5.2   GROWING DIVERSITY

How should the political dynamism be interpreted against this background? First there appears to be growing diversity. Since the 1979 Iranian revolution more and more different movements have arisen that defy a simple division into fundamentalist or moderate, violent or peaceful, *Ummah*-wide or oriented to the nation state (ICG 2005).[15] In an attempt to chart the current landscape, a distinction must be made, following the example of the ICG, first between Shiite and Sunni movements. At least eighty percent of all Muslims are Sunnis. Although, in the West, Shiite movements since the Iranian revolution are usually associated with radical movements directed to the restoration of the *Ummah*, most of them today are active exclusively within the national context. This applies to Azerbaijan, Bahrain, and Iraq, where the majority of the population is Shiite. It also applies to Lebanon, Yemen, Kuwait, Pakistan, Afghanistan, Saudi Arabia, the United Arab Emirates, Syria, Turkey, India, Sri Lanka, Burma, and eastern and southern Africa, where Shiites are in the minority. Shiite minority activism is characteristically chiefly directed at the defense of the interests of the Shiite group against those of other population groups and the state. For this reason, the specific goals, the political discourse, the forms of expression and the instruments of Shiite movements vary according to the national and local political contexts (ICG 2005a). In Pakistan, for example, where about fifteen to twenty percent of the population is Shiite, Shiite activists traditionally promote the interests of their community in the areas of education and legislation, witness also their advocacy of separate textbooks for religious education in state schools.

Under the broad umbrella of Islamic activism further general distinctions can be made on the basis of strategies, orientations, and resources (see table 3.3): movements that emphasize *evolutionary political* activism, *revolutionary* (jihad) activism, movements that employ chiefly *social* activism, and those that focus on *missionary activities* (Yavuz 2004: 274). The first two strategies aim at a top-down Islamization, using the state and the political and judicial systems. They make use of a political vanguard that strongly influences the strategy, tactics, resources, and discourse of the movement. The other two types of activism strive chiefly for Islamization from the bottom up, through social groups, organizations, and individuals. They try to change society from the inside out. The more group-oriented variants do this by mobilizing the communities in which debate takes place. Since the economic (and in a number of countries political) liberalization of the 1980s they chiefly make use of their own media and means of communication (newspapers, publishing houses, Internet, TV) and economic and social networks (banks, social services, associations, schools) to create free spaces for their Islamic discourses. The more individualistic, spiritual, and missionary-oriented variants regard changes in one's inner self and spirituality as the key to social transformation. They are exponents of the increasing fragmentation of the authority of the traditional ulama that, through their close ties to the authoritarian state, often have lost credibility and face competition from self-declared religious leaders, Sufi movements, and religiously inspired intellectuals (Piscatori 2000: 4). If these spiritual groups close themselves up even more strongly in their own communities of believers, there is a chance that they will withdraw from the legal political and juridical framework of the national state. But by engaging with, and integrating into society through missionary work, they can also transform into socially and politically oriented organizations.

Politically activist groups can have, in addition to an evolutionary program, social and religious organizations and a militant revolutionary branch. Depending on the obstacles in the external environment, such as the space to maneuver in the political arena, they will employ alternating mobilization strategies and resources and also adjust their frames of meaning and political discourse. The classifications in table 3.3 thus do not suggest that these strategies and orientations are mutually exclusive or immutable; changes in the mobilization factors described above (sec. 3.2.2) often lead also to changes in the orientation, strategies, and direction of development of activist movements.

Table 3.3   Orientations of Islamic activist movements

Vertical	Evolutionary	Revolutionary
State-centered Vanguard movement Top down	Participating with the goal to controlling it or influencing policy through the formation of their own political parties or through coalitions with other parties	Directed against the the system, taking over the state
Directed at	Political arena, juridical and constitutional system, social services, education	The state/states
Most likely development	Accommodation	Confrontation
Examples	Refah Party, AKP	Tanzim al Jihad, Islamic Jihad
Horizontal	**Social, daily life**	**Missionary, spiritual**
Socially directed Associations Identity-oriented Bottom up	Groups use their own organizations, associations, the media and communications networks to create debate space for the construction of an Islamic identity; Islam considered as cultural capital; market-oriented and directed at networks and associations to mobilize the community	Striving for inner purity and religious self-awareness
Directed at	Media, economy, (private)education, social services	Religious communities, mosques associations, education
Most likely development	Integration	Isolation, parallel autonomous communities
Examples	Islamic NGOs, etc	Tablighi, Salafiyya

The growing diversity within the Muslim world means that more and more competing Islamic movements present themselves on the national political and social stage. The largest political activist movement in the Middle East and North Africa is the Muslim Brotherhood, which has branches in Jordan, Lebanon, Kuwait, Sudan, Iraq, and Yemen. The Brotherhood also supports other national organizations including the Tunisian Nahda party, the Moroccan Justice and Development Party (PJD), and – the exception to the rule regarding nonviolence – Hamas in Palestine. Other movements are linked to the Jamaat-i-Islami. In addition to their home base in Pakistan, these can be found in India, Bangladesh, Central Asia and North Africa. Elsewhere in the Muslim world we encounter politically oriented tendencies in countries like Turkey, Indonesia, Pakistan, Malaysia, Turkmenistan, Nigeria, and Sudan.

3.5.3 FROM REVOLUTIONARY PAN-ISLAMISM TO EVOLUTIONARY RELIGIOUS NATIONALISM

In addition to a growing diversity, a second trend is visible. The *politically* oriented activist movements have mostly abandoned their revolutionary and militant aspirations for an evolutionary, moderate path within the national state. Instead of striving to replace the secular national state, by violence if necessary, with an (*Ummah*-wide) Islamic state, they aim at participation in the political order and taking part in elections as a regular political party. That means that the revolutionary power of Islamic activism has largely past its peak. This change is in part the result of a realization that the social costs of anarchy and of possible state failure are enormously high, including the possibility that the mobilized population could, in such a case, easily turn against the revolutionary leaders. In part it also reflects a more recent political learning process of Islamic movements, their leaders, followers, and the governments in Muslim countries. In most countries where activists have acquired any access to the political arena, the benefits of using political channels have appeared in general greater than the costs of armed confrontation with the state that controls a powerful and experienced security apparatus. Therefore the activists stand less and less of a chance of taking over the state. The state, however, pays the price of a diminished grip on the public arena and the social manifestations of Islamic activism (Fuller 2003: 126, 169).

The development of the Egyptian Muslim Brotherhood exemplifies this evolutionary process. Begun as a fundamentalist, explicitly anti-state movement, the Brotherhood has now turned into a more moderate political opposition force that functions as a political party. The Brothers recognize not only the legitimacy of the Egyptian state but also the current government. The electoral success of the leaders of the Brotherhood has also brought the imprisoned leaders of the once-so-radical Jamaa to the realization that social Islamization from the bottom up and a future role in the electoral system are more effective than armed resistance (al-Sayyid 2004: 22). A comparable development process has taken place among the Muslim Brothers in Jordan, the PJD in Morocco, al-Nahda in Tunisia, and Refah in Turkey. We also see a preference for evolutionary politics among Shiites in Pakistan. Although Pakistan's first Shiite political party was founded immediately after the Iranian revolution, its revolutionary fervor has in the meantime lessened. Just like most Shiite minority communities, the vast majority of Pakistan's Shiites have come to accept the legitimacy of the national state. Their political activism is largely directed to the advancement of their own position within the state, especially since sectarian violence has grown in the last twenty years. This explains in part why their political discourse is pervaded by modern interpretations of pluralism, human rights, and a concept of citizenship that is independent of religious identity (ICG 2005a).

In general it is true that *politically* oriented and institutionalized activism is the least fundamentalist and violent and therefore also appears to be the least vulnerable to processes of radicalization in the direction of jihadist groups (ICG 2005a). But armed resistance, military takeovers, and terrorism have not disappeared as activist strategies. Nor does it mean that such activism cannot still return. In countries or regions where liberation movements motivated by nationalist or separatist goals are active, Islamic activism can expand into a broad national resistance movement that sometimes can make things very difficult for the state. We have seen this in the conflicts in Palestine, Chechnya, Kashmir, and in the Philippines, among other places, where Muslims are fighting against non-Muslims (Fuller 2003: 126). Sometimes local Islamic activists in these places are spurred on by cells and groups that operate transnationally and are thoroughly radicalized. Conflicts like the wars formerly in Afghanistan and Bosnia and currently in Iraq work then as catalysts for further escalation of violence. There are conflicting forces at work here which makes it difficult to assess the dynamics. The ease by which transnational and international contacts can be maintained and resources can be transferred explains in part the dissemination of conservative Wahhabism from the Arab world to other parts of the Muslim world, Europe, and the US. However, after reaching a peak in the early 1990s this influence seems to be on the decline again, especially since Wahhabism in Saudi Arabia itself is showing cracks (see below) and the international battle against terrorism has been intensified (ICG 2005a). Against these conservative fundamentalist forces that have spread to the rest of the Muslim world there is also the gradual spreading of the ideas and political practices of enlightened Islamic political thinkers from countries like Iran, Indonesia, and Malaysia (see Chapter 2).

99

In countries where Islamic activists have succeeded in attaining positions in the army or where the state is losing its grip on the government apparatus, attempts at military takeovers cannot be excluded. This applies, among other places, to Pakistan, Saudi Arabia, Bangladesh, and Morocco, where the regimes have not managed to keep Islamic activists out of the army (Fuller 2003: 169). As we have seen, Pakistan also wrestles with the problem that Shiites are threatened by puritanical Sunnis, like the Deobandi who are affiliated with Wahhabism (ICG 2003a).[16] As in so many developing countries, the regimes are very dependent on the army for maintaining social and political stability. However, that also makes them vulnerable to military coups.

3.5.4 POLITICAL RAPPROCHEMENT WITH CONCEPTS OF DEMOCRACY AND HUMAN RIGHTS

In addition to the moderating of the mainstream of political activism, many political activists have a growing inclination to employ a political vocabulary in which political parties, elections, and terms like democracy, human rights, and pluralism play an increasingly prominent role (Fuller 2003: 25). In this regard they are clearly influenced by the confrontation with Western political ideas and debates that, as we saw in Chapter 2, have a very long history. That does not mean that they have abandoned their own Islamic discourse nor that these concepts have the same significance and support in every context or for every group. But it does appear that through this Islamic vocabulary they are engaged in re-evaluating traditional ideas about the relationship between state, society, and politics. Thanks to the banner of Islam and the Islamization of political discourse, a bridge can be built between culturally familiar Islamic categories and concepts (like shura, baya, Sharia) and concepts of democracy and law that formerly had been employed only by a small, Western-oriented secular elite. In most Muslim countries Islamic activism is socially more deeply rooted. It also has greater potential to bring about changes than other reform movements and ideologies that are led from the top down such as Kemalism in Turkey or secular nationalism in Egypt (Yavuz 2004).

How powerful the vocabulary of Islamic political activism can be as a motor for change is especially apparent in political systems that are almost completely closed. Recent developments in Saudi Arabia are illustrative. The stationing of American troops on Saudi territory during the first Gulf War (1991-1992) was the immediate cause for the quietist Wahhabists, whose actions had been directed at the private sphere, to openly act in public as Salafiyya political activists. Religious leaders, judges, and intellectuals drew up a petition in which they called upon the regime to restore Islamic values. The petition listed all sorts of concrete proposals for politi-

cal reform, including the instituting of a consultative assembly, fair administration of the law, redistribution of wealth, and the primacy of religious
law. Only the Islamic vocabulary and Islamic authority made it possible to
abandon the strong norm of self-censorship and to of express the kind of
political criticism unheard of in the Saudi context. It is more difficult for
the regime to outlaw criticism that comes under the banner of Islam
because it is Islam that gives the regime its legitimacy. The Islamic frame
of thought and discourse is also more effective than any other because it is
shared by all the groups in the society, whether they are women, national-
ists, city or rural dwellers. It functions as a crowbar that can break open
the closed political climate so that criticism can be expressed and debate
started. Other critical groups can 'hitch a ride' in the wake of this Islamic
frame of thought (Okruhlik 2004: 261-262). In Saudi Arabia we see indeed
that a number of liberal and Islamic activist intellectuals increasingly dare
to speak out more sharply against the excesses of Wahhabism. These
excesses include terror by the religious police, the ban on women driving
cars, and also militant jihadism that, since the attacks of September 11, 2001
in the US and those of 2003 in Saudi Arabia, is increasingly heavily criticized. One thinker has even called for a return from Wahhabism to the
'true', more tolerant Salafism. He considers Salafism a good theological
underpinning for his pro-democratic activism (Lacroix 2005).

The growing significance of electoral channels and processes and concepts
like democracy and human rights is also evident from the lack of sharply
defined notions of Sharia and the Islamic state in the political arena.
Slogans like 'Islam is the solution', 'the Quran is our constitution' and also
the striving for an Islamic state following the Iranian model become scarcer
as Islamic movements commit themselves to programmatic politics.
Instead they call for justice, freedom, independence, recognition by the
state of pluralism and Sharia (see Chapter 4). The Egyptian Brotherhood,
for example, now employs the slogan 'respect for the constitution', and the
once-so-revolutionary Lebanese Hizbollah advocates a policy of openness
(infitah) and integration within the national state (Perthes 2004a: 134;
Alagha 2006). Moreover, political activists increasingly link their call for
Sharia to two important conditions. The first concerns the need to
acknowledge that everyone has the right to interpret Islam (ijtihad) in
order that legislation can be fitted to the needs of a modern society. The
second qualification follows from the first, namely that ijtihad implies an
acknowledgment of actual differences of interpretation over the place and
position of Islam in society and thus also over the right to and the need for
political debate and consultation. At the same time there is a role reserved
for programmatic politics and representative parliaments in the legislative
process (ICG 2005a: 7).

When these Islamic political parties and movements gain access to the system, they are often inclined in practice to acknowledge a *de facto* difference between politics and religion as more or less separate domains within the modern state. The developments in Iran are illustrative. The establishment of the Iranian Islamic state through a popular uprising against the authoritarian regime of the Shah led to a further Islamization, from the top down, of the political arena, political discourse, and Iranian society. This process has, however, also led to further pressure to separate the political from the religious domain. Already under Khomeini it was decided in Iran that the national interest superseded that of Islam, but now even influential religious leaders are trying to 'rescue' Islam from the hands of the rulers (Roy 2004: 91). At the same time, for a growing proportion of the population religion is a personal matter, by which they mean that the state should stay out of it. Especially youths, who make up more than fifty percent of the eligible voters, have become cynical about the stifling 'Islamic' social norms that are enforced on behalf of the state and the repression and corruption in the name of theocracy. In Iran there is also a lively debate over democracy, human rights, and pluralism, in spite of the Islamic vocabulary that even Iranians who are hardly religious feel in part compelled to employ and in spite of the recent victory of conservative political forces. The intellectual and social debates in Iran also stimulate discussions elsewhere in the Muslim world over the value of the autonomy of mosque and state as a safeguard against the misuse of religion by the state.

We can see in Turkey, a secular republic *par excellence*, how Islam has become the discourse of the resistance of the marginalized periphery against the strongly centralized state. This 'opposition Islam' from the bottom up is not a closed front but one that, because of internal and external economic changes, has broken down into various social movements and groups that have developed their own identity via Islam. Thanks to the economic liberalization of the 1980s, for example, a new bourgeoisie arose that found a new modern discourse based on the Quran and the hadith as opposed to the enlightened fundamentalism of the elite and equally opposed to the 'primitive' 'folk' Islam of the lowest classes (Yavuz 2004: 273). The Islamic modernity of these groups also produced its own 'high culture' in fields like music, fashion, literature, and cuisine, which competes with other Islamic cultures and identities. In this way, the integration of some religious groups and social classes comes about through participation in consumer culture, while others are marginalized, and thus we see growing differentiation among Muslim cultures. Similar complex processes are taking place in many locations within the Muslim world and outside where Muslims live in a minority situation.

As Yavuz shows, processes of emancipation and integration lead to a far-reaching objectification and therefore secularization of religious identity through the mass production of Islamic goods and symbols, ranging from stylish head scarves to halal foods, hotels, and vacations. Through these new 'Islamic' consumption patterns large sections of the modern public space, including the media, education, the market, and fashion, are redefined. For example, female students can, thanks to an ultra-stylish head scarf, participate in the public space without having to deny their religious identity. The head scarf, which represented for the Kemalists a symbol of backward, peasant identity, has been upgraded to a symbol of new chic, social mobility, emancipation, and individuality. The secular elite in Turkey, however, interpret this item of clothing as a provocative expression of Islamic radicalism and undesirable Islamization (Yavuz 2004: 280-281).

In many countries where Islamic political parties have meanwhile gained access to the electoral process and, thanks to their social roots and associations, have maintained contact with the population, it appears that these parties experience a learning process in which they can also bring along their grassroots supporters. They gain experience with gradual, step-by-step political liberalization, how to deal with political institutions, how to reach compromises and make alliances within a pluralistic environment, and how to formulate concrete political programs that connect with broad layers of the electorate. Through this process they distance themselves from fundamentalist dogmas or undefined forms of 'opposition Islam', which appeal above all to radicals. Moreover, they learn from experience the lessons and principles of electoral competition; they know that Islamic political parties, just as the others, are ultimately judged by their accomplishments not in the area of Islam but in concrete tasks like combating unemployment, corruption, lawlessness, and the arbitrariness of the regime. In short, in a number of Muslim countries, in addition to threats, there are also opportunities for further political institutionalization, gradual political liberalization, and the strengthening of human rights. Chapter 5 examines whether and how Dutch and European policies can support these processes.

3.6   CONCLUSION

In many parts of the Muslim world Islamic political parties have for a considerable time been among the most important mobilizing forces. There is not one political activism; activist political movements come in a number of shapes, coalitions, and contexts, and represent a vehicle for countless aspirations. The primary political playing field of these movements might be the national state, but it could also be international or transnational politics; their orientation might be pan-Islamic, anti-West-

ern, or anti-Shiite. Movements oriented to domestic politics have numerous diverse goals, such as the introduction of an Islamic state and constitution, the countering of Western interference in national or regional politics, the spreading of belief and the provision of social services, the
combating of corruption and the exposure of failed government policy, the
advancement of human rights and the position of women, and the eleva-
tion of the emerging religious middle class. Additionally, these movements
alter their strategy and tactics often, while they also use multiple tactics at
the same time.

The Islamic activists who seized power in Sudan, Afghanistan, and Iran
after 1970 all tried to base the state and society on an Islamic model. They
remained in general stuck, however, in a superficial, conservative Islamization: the heavy-handed imposition of strongly anti-modern vocabularies,
behavior codes, and prescriptions labeled as Islamic (Bayat 1997). That
especially applies to Afghanistan under the Taliban, where the regime
linked literal interpretations of the Quran to traditional tribal codes. Iran
represents an exception to the resorting to a distant Islamic past because
that country has, like no other, experimented with new forms of politics,
government, and law based on Islam. It is a hopeful development that
precisely in this Islamic theocracy one can find among large segments of
the middle class support for an extremely pragmatic, *de facto* secularization of Iranian politics and social life. This offers opportunities in the
longer term to link Islamic principles with democratic politics and the
improvement of human rights.

In many other parts of the Muslim world the agenda of Islamic activists has
led to a redefinition of the state, the society, and the public space in
'Islamic' terms. Sometimes this took place directly as Islamic movements,
organizations, and parties could implement their political agenda through
the political and social arena. More often it occurred indirectly as the
incumbent regimes tried through a policy of Islamization to take the wind
out of the sails of rising religiously inspired groups. At the same time they
tried to play these groups off against one another to prevent them from
forming broad, reform-minded coalitions. This resulted in an intensified
control of the exercise of religion and religious education, the use of Islamic
religious symbols and the taking over of the agenda of reactionary Islamic
political movements in areas such as law, morals, and the position of
women. It is precisely these top-down Islamization processes imposed by
strongly authoritarian regimes that have few correction mechanisms in
politics or society. They run the risk of serving the most conservative,
fundamentalist agendas and of excluding the more progressive Islamic
political movements that are oriented toward political liberalization and
good government.

The growing presence of activist movements oriented to the national political order, however, offers opportunities for democratization and the
advancement of human rights. Many leading revolutionary activists have in
the 1990s chosen an evolutionary, constructive agenda within the constitutional limits of the national state. Instead of striving to replace the secular
state, by violence if necessary, with an (*Ummah*-wide) Islamic state, they
aim at participation in the political order and taking part in elections as a
regular political party. Just like other movements, they are exposed to
diverse transnational and global forces, such as the international media,
companies, and NGOs, global terrorist networks and money flows from
Saudi Arabia. And, of course, their political thought, discourse, strategies,
and agenda are in part determined by international issues that are important for Muslims, such as the war in Iraq and the Israeli-Palestinian problem. But it is remarkable that many of them increasingly are guided by
issues like economic development, political reform, good government, and
cultural and social emancipation in their own political arena. Wherever
these developments contribute concretely to democratization and the
advancement of human rights, they deserve support from the Netherlands
and Europe.

105

NOTES

1 For example, the Afghan political and spiritual leader of Hizb-i Islami, Hikmatyar, demanded unconditional loyalty from his followers and the exclusive right of religious interpretation (*ijtihad*). Thus he put himself above the authority of the ulama with respect to religion.

2 Examples of similar movements include the fundamentalist movements Tabligh Jama'at and the Nur. The first arose in India in 1927 as part of a broader movement that had groups of laymen travel around to convey to fellow Muslims the essential values and rules of the faith. The most important ceremonial event in the Tablighi calendar is the so-called Raiwind, the yearly mass gathering of more than a million Muslims in Pakistan. Outside of Pakistan the Tablighi has developed an extensive global network of sister organizations in the US, Canada, the UK, and the Netherlands, among other places. Although the Tablighi is explicitly apolitical, the movement represents for some young people a step towards (sometimes violent) Islamic political organizations. The Nur movement of Said Nursi (created in 1926) and its successor, the neo-Nur movement of Fethullah Gülen of Turkey, are among the largest Muslim movements in the world. The movement carefully stays out of the political arena, regards education and knowledge as the most important means to attain religious insight, and in particular directs its activities to the building of schools within and outside Turkey, especially in Central Asia. At the same time, the group's leader Gülen is known as a fierce anti-Communist. In the past he criticized the Turkish Islamic Refah party and regularly gave advice on how to vote. Since the 1960s the Nur has succeeded in playing a more important role in the ideological and political mobilization of parts of the new Turkish middle class and the traders from Anatolia, who discovered their own version of modernity (Yavuz 2003).

3 Half of the members of this Council of Guardians are chosen by the parliament (from a list of candidates of the High Council of Justice which is appointed by the Supreme Leader) and half are appointed from the ranks of the clerical elite (*fuqaha*).

4 In 1997 Pakistan, Saudi Arabia, and the United Arab Emirates officially recognized the Taliban regime. However, the latter two countries withdrew their support after the attacks by al-Qaeda on September 11, 2001. The regime did not succeed in occupying the Afghanistan seat in the UN and the OIC.

5 Article 149, Chapter 10 also states: "The provisions of adherence to the fundamentals of the sacred religion of Islam and the regime of the Islamic Republic cannot be amended." (International Constitutional Law: Afghanistan, undated)

6 At the same time there are no limits proposed for the ethnic, religious, or cultural composition of the parliament (see Art. 83).

7 The first commotion surrounding Article 3 arose in January 2005 when Afghan state television broadcast images of a once-beloved Afghan female singer. It was the first time since the Taliban regime took over Kabul that a female singer had appeared on the screen. Conservatives cried that this was in conflict with the Islamic code and the constitution, a claim that was adopted by the Minister of Justice but was contested by the Minister of Information and Culture, who referred to the constitutional equality of men and women. President Karzai aimed at a compromise with his statement that the Afghan radio and television had allowed female singers for more than sixty years, but that all parties simply must work in the context of the current cultural and social climate and must act in agreement with it (Tarzi 2004).

8 Between 1976 and 1986 the professional population in Egypt increased by 2.2 per cent annually and the number of graduates rose by 7.4 per cent annually. The average waiting time for a recent graduate to obtain a government job increased from three to ten years in the period 1979-1985 (Rosefsky Wickham 2002).

9 The statement of a former party leader of the leftist National Progressive Union Party, the NPUP, is telling: "All the political parties are isolated from the people. We are like boats floating on a river. Some of us trail longer anchors than others, but we are all floating on the surface, even the Islamic associations. The overwhelming majority of the citizens are simply not politicized." (Quoted in: Rosefsky Wickham 2002: 69)

10 Zumur's party newspaper concluded: "All the peacefulness and gradualism upheld by the [Muslim] Brothers during their political struggle, and their work through the regime's legitimate, legal [channels] did not save them from being handcuffed, tried in front of military courts, and dragged to prison. All the while their preachers declare that they will not be provoked and will not attempt confrontation" (Hafez 2003: 55).

11 The FIS obtained more than 47 per cent of the votes (or 188 seats) in the first round of the 1991 election. To gain an absolute majority in the parliament they would have needed to win only 28 more seats in the second round.

12 During a 1982 uprising, for example, between 15,000 and 25,000 Syrians were killed within a week in battles with the army.

13 According to estimates Saudi Arabia alone funneled 3.5 billion dollars to the Pakistani army for weapons and additional support for Sunni groups on the border between Pakistan and Afghanistan (ICG 2005d: 12).

14 In Mernissi's words: "Others feel their interests to be terribly threatened by that *dimuqratiyya*. This is apparently the situation of all those excluded from the good things mentioned above. Can it be that the most dispossessed in our societies cling to Islam because they fear being forgotten by

their own people, who have found another identity and are involved in other networks, especially those very strong ones that create profit on an international scale?" (Quoted in: Noyon 2003: 43).

15   Olivier Roy, in his sketch of twenty-first-century Islamic activism, makes a distinction between Islamism, neo-fundamentalism, and jihadism. The International Crisis Group employs a three-part division of political Islamism, missionary activism, and jihadism to describe contemporary Sunni tendencies, while an author like Graham Fuller uses the terms political Islam and Islamism as interchangeable concepts. In Fuller's definition it concerns a broad spectrum of movements that assume that Islam has an important mission regarding the organization of contemporary politics and culture, and that want to implement this basic principle in one way or another. Within this he makes a distinction among traditionalism, fundamentalism, and reformism (Fuller 2003: xi and 47-49). All these authors recognize, however, the relativeness of these labels; the changes in the Muslim world go too fast, the (national) diversity of these movements is simply too great, and also the border between national and transnational orientations is becoming ever more porous.

16   More than seventy per cent of the victims of sectarian violence since 1985 are Shiite. See ICG 2003b.

4 THE DEVELOPMENT OF LAW AND LEGAL SYSTEMS

4.1 INTRODUCTION

This chapter examines the development of law and legal systems that has
taken place in Muslim countries in recent decades under the influence
of Islamic activism. An important question in this regard concerns the
relationship between the Islamization of national law and the concept of
human rights – and the possible rapprochement between them.

In Muslim countries perhaps the most central aim of movements that are
oriented toward Islamization is to introduce Islamic law – Sharia – into the
national legal system. Islam is a religion that in its development has been
strongly based on a just life: that is, on religious codes of behavior for the
individual believer in his relationship towards God and the community of
believers (Platti 2004). Thus, for many Muslims 'Islam' and 'Sharia' more
or less converge (Kadhim 2003). This also means that Muslims view 'law'
more broadly than is common in Western legal traditions. Certainly in
many Muslim countries the state is granted an important role to support,
through law, the individual in his or her realization of religious duties, but
the relevance of Sharia goes further still. Pleas for the honoring of Sharia
can refer to the national law but also to norms of behavior outside of the
sphere of the state, for example in informal social and cultural groupings.
In this chapter, however – in keeping with the issues of concern in this
report – we are concerned primarily with national law, though we do not
ignore the competition between government and religious authorities
regarding control over that law.

Many in the West as well as in Muslim countries regard any development
toward Islamization of law with great suspicion. Alongside *jihad*, in the
sense of armed struggle, Sharia is for them a central factor in the confrontation between the West and the Muslim world. Movements oriented toward
Islamization are seen as always wanting to replace the formerly secular law
in Muslim countries, which was derived from the West, with Sharia or with
legislation based on Sharia. 'Sharia' is therefore an extremely loaded concept,
which in the eyes of many people contains many of the negative characteristics they ascribe to 'Islam,' such as the rejection of the separation of religious
community and state, rejection of universal human rights, re-introduction
or maintaining of antiquated views about the relations between men and
women, and the application of draconian punishments, such as stoning and
amputation of body parts. The experience of the application of law in Saudi
Arabia, Iran, and – during the Taliban regime – Afghanistan, three countries

109

that actually put Sharia into practice, of course also gives little reason for minimizing the differences with law in force in the West. One could add that the efforts to bring Sharia into force are not limited to Muslim countries. Also in Western countries Muslims or Islamic movements sometimes declare that for them only one law holds, namely that of God. Or they advocate the idea that elements of the Sharia should be honored in the prevailing laws and/or in the legal system, as some Muslim groups in Canada and Great Britain have urged. This fuels the notion that Muslims in the West, too, reject the existing constitutional state and would like to replace it with Sharia. Therefore the question regarding what Sharia in theory and practice entails, how both these aspects relate to Western law, and whether Western perceptions and fears are justified, is a significant one.

The rise of movements oriented towards Islamization is not the only factor that has influenced the development of law in Muslim countries in recent decades. In the same period that Islamic activism increased, the importance of human rights also received new impulse, and scores of multilateral institutions and (trans)national non-governmental movements were founded, exerting pressure on Muslim states to conform to standards of human rights and acting as watchdogs to oversee compliance. Therefore, national law and legal systems, which first and foremost have their own dynamics, are exposed to forces from within and without. And just as Islamic activism in Muslim countries is nourished internationally, international pressure to respect human rights has resonated among many national and local human rights movements in Muslim countries.

Against this background of national and international influences, section 4.2 examines the scope of Islamization of national law that has occurred in recent decades in Muslim countries. We will see that this scope is limited and, besides constitutional aspects, mainly affects criminal law. Family law in many Muslim countries has long been based on Sharia. In both cases, there exist important areas of conflict with universal human rights. Section 4.3 discusses the theme of 'Islamic' and 'universal' human rights and the dynamism that can be observed. Section 4.4 attempts to characterize and interpret this legal dynamism in Muslim countries. Finally, some conclusions are drawn in section 4.5.

This chapter is based to a large extent on a comparative law study conducted explicitly for this report by the Van Vollenhoven Institute for Law and Administration in Non-Western Countries of the University of Leiden; where use has been made of other sources, this is indicated. The research analyzes the developments of national law in twelve Muslim countries, meaning countries in which the majority of the population is Muslim. The study covers Egypt, Morocco, Sudan, Nigeria, Mali, Turkey, Pakistan,

Afghanistan, Iran, Saudi Arabia, Indonesia, and Malaysia. Thus, all of the core countries are represented, and the selection also encompasses the important regions. The three publications resulting from this study delve deeply into questions of theory and terminology which are important for comparative law (Otto 2006; Berger 2006; Otto et al. 2006). They were issued simultaneously with the Dutch version of this report.

4.2   RECENT ISLAMIZATION OF LAW AND LEGAL SYSTEMS

4.2.1   MEANINGS OF 'SHARIA'

Before we go into the nature of Islamization, it is worthwhile to provide clarity about the concept of 'Sharia' that is so often employed in relation to 'Sharia' law. To what extent is Sharia an unambiguous concept that refers to a firm collection of prescripts which apply to all Muslims? Despite the many seemingly self-evident references to 'Sharia', the term is used with many different meanings that are of great importance for judging the nature and scope of the Islamization of law. Distinctions can in fact be drawn between Sharia as an ideal, as a classical system of law, as a contemporary interpretation of this law (Otto 2006; Berger 2006) and as a 'lived' practice of law.

Sharia as ideal alludes to the religious and metaphysical principle of a divine plan for human beings and their society. In this sense, the term has a strong motivating and mobilizing meaning, for example, as a plea for greater justice or against corruption, but it says little about concrete rules of law that would serve this end.

As a classical legal system, Sharia refers to the body of legal rules laid down in the so-called *fiqh* by legal scholars and theologians. The most important written sources of Sharia are the Quran and the Sunna (the recorded acts and sayings of the Prophet). In these sources themselves, there are few statements to be found that could be interpreted as rules of law; those statements that can be applied, concern mainly family and inheritance law and rules about a limited number of offenses. Through various techniques, concrete precepts are laid down in the fiqh for these and other areas of law. Important differences of interpretation have arisen, including between Shiites and Sunnis and among schools of law. The concrete differences also correspond to the enormous geographical spread of Islam, whereby local legal practices and royal decrees are included in the fiqh in various areas. Sharia in this sense thus incorporated many rules of behavior that were not originally Islamic. The Sunni world recognizes, along with many smaller ones, four large schools of law, which mainly differ in ways of applying the legal rules. The *Hanafite* school is the most liberal of the four and emphasizes systematic consistency and consensus among recognized jurists.

111

Reasoned insight plays a large role as well; this school of law is the least puritanical of the four and also the most widespread. It prevails mainly in the former Ottoman Empire, in Pakistan, India, and China. The *Malikite* school of law emphasizes the Quran and the Sunna as sources of law and can be considered as traditionalist and conservative. It prevails chiefly in North and West Africa. The *Shafite* school of law stands somewhere between the Hanafite and Malikite schools and appears especially in Egypt, Jordan, East Africa, Sri Lanka, Malaysia, and Indonesia. The *Hanbalite* school of law arose as a legalistic and conservative offshoot of the Malikite school. It holds that Sharia can only be based on the literal texts of the Quran and the Sunna. This very puritanical school is found especially on the Arabian peninsula; it also later produced the Wahhabism prevailing in Saudi Arabia (Berger 2006: 21-25). Within each of the schools of law, there exist yet again differences between more orthodox-classical and more liberal or modern interpretations. Thus, compared to the contemporary national rules of law in Muslim countries, the area in which unanimity about the legal rules themselves exists is very small.

Due to its casuistic character, the fiqh is often compared to Anglo-Saxon jurisprudence. But there also are great differences: Anglo-Saxon jurisprudence has been developed by practicing jurists and is based on the practice of law, while the fiqh has been developed by scholars and to a considerable extent has a theoretical character.

In orthodoxy the fiqh was rather quickly, after two centuries, considered completed and seen not so much as *human* elaboration of Divine Law but as the Law itself. In this way, the interpretation took on a status of infallibility and immutability, valid for every place and time. Because the development of the law was considered completed, from the tenth century the legitimate right of interpretation – ijtihad – was taken away from scholars and believers. In this manner, the path toward modernization was closed, and the legal system was fossilized for a long time. Only from the nineteenth century has ijtihad again been applied, although the permissibility of reopening the gates of interpretation has been very controversial.
In the present time, too, new interpretations occur everywhere, which often meet sharp opposition – although certainly not always on the same grounds – from the orthodox ulama and radical Islamic movements (Berger 2006). So it was that when a new family law, the Muddawana, was adopted by the Moroccan parliament in 2004, the proponents of the changes justified their position by continually referring to ijtihad. Appealing to the fact that he as 'sovereign of the believers' represented the highest authority regarding the right to ijtihad, the king, against all opposition, played a breakthrough role in bringing about this law. The result is a sweeping break with the patriarchal family model; henceforth men and women are

together responsible for the family, instead of only the man, as had been the case previously (Buskens in Otto et al. 2006). Total application of the classical fiqh no longer exists anywhere, not even in Saudi Arabia. While according to classical Sharia slavery is permitted, it was outlawed in Saudi Arabia in the 1960s. As we will see, despite the recent Islamization of certain areas of law, including in core areas that in most Muslim countries always were determined by Sharia, there exist great differences from country to country.

In addition to the principle of ijtihad, that of *siyasa* is also an important avenue toward modernization of law. The classical Sharia recognizes in the ruler his own freedom of discretion (siyasa) to regulate everything necessary to execute God's plan, provided it does not conflict with Sharia. This right already implied *de facto* a certain separation between religious and secular power in the Islamic kingdoms. So it was that the Ottoman state of old formed in practice a secular government apparatus long before the reforms, based on a European model, began in the nineteenth century (WRR 2004: 43). That area of discretion obviously has increased strongly virtually everywhere with the rise of the modern state. The formal requirement that law developed in this domain not be in conflict with Sharia usually causes no problem, so that national law in Muslim countries often can closely dovetail with law in other parts of the world, such as with Common Law or Civil Law structures.

The fourth meaning of Sharia relates to law as lived. Sharia is religious law and therefore concerns precepts of belief. Even where this finds expression in formal, national law, the individual believer or an Islamic movement can find his/her/its own interpretations for rules to live by and be able to employ them in fulfillment of – or in deviation from – the formal law in place. In many Muslim countries the state has not yet won the battle over the monopoly of law over all areas. This holds true not only in states with large ethnic diversity or religious differences. In various Muslim countries, such as Pakistan and even Egypt, religious movements have sometimes managed to 'hijack' sections of cities and have actually proclaimed and imposed their version of Sharia (Roy 2004). Also, customary practices, forbidden by national law, nevertheless can be regarded by believers as 'Islamic' or as conforming to their interpretation of Sharia. This holds, too, where it concerns customs, such as female circumcision, that in some areas are also observed by followers of other religions. Certainly in regions far removed from the seat of government in a country that is barely controlled by the state, there reigns a mixture of unwritten Islamic law with customary law. This also applies in cases where the state apparatus has collapsed or is barely functioning, as currently in Afghanistan and Iraq. The informal forms of law which may be resorted to, are then often exercised by people who still have authority or power, and these often are religious functionaries and local war lords (UK Home Office 2004).

Because this report concerns the relationship between Islam and *national law*, Islamization of law here refers to the first three meanings of Sharia. The differences among these, and also the large differences of interpretation that exist within each meaning, indicate – unlike what is often thought – that Sharia is no unambiguous system of legal rules and behavior codes. Given the large differences, it is actually a mistake to speak of 'the' Sharia. It is not at all clear in advance what is meant by pleas for the introduction of Sharia or what the effect will be of amending systems of law according to Sharia. Such pleas or references do not automatically mean a return to orthodox precepts of behavior. Islamic activism of the last decennia must partly be seen as a reaction against the mindless following of traditional rules of behavior. When a plea is made for the incorporation of Sharia into national law, this can refer to a modern as well as a puritanical interpretation. It certainly is true that a pious Muslim would give a sacred and positive connotation to the concept of Sharia as such. Most Muslims view the Quran, as the most important basis for Sharia, as the Word of God. The positive connotation of Sharia that is derived from this sacred nature – the first meaning – closely resembles 'social justice'. It can be compared with the positive sentiments that most Westerners associate with 'liberty, equality, fraternity.' But as with this trinity of values, referring to 'the' Sharia does not say much about the concrete laws and duties that issue from it.

4.2.2   ISLAMIZATION OF THE LAW IN MUSLIM COUNTRIES

The present-day call in Muslim countries to Islamize the law dates mainly from the 1970s. There were certainly always movements that stood for this cause, but in many Muslim countries the ruling elites in the decades prior to the 1970s were mainly concerned with nationalism and modernization. Both colonized countries and countries without a colonial past such as Turkey, Iran, and Afghanistan, in many areas witnessed the introduction of Western-inspired law. From the 1920s onward, there was a heavy-handed push toward national unity and modernization, often also colored by socialism. Religion was either paid little attention or its public influence was curtailed, as in Turkey and Iran. The rising call for Islamization of law at least in part emerged from this forced modernization and the marginalization of Islam and its authorities, the legal scholars. This resistance was directed against failing authoritarian regimes and their programs of modernization. It also had a strong anti-Western content due to Western support of and influence on these regimes and their attempts at modernization according to a Western model.

In many cases, the desire to introduce Sharia should therefore be seen as a striving toward restoration of the connection with one's own heritage, i.e. from 'Islam is the problem' to 'Islam is the solution.' Nevertheless, this does not imply any discontinuity across the board or the complete re-introduction of earlier legal systems. Thus the international order of nation states, which emerged from the two world wars and the wars of independence, has remained unaffected. As a constitutional concept, the Quranic unity of the entire community of belief – the *Ummah* – could not match the nation state (An Na'im 1990; ICG 2004a). Law and legal systems are tied therefore to individual states, and on that basis alone they already exhibit great differences. This incorporation of law by the state also implies, that the principle of codifying law that was introduced by the colonial powers or copied from the West, has been retained. This is also true for nearly all the Sharia core countries. All Muslim countries have a written constitution, even – since 1992 – Saudi Arabia, which is called the *Basic Regulation*, because the Quran and Sunna are regarded there as 'The Constitution'. But in this country, the law of persons, for example, is not codified. Apart from Saudi Arabia and Afghanistan in the Taliban phase, Islamization of the law plays itself out within the framework of national law, through amendment of legislation and jurisprudence. The same holds for the entire legal system, that was modeled more or less everywhere on European examples of the nineteenth and twentieth century, particularly those of Great Britain and France. Islamization can thus lead to an extension of the formal structure of courts and courts of appeal with Sharia tribunals.

Similarly, if we look at the content of the law, there is considerable continuity. In most Muslim countries, family and inheritance law for Muslims was always based on Sharia and on customary law – and this has not changed. But in many other areas, despite formal Islamization, existing laws have been maintained, including those laws derived in the past from the West or shaped on Western models. This was and is possible because of the siyasa described above, which grants to the ruler legislative authority in areas which the Quran or Sunna do not cover, provided such legislation does not conflict with these texts. In areas such as, for example, general and private contract law, torts, labor law, property law, procedural law, partnership law, bankruptcy law, transportation law, intellectual property, electoral law, information law, general administrative law, public planning law, environmental law, education law, postal and telecommunication law, and large sections of criminal law, the Sharia has no, or scarcely any, substantive influence. Measured against the entire body of national law, the potential scope of Sharia is very limited. This holds true also for countries that advocate the *general* introduction of Sharia. But the limited substantive scope naturally does not mean that the influence in areas of law that do indeed fall under the Sharia would be limited. In the following sections, we examine successively the constitutional aspects, criminal law, and family law.

4.2.3   CONSTITUTIONAL ISLAMIZATION

The concepts of state, state law, and constitution do not appear in classical Sharia, and their equivalents also receive little treatment. The starting premise of classical Sharia is that of a community of belief with a leader. Relations within a state context hardly receive any attention. The state and administrative law have long been regulated by the ruler himself on the basis of siyasa, which grants him freedom of policy. The independent states that arose in the twentieth century built further on the older Muslim empires but also on the colonial or Western-inspired conceptual frame-work of public law, such as head of state, government, ministers and parlia-ment. The Islamic activism of the 1970s also had 'Sharia-zation' of consti-tutional aspects on its agenda, for which there were therefore few historical models available. For example, the Caliphate is an *Ummah*-wide rather than nation-state concept; besides which, as we have seen in Chapter 2, its Islamic foundations are very controversial. Thus, constitutional Islamiza-tion' is truly experimental, involving many juridical ambiguities and uncertainties.

The British legal philosopher Hart points out that constitutions include so-called *rules of recognition*: rules that define that a rule is a legal rule. The appearance in constitutions of such basic norms of positive law is not, however, sufficient 'proof' for their actual functioning. According to Hart, whether such a ground rule can be accepted, should mainly be derived empirically, from the conduct of judges, legislators, and the administration. Besides, in the text of a constitution itself, there can be various 'highest' norms; on that basis alone, their factual meaning requires empirical exami-nation (Hart 1997). When one wants to study the role of Islam in connec-tion with the state, the constitution is the obvious document. After all, such a text always shows how a country defines itself. An important form of 'constitutional Islamization' – at least on paper – concerns the explicit changing of the state into an Islamic one. It is also important whether or not Islam is regarded as a state religion. In addition, Sharia can be included in the constitution as source of legislation.

Below we will first analyze these issues for all Muslim countries, meaning countries in which Muslims make up a majority of the population (see appendix 3). From the classification employed, it appears that the constitu-tional position of Sharia (or Islam, Quran, Sunna, fiqh) in regard to legisla-tion can vary widely, namely from 'the', 'the most important', 'an impor-tant' to 'a' source of legislation. As the formulation becomes weaker, the constitutional room increases also for other sources of legislation and therefore also 'highest' norms. Of the 45 Muslim countries for which we have data, ten appear to define themselves constitutionally as Islamic states. In these ten countries, Islam is at the same time the state religion; it is also the state religion in eleven other countries. In eight Muslim countries, Sharia is 'the' or 'the most important' source of legislation, and in nine countries Sharia counts in the constitution as 'an important' or 'a' source of legislation, therefore along with other sources. In total, 17 of 45 Muslim countries thus give Sharia some sort of constitutional role as a source of law and legislation (appendix 3). Obviously, this holds for nearly all the states that define themselves as Islamic. Morocco represents an exception; this country is an Islamic state, Islam is the state religion, but Sharia is not considered a source of legislation. Morocco's constitution speaks of 'the will of the nation' that must be expressed in the law. In the preamble reference is made to human rights.

Clearly, then, there is no one-to-one correspondence between 'Muslim country' and 'Sharia'; Sharia has a constitutional position in only about one-third of all Muslim countries, while in about one-sixth of Muslim countries it is recognized as having formal supremacy as source of legislation. This does not mean, however, that the substantive influence of Sharia is great in these countries. Nor, on the other hand, does it mean that substantive influence is lacking in countries where Islam constitutionally has no influence.

For more insight into constitutional Islamization in recent decades, we will now begin by examining the twelve countries selected for closer research. First we look at their form of government. Defining a state as Islamic means that state power itself and not only law is legitimized religiously and made sacred. In such cases, criticism of the state can easily be made equivalent to criticism of the religion itself and be considered as heresy, as has been the case in Iran (Hajjar 2000). Of the twelve countries, there are four where in the last three decades the form of government was changed (temporarily) into an Islamic one, namely Iran, Pakistan, Sudan (now no longer), and Afghanistan. Saudi Arabia and Morocco were already Islamic from their formation as independent states. Below we look at each of the four (permanently or temporarily) Islamized states.

Iran

The establishment of the Islamic Republic in Iran in 1979 definitely involved the most radical formal change of form of government in the Muslim world, from a secular monarchy to a theocracy. At the same time it is striking that, from the very beginning, this theocracy ascribed a formal place to democracy; in this respect as well as with regard to constitutional rights, the founders allowed themselves to be inspired by France. The Islamic Republic, therefore, can be seen as a sort of 'theo-democracy,' the term that Mawdudi reserved for the system that he advocated for Pakistan (Mawdudi 1980). The constitution has two basic norms: supremacy of God and supremacy of the people, with the first determining the borders of the second. The institutions whose members are chosen by general election – president and parliament – are subject to the supervision of the Supreme Leader, de *vila yat-i faqih*, and the Council of Guardians, consisting of religious scholars and professional jurists, which stands in service to the leader. Constitutionally, primacy belongs to Sharia, and the Council of Guardians has the task of testing all legislation against it. In spite of the explicitly hierarchical structure, the last 25 years reflect a history of regular clashes between the two constitutional basic norms. Although parliament, on the basis of the Sharia adhered to in the constitution, has the status of a consultative assembly, it has regularly sought to strengthen its authority to the disadvantage of the theocratic institutions. The most important result of these confrontations has been the creation of a new state body, the Expediency Discernment Council for the System. This council arbitrates between parliament and the Council of Guardians, a practice which thus far has led to approval of seventy per cent of the legislation proposed by parliament. The new council is based on some fatwas (juridical instructions) issued by Khomeini, which indicates that the state's interest can prevail above Sharia. All the same, if differences persist, the last word is given to the faqih (Dekker and Barends in Otto et al. 2006).

Shiite Iran is thus, along with the Sunni Saudi Arabia, the most marked example of a constitutional Islamic theocracy; both countries have a system of law that in principle is based on classical versions of Sharia. There is still an important difference between these two countries: unlike in Iran, the theocracy in Saudi Arabia is absolute. Saudi Arabia has no written constitution and thus, constitutionally, has no place for democracy. The members of the advisory body (shura) are appointed, and not – as in Iran – chosen by universal suffrage (Barends and Van Eijk in Otto et al. 2006). In 2005, under American pressure, the first local elections were held; only men were given the right to vote. The theocracy is constitutionally anchored in Iran, but space is also created in the constitution for many modern rights (education, etc.).

Pakistan

Pakistan, since its founding as an Islamic state, has been exposed not only to forces that wanted to found a theocracy (Mawdudi, mentioned in Chapter 2, was an important exponent of one of these, the Jamaat-i-Islami-movement) but also to forces directed toward democratization. The vacillating power relationship between these forces was expressed in successive constitutions. The constitution of 1956 mentioned 'the Islamic Republic' and had a strongly religious character. That of 1962 dealt with the 'Republic of Pakistan' and instead of speaking of 'the holy Quran and Sunna,' spoke of the wider concept, 'Islam.' This illustrates how Pakistan has struggled and still struggles over determining the priority between a clearly Islamic and a more secular system of norms. In the third constitution of 1973, the first drafted by an elected representative body, place was also created for Islam (art. 1: "Pakistan shall be a Federal Republic to be known as the Islamic Republic of Pakistan"), as well as for democracy, freedom, national unity, equality and solidarity. General Zia ul-Haq suspended this constitution in 1977 and sought support for retaining power in the radical Islamic groupings that were growing in membership. He considered Islam irreconcilable with democracy on a Western model and assigned to himself a special status. During Zia's dictatorship (1977-1988), Pakistani law was extensively Islamized, including the introduction of an Islamic criminal law and the notorious blasphemy law, both of which remain in force. A new constitutional article, introduced by decree, stated that the precepts of Islam shall be the highest law of the land. This was in contradiction to other constitutional articles that designated the constitution as the highest norm. A special legal body was charged with testing legislation and legal judgments concerning some crimes cited in the Quran against Islamic precepts. This ambiguity led to great controversy within the judiciary. The contest between forces directed toward Islamization, on the one hand, and secular forces, on the other, has continued since 1988. Nevertheless, it appears as though the Islamization project lost a lot of its fervor in the 1990s. Since 2003, the constitution of 1973 is again in force (Barends and Otto in Otto et al. 2006).

Sudan

Sudan's temporary, secular constitution of 1956 laid great emphasis on parliamentary democracy but, from the very start, strong forces manifested themselves, directed toward an '*Islamic* parliamentary republic,' with Sharia as the most important source of legislation. The high point of Islamization was reached in the 1980s when the attempt was made, by amending the constitution, to bring the constitution into line with 'the' Sharia. The president was given a new name as 'leader of the believers,' the parliament was changed into a consultative council (in conformity with the Quranic shura), its members were obliged to be loyal to the leader, and Sharia became the only source of law. These changes effectively put the 'permanent' constitution of 1973 out of use. In this constitution, as in that of the provisional one of 1956, Sudan had been designated a parliamentary democracy. The Christian south received a form of self-government. The new constitution was granted only a short life and was unable to prevent bloody conflict between the north and the south. From the time of independence in 1956, the non-Islamic south, rich in raw materials, had tried to withdraw from the (legal) hegemony of the Islamic north. The constitutional struggle, however, not merely concerned the role of Islam throughout Sudan but also whether to adopt an orthodox or liberal interpretation of Sharia. In the constitution of 1998 currently in force, Sudan is not defined as an Islamic state, but as a country in which "(…) religions conciliate. Islam is the religion of the majority (…)" (art. 1 of the Constitution). Other provisions also secure Muslim dominance. Whether this constitution is meant to be valid until the 2011 referendum on the possible separation of South Sudan is still unclear (Köndgen in Otto et al. 2006).

Afghanistan

In the new constitution of 2004, Afghanistan is held to be an 'Islamic republic,' Islam is 'the sacred religion,' and the head of state is designated as patron of Islam with the task of guaranteeing the basic principles of the holy Islamic religion, the constitution, and other laws. Because the constitution also employs sources other than Sharia, its theocratic character is less explicit than during the period 1994-2001, when the Taliban gave Islamization a completely forbidding face. During that time, all the laws and regulations that the Taliban found to be in conflict with the strict Islamic interpretation of traditional Deobandi and Afghan-Islamic tribal traditions were abolished; government ruled by decree and a very stringent version of Sharia was implemented (Yassari and Saboory in Otto et al. 2006).

The remainder of the twelve countries researched do not define themselves as Islamic states. However, constitutional Islamization can also manifest itself in the adoption in the constitution of Islam as state religion and/or designation of Quran and Sunna, fiqh or Sharia as sources of legislation. Thus, unlike in a theocracy, the state does not base its authority on the Islamic law itself, although it does link state power to applying and enforcing compliance with Sharia. With regard to this category one could speak of 'nationalization' of religious legislation and jurisprudence (Hajjar 2000). Since the 1970s, other than in the countries already mentioned, Islam has only been (re-)installed as the state religion in Egypt (1980) and Turkey (1982). In Morocco, Islam had already long been the state religion, as in Malaysia since the first constitution of 1957. In Nigeria, Mali, and Indonesia, Islam is not the state religion (Otto 2006; Otto et al. 2006).

As is evident in the overview of all Muslim countries in appendix 3, terminology is very important with regard to the source of legislation. The sources may involve (principles of) Islam, the Quran, Sunna, Sharia or the fiqh, and the degree of exclusivity granted to the source can vary strongly. If we speak of 'a' source, there are also by definition other sources, as laid down in other articles of the constitution. We can thus speak of a double, or at least an ambiguous, constitutional basic norm. Since most constitutions also contain provisions about fundamental rights, such as the principles of equality and of freedom of religion, there is ample room for conflict. The extent to which this is the case, is evident from the fervor with which the discussion over these questions has been or is conducted from time to time. Recently the conflict also occurred in Iraq, when the question arose whether in the new constitution Sharia should be designated as 'a' or 'the' source. The outcome in Iraq is that Islam is a fundamental source for legislation and that no law can be adopted that is in conflict with its undisputed stipulations. It is up to the supreme court to interpret this stipulation (Coleman 2006: 30).

The situation in the countries more closely studied for this report is as follows (Otto 2006; Otto et al. 2006). Iran employs a strict formulation in the constitution of 1980: all laws and rules must absolutely be based on Islamic criteria and classical Sharia takes precedence above any form of customary law and international law. The formal position of Pakistan seems to be somewhat less stringent: the constitution of 1973 stipulates, on the one hand, that "obedience to the Constitution and law is the [inviolable] obligation of every citizen" (art. 5.2), but, on the other hand, all laws ought to be line with "the Injunctions of Islam as laid down in the Holy Quran and Sunnah" (art. 227). In 2002, however, the introduction of a puritanical interpretation of Sharia was proposed in one of the Pakistan's provinces. In Egypt the principles of Sharia were set down as the only source of legislation in 1980. The testing of legislation against this constitutional stipulation is reserved to the High Constitutional Court of Justice. The Court has determined, however, that only legislation from after 1980 must be in agreement with the principles of Sharia. Furthermore, these principles are interpreted in a very restricted fashion, namely, it considers only the rules of Sharia that are indisputably established in the Quran and Sunna. In this way, laws can still be adopted that meet all Western standards. The empirical test of Hart (1997) shows, therefore, that even if the constitution considers Sharia as the exclusive source of law, this may in concrete terms have only a limited meaning. The Sudanese constitution of 1998 states: "Islamic law and the consensus of the nation, by referendum, Constitution, and custom, shall be the sources of legislation and no legislation in contravention with these fundamentals shall be made..." (art. 65). This plurality has been chosen for the sake of restoring national unity, after twenty years of Islamization of law along orthodox lines, and resistance against it, especially but not exclusively in the Christian south. In the Afghan constitution (2004) it is stipulated that no law can be in conflict with the precepts of "the the sacred religion of Islam and the values of this Constitution" (art. 3). Formally, the law is based on a dual structure of norms: Sharia as well as human rights. Only when no legislative stipulation exists, should courts directly follow the principles of Sharia and of jurisprudence according to the Hanafite school of law (art. 130). In the constitution of Malaysia, Sharia is not indicated as a source of legislation. Furthermore, in 1988 it was determined by the highest judge that Sharia does not apply to public law but only to the law of persons and family law. Moreover, under the constitution legislative authority in matters of Islamic law does not lie at the level of the Federation but of the states. In a couple of states, with Islamic political parties in power, this led in the 1990s to criminal legislation based on Islamic principles. This situation is, very controversial however, including from the point of view of division of jurisdiction within the Federation. In Indonesia and Nigeria Islam plays a role as source of legislation on the decentralized level. Attempts in Indonesia to Islamize the national state and to introduce Sharia have up until now had no success. However, in the framework of decentralization legislative authority has been granted to some districts. National law grants Aceh the possibility of introducing certain elements of Sharia. Whether the recent Nigerian constitution (1999) grants the states competence to enact criminal legislation is a controversial question. The jurisdiction of Sharia on state level is, however, as in Malaysia, limited to the law of persons and family law. Despite increasing political manifestation of Islamic movements, the constitution of Mali (1992), because of the secular character and the balance of power, carefully avoids naming Sharia or Islam as source of legislation. We have already seen that although Morocco is an Islamic state, Sharia is constitutionally no source of legislation. In Turkey, finally, there is no constitutional reference to Islam or Sharia as source of legislation. In this secular state, an Islamic political party in fact was banned in 1997 because of suspicion that it wanted to introduce elements of Sharia (WRR 2004).

Conclusion

The Islamic activism that has appeared in all Muslim countries in recent decades has led to diverse consequences from a constitutional point of view. The role of Islam and Sharia in state and law was controversial in most of the twelve countries studied and sometimes led to unusually fierce conflicts, as in Sudan, Nigeria, and Pakistan. As we saw in Chapter 3, the conflicts were not only between those motivated by Islam, on the one hand, and Christian or secular forces, on the other, but also conflicts between radical and moderate Islamic groups or between Islamic schools of belief. The result is that Muslim countries display great differences with regard to the constitutional place of Islam and Sharia. Only a minority of Muslim countries define themselves as Islamic states, and Sharia is formally the most important source of legislation in only a minority. Also, if a country defines itself as an Islamic state, it is not always a theocracy (e.g. Pakistan). Neither does being an Islamic state wholly exclude democracy in principle, nor does it imply that the system of law in these countries is per se wholly determined by Sharia.

The constitutional variety we have observed can be summed up in three parts, namely theocratic systems, secular systems, and mixed systems. Of the countries examined more closely, Saudi Arabia and – to lesser extent – Iran are closest to theocracy, and at the other extreme stand secular states like Mali and Turkey. In between is a large group of mixed systems, which also can be further subdivided. First, there are three states with a predominantly secular constitution, namely Nigeria, Indonesia (not even a single reference to Islam in the constitution), and Malaysia. None of these countries defines itself as an Islamic state, Sharia does not serve as a source of legislation, and, except in Malaysia, Islam is not the state religion. This country illustrates that even when Islam functions as the state religion, this does not have to exclude a secular form of government (WRR 2004). Finally, there are five countries where Islam constitutionally has more influence because it is the state religion; they define themselves as Islamic states and/or Islam/Sharia are 'a' or 'the' source of legislation. This group consists of Egypt, Morocco, Sudan, Afghanistan and Pakistan. But that is not the whole story. Proclamations of Sharia as sources of legislation can have great influence, but not necessarily. Given the various meanings of the concept, Sharia can have a high 'declaratory' or 'preambulatory' content, without a lot of demonstrable influence on positive law; this is the case in Egypt. Again this does not imply that placing law under the symbol of Sharia is wholly without meaning; we will return to this point later.

Finally, it also can be concluded that Islamization of state and law is not a unilinear process that is going to occur in an ever greater part of the Muslim world, neither is it an irreversible process. Certainly each of the twelve countries studied has been exposed to sometimes heavy pressure from Islamic activism, but in countries like Turkey, Pakistan, Iran, Indonesia, Malaysia, Sudan and Egypt counter movements also have (had) a place. These could result in a weakening of the role of Islamic law or in more liberal interpretations. Furthermore, it seems that the sharpest phases of constitutional Islamization took place through revolutions, coups d'etat, or during states of emergency (Iran, Sudan, and Pakistan respectively). When populations in the last few years could express themselves in elections, moderation was fairly often chosen (Iran, except in 2005, Egypt, Morocco, Pakistan, Turkey, Indonesia, and Malaysia). Therefore there is no unambiguous process supported by the mass of Muslims, directed toward Islamization of state and law according to the classical model. Here, however, it must immediately be noted that – as was shown in the preceding chapter – elections were not always possible nor always allowed to proceed fairly; thus one can only speculate about the outcome of honest elections.

4.2.4   CRIMINAL LAW

The area of law where Islamization in a number of countries most comes to mind is certainly Islamic criminal law. Because of the cruel punishments, it is precisely Islamization in this area of law that stands as a model for the perception of 'regression to the Middle Ages,' which the concept of Sharia evokes for many.

Classical Islamic criminal law consists of three parts:
- The *hadd* crimes: this concept involves five offenses described in the Quran and the punishments prescribed, namely theft (amputation), highway robbery (from banishment to crucifixion, dependent on the seriousness), consumption of alcohol (whipping), *zina*: sexual relations outside of marriage (from lashing to stoning), and false accusation of *zina* (whipping). There exists controversy over whether or not apostasy in regard to Islam also is a *hadd* crime. The classical schools are in agreement regarding the measure of punishment for apostasy: the death penalty, in cases where the apostasy is not retracted. The schools of law vary on homosexuality and its sentence. In the fiqh, legal scholars have laid out stringent procedural conditions in such a way that applying the *hadd* punishments on the basis of provable evidence is always very difficult.
- *Jinayat*: rules for the application of the pre-Islamic principle of retribution 'an eye for an eye, a tooth for a tooth', or compensation with blood money in the case of murder, manslaughter, or assault and battery.
- *Siyasa*: the authority of the government to set rules for the remaining category of criminal offenses that cannot be counted among the above.

In the nineteenth and twentieth centuries, in most of the Muslim countries Islamic criminal law had made way for a Western form of criminal law; only in Saudi Arabia, Yemen, and Qatar was it retained. According to Berger (2006), beginning in the 1970s the following countries re-introduced Islamic criminal law: Libya (1972), the United Arab Emirates (1978, though not implemented), Iran (1979), Pakistan (1979), and Sudan (1983). The current situation regarding the *hadd* punishments in the twelve countries more closely studied is shown in table 4.1. The table reveals that the examples of Pakistan, Iran, and Sudan are not followed in Turkey, Egypt, Morocco, Indonesia, Mali, Malaysia, or Nigeria. However, some states in the federations of Nigeria and Malaysia have introduced Islamic criminal law (Nigeria in 2000, in Malaysia in 1993, where it has not yet been implemented).
The fact that Islamic criminal law has not been introduced even though the basis for it exists in the Quran and the fiqh, does not mean though that this was not on the agenda or is not still on the agenda for some Islamic groupings. In countries like Malaysia, Egypt, and Nigeria there are proponents of

incorporating Islamic criminal law into formal law. Table 4.1 makes it clear the adoption of hadd punishments in criminal law does not always imply that these are also carried out; indeed, it seems that this is increasingly less the case.

Table 4.1   Hadd punishments according to the law and in reality

	Hadd punishments in the law1[1]	Execution of stoning and/or amputation[2]
Egypt	No	No
Morocco	No	No
Saudi Arabia	Yes	Regulated
Sudan	Yes	Sharply decreased
Turkey	No	No
Afghanistan	Yes, but legitimacy disputed	No
Iran	Yes	Sharply decreased[3]
Pakistan	Yes	No
Indonesia	No	No
Malaysia	No, except some states	No
Mali	No	No
Nigeria	Yes, in northern states	Stoning no, amputation sharply decreased

1 The criminal law of Saudi Arabia is completely based on classical Sharia, including hadd punishments. In the other 'yes-countries' these punishments were adopted through legislation: Sudan, criminal law of 1991; Afghanistan, 1976 code of criminal law; Iran, 1996 code of criminal law; Pakistan, hudud ordinances of 1979; Malaysia, hudud laws of two provinces, Kelantan and Terengganu; Nigeria, code of criminal law of eleven northern states.

2 It must be noted here that in some countries whipping is regularly imposed, for example, in Pakistan particularly in the early 1980s.

3 In July 2005 two boys were hanged in Iran after being convicted of homosexuality. This sentence was shocking and remarkable because since 2002 Iran had dropped the most severe forms of corporal punishment – stoning, amputation – for hadd offenses. Moreover, the punishment did not correspond to the hadd punishments stipulated in the classical Sharia.

Source: Otto 2006

One must not take lightly the abandonment of the hadd punishments or the failure to implement them by countries that constitutionally have placed their law under the banner of Sharia. Exactly because the Quran enjoys such high status and is so explicit about some crimes and their punishment, the relevant Quran verses cannot simply be ignored. The deviation from the literal text demands – always controversial – interpreta-

125

tion, ijtihad. Via this method, the hadd punishments are interpreted alle-
gorically or as something clearly to be considered as a theoretical maximum
for the punishment or as punishments that are only valid in an – alas, not
yet realized – ideal Islamic society. There also is the possibility, when hadd
punishments are indeed part of the country's criminal law, to tie implementation to very stringent procedures for furnishing proof of the crime
(Shahrur 1992 in Trautner 1999a: 19; Bielefeldt 2000: 107).

The equally harsh punishments for jinayat crimes are in force in Iran,
Afghanistan, Sudan, Pakistan, Saudi Arabia and northern Nigeria. Behavior
subject to public prosecution on the grounds of siyasa may relate to
offenses against religion and violation of religious prescriptions, in so far as
these are not punishable as hadd offenses. They can involve apostasy
(rejection of the faith); insults in addressing religion (such as the infamous
blasphemy laws in Pakistan); missionary activity by non-Muslims; religious practice and proselytizing by Muslims with inadmissible religious
beliefs; sexual behavior considered sinful such as adultery or physical
contact in public; immoral cultural behavior such as dancing and singing;
failing to observe religious duties such as Friday prayer, abstaining from
alcohol, and fasting during Ramadan (Otto 2006; Berger 2006). In Saudi
Arabia, Iran, Sudan, and Afghanistan during the Taliban period, public
morals were guarded by the morality police, who often came under an
'office for promotion of virtue and prevention of vice'. The situation in
regard to the law and actual punishments concerning rejection of the faith
is reflected in table 4.2.

Apostasy is threatened with very heavy punishment in Saudi Arabia,
Sudan, Afghanistan, and Iran, with a lighter punishment in Malaysia. In
seven of the twelve countries studied more closely, apostasy is not
addressed in the criminal code; in Afghanistan and Iran the subject is
disputed. The death penalty for apostasy has not been carried out in recent
years in Saudi Arabia and Iran, and in Sudan it is carried out only occasion-
ally. According to Otto (2006), Beke's observation in the 1990s still applies:
while actual punishment for apostasy is an exception nowadays (Beke
1996), the threat that arises from the penalization of this offense is, of
course, exceptionally high.

The summary above indicates that it is especially in the countries with an
Islamic state that Islamic criminal law is introduced, but this does not hold
true for all cases. In Afghanistan, after the period of the Taliban government, the criminal law code from the 1970s is again being applied. A new
criminal code is being prepared; it is unclear to what extent the hadd
punishments appear in it (Yassari and Saboory in Otto et al. 2006: 195). At
the same time it is worth considering that in Afghanistan the legal system

Table 4.2   Apostasy: penalization and actual punishment

	Penalization of apostasy[1]	Conviction for apostasy and execution of punishment
Egypt	No	No
Morocco	No	No
Saudi Arabia	Yes	Not recently[2]
Sudan	Yes	Occasionally
Turkey	No	No
Afghanistan	Disputed	No
Iran	Yes, legitimacy disputed	Not recently[3]
Pakistan	No	No
Indonesia	No	No
Malaysia	Yes	Very rarely[4]
Mali	No	No
Nigeria	No	No

1 Criminal law in Saudi Arabia is completely based on Sharia. Apostasy is a capital offense. If the crime is proven, the punishment is imposed. In Sudan (article 126 of the criminal code) apostasy is also a capital offense.

2 According to the US International Religious Freedom Report 2004 there have been no executions for apostasy in recent years.

3 According to an official report by the Dutch Ministry of Foreign Affairs in 2005, p. 31, there have been no persecutions of individuals in recent years for conversion to Christianity. No executions for apostasy have taken place recently.

4 Here this refers to very rare actions on the basis of state legislation, where the maximum punishment is three years imprisonment.

Source: Otto 2006: 107

under construction still finds itself in a chaotic situation. Where the formal system has not been working for a long time, there has been a resort to the informal customary law that in practice is interwoven, in incorrect ways, with stipulations from Sharia. In practice, then, hadd punishments will certainly be carried out (UK Home Office 2004). Among the countries where hadd punishments are now formally in place, there are great variations in interpretation and application. In addition to Saudi Arabia, in Iran and Sudan the stringent forms of hadd punishments are actually employed in such a way that even the religious scholars sometimes protest that the conditions formulated in the fiqh for the furnishing of proof are insufficiently brought into consideration. Corporal punishment may sometimes also be introduced 'for the sake of convenience' for offenses that fall outside of the Quranic hadd definition. At present it seems, however, that in Iran and Sudan, as well as northern Nigeria, the application of hadd punishments is decreasing; sensitivity to international protests has something to with this decrease.

It is remarkable that, with the exception of Saudi Arabia and Iran (up until 1982), the issuing of rules follows the model of national legislation and is applied by a national judicial power. At the same time, through this hybrid construction, brakes are built in against applying hadd punishments. Judgments by lower courts, staffed by conservative judges, often are overturned at higher levels. Higher judges, in particular, apply their authority – sometimes also with the effect of limiting the political power of the regime – to limit the range of hadd punishments and/or to make more demanding the furnishing of proof so that it is made more difficult for an offence to come to judgment as a hadd crime. Even in Libya, in the space of thirty years, only once has the most severe punishment been carried out, while in Pakistan, where the relevant highest law court consists of a majority of professional judges, the most severe punishments (stoning and amputation) have not to date been implemented (but punishments with lashings and also the jinayat-punishments have been carried out). Islamic criminal law is applied in a limited way on the level of individual states in northern Nigeria, but in Malaysia it is not yet or rarely applied in certain states. In both countries the authority to apply Islamic criminal law is very controversial due to the constitutional division of authority over criminal law between the federation and individual states; in Nigeria, criminal law is explicitly reserved to the federal level. Non-implementation of the most severe hadd punishments does not mean, though, that these offenses are not punished at all. The perpetrators of these 'crimes' can in general count on lighter physical punishments (whipping) or imprisonment.

Conclusion

We can conclude that Islamic criminal law is implemented only by a limited number of Muslim countries, namely eight of the 48, as well as by individual states/provinces in two Muslim countries. There is thus no foundation for ideas based on the assumption that in a Muslim country Islamic criminal codes always apply, nor for the opinion that such law is applicable in all the countries where law is formally (partly) based on Sharia. Moreover, formal implementation still does not mean that this criminal code also is actually implemented according to classical Sharia. In some countries the professional judges and higher bodies of law function as a brake on its implementation. The implementation of classical Sharia occurs in only a few countries; furthermore, in some of these countries it is limited to less extreme punishments (whippings). Other than in the case of some individual states, this criminal law is not introduced by normal democratic procedures but by the decree of rulers in coalition with the army or militias and radical Islamic groups. Such rulers avail themselves of this criminal law, either to take the wind from the sails of radical Muslim movements or to create an extra instrument of repression against opponents, all the better if it can be done 'in the name of Islam.' That this criminal law is implemented undemocratically does not, incidentally, mean that it is always rejected by the people. Certainly in situations of very high criminality and supposed harm to public morals accompanied by a weak or corrupt criminal investigation and trial apparatus, populations can feel the need for a firm hand (Otto 2006).

4.2.5 FAMILY AND INHERITANCE LAW

Family and inheritance law are the areas of law that in most Muslim countries have long been determined by Sharia; even under colonization this Sharia law was retained for Muslims. Conversely, these areas of law clearly represent the kernel of classical Sharia and are the most fully developed Islamic legal sources. Therefore it is not surprising that more or less immediately after the Islamic revolution in Iran in 1979, previous reform laws were abolished and replaced by the uncodified Sharia (1931: abolishment of polygamy, required marriage registration; 1967: equality under law for men and women; 1975: Family Protection Act). When the Taliban came to power in Afghanistan, the existing legislation was also abolished, and it was proclaimed that the laws could not be in conflict with the interpretations of the classical Hanafite school of law. But new national laws failed to appear; in practice there prevailed a very crude form of discrimination against women, who were almost completely excluded from the public domain and, through the religious police, also strictly controlled in their behavior in the private sphere (Yassari and Saboory in Otto et al. 2006: 187-188). Therefore, with the exception of these two countries and also Sudan, where the existing Islamic family law has been codified, there has been no recent Islamization in this area of law, at least in the sense of replacement of secular law by a specific version of Sharia. At the same time, this area of law encompasses subjects involving tensions with important conventions of human rights. Although family law forms only a small part of the whole body of present-day law in Muslim countries, it is naturally a very far-reaching area of the law, as it restricts the position of women, half of the population.

Where Sharia family law is in effect in Muslim countries, minorities who are members of another religion often have 'own' law in this area, frequently also with their own courts (Berger 2006: 37). This represents an important difference with *secular* systems of law, which are based on equal rights and duties for all. When *religious* law is the starting point for family law, legal pluralism is to be expected in religiously mixed populations: group rights in a given area for one group elicit group rights for others.

Just as in many other religions, in Islam the family is viewed as the sacred cornerstone of society. In Article 5 of the Cairo Declaration of Human Rights in Islam (see sec. 4.3) the family is quite explicitly referred to as the cornerstone. The reasoning is that men and women are equal in human value, but not in rights and duties. According to Dr. Yousuf al-Qaradawi in an explanation of the position of women in Islam, they are created in complementarity, and from their differences in natural disposition, different rights and duties follow. By nature, the woman is relatively weak, instinctive and seductive, and therefore limitations are placed on her behavior; it is also up to the man to protect her dignity (al-Qaradawi undated). In the classical view the man has the obligation to support his wife/wives financially from the moment the marriage is 'consummated', whereas the woman is responsible for maintaining the household and caring for children and for protecting the honor of her husband and his family. In this view the woman falls under the authority of her spouse, and therefore ought to be obedient, an obedience that may be compelled finally with 'not dishonorable beating'. The schools of law differ about the content of the demands for obedience, but in every case the woman cannot leave the conjugal house without the husband's permission. A notoriously controversial point is that a Muslim woman is forbidden from marrying a non-Muslim. The reverse is indeed possible; these marriages and the children born of them fall automatically under Islamic law. Other points of conflicts are the right of the man to have up to four wives at the same time and also the law on divorce. While the husband has the right to end, unilaterally and without giving a reason, the marriage by casting off the wife, in the classical view the woman is not granted the same right of divorce. She does have available some possibilities for dissolving the marriage, such as in the case of the man not fulfilling his conjugal duties, contractual conditions (dissolving in the case of a man's second marriage), and 'divorce with mutual consent' (Berger 2006: 38-41). All in all, classical family law reflects very patriarchal relationships, in which women occupy a position derived from that of the man. Although in the seventh century the Quranic rules represented an improvement in position of women who had previously been without any rights at all, from the present-day point of view of individual rights, the legal position of women according to classical Sharia is an anachronism.

The law of inheritance, too, belongs to the core of Sharia and is also developed in a very detailed manner. Just as marriage law, it reflects the classical tendency to closely guard the borders of the group. Muslims and non-Muslims are by law not named as one another's inheritors; it is in fact possible for a non-Muslim to inherit from a Muslim by testament, for no more than a third of the legacy. The inheritance right of women – divided into eight categories of claimant – is established by the Quran; they are considered as the 'Quranic' inheritors and receive their part first. The portion to be received by the diverse categories for women is always half that of her male counterpart (Berger 2006: 41-42). Here, too, the law represented a positive improvement at the time of its first introduction, but today implies discrimination in terms of the standards of international law.

Because family and inheritance law are so central to the classical Sharia and the rules concerned have such a high Quranic content, one would expect that exactly in these areas of law little would change or that, under the influence of the Islamization movement, they would in fact be further purified, as took place in Iran right after the revolution. However, in many countries we can actually observe a dynamism in law, and this often implies an improvement in the legal position of women. Still, this applies more to family law than inheritance law; large change did not occur in this latter area. A first factor that contributes to an improvement in the legal position of women is the codification of this part of Sharia in the course of the twentieth century in nearly all Muslim countries. The legislation and application of law were thus at least partly taken away from the ulama. Legislators use this formalization of Sharia in national systems of law for all kinds of improvements in the legal position of women. Thus it is the legislators themselves who take control of the interpretation of Quranic stipulations (ijtihad). This new 'state-regulated' reading or interpretation of the holy sources led in Tunisia to a ban on polygamy; in Egypt, Pakistan, Iran and Algeria to an expansion of the divorce possibilities for women (Berger 2006; Otto 2006). In Morocco, through application of the Quranic principle of ijtihad, sweeping changes were brought about. The break with the patriarchal model in the new family law of 2004 expresses itself, among other ways, in full freedom in the marriage contract and in regard to the custody of children after divorce (Buskens in Otto et al. 2006). Moreover, one of the forms of separation introduced, unknown in classical Sharia, places women in a position to request divorce on the grounds of 'structural breakdown' of the marriage (Berger 2006).

This 'secularization' of Islamic law (Baelz 1998) also expresses itself in other ways, this time via siyasa. Where Sharia family law is founded to a great degree on explicit rules in the Quran or Sunna – rules therefore that are supposed to have eternal validity and are thus seen as immutable – the governments of by far most Muslim countries use their free policy space – siyasa – to create all sorts of administrative and trial law conditions, procedures, and legal consequences that build a dam against automatic

131

application. Polygamy is, if not abolished as in Tunisia, linked to all kinds of conditions, such as agreement by the first wife and the requirement to report to the wife or a court that the man is capable of sustaining two or more households. Casting off of a wife is only permitted after settlement of financial conditions and/or after a required attempt at reconciliation through the court. This latter mode is not unknown in classical Sharia; the Sharia courts for family matters often follow the traditional line, where great attempts are made to move the two parties of the marriage toward reconciliation (Berger 2006: 71-73). Similar negotiation or mediation, furthermore, is also becoming increasingly significant in the pre-judicial stages of divorce proceedings in the West.

The result of the various Islamic modernization techniques is that in Saudi Arabia, Mali, Sudan, Nigeria, Iran and Afghanistan there are still few limits to polygamy; in Mali, Nigeria and Sudan, furthermore, polygamy is seen not primarily as an Islamic right but as stemming from customary law. In the remaining countries either all sorts of limits have been imposed upon this Quranic right (for example the requirement of approval in advance from the judge or another body and/or approval by the present wife or wives and the new one entering the marriage) or polygamy is forbidden (Turkey, Tunisia and – for government officials – Indonesia). In the countries where it is tied to conditions, the requirement based on Sharia of sufficient means of support and equal treatment, is often set by law. Relaxation of conditions occured in Malaysia. In this country the requirement for prior legal advance approval of polygamy, in force since 1984, lapsed in 1994. Casting off of a wife meets with few restrictions in Saudi Arabia, Sudan, and Afghanistan or – based on customary law – in Mali and Nigeria. In Egypt, Morocco, Iran, Pakistan, Indonesia and Malaysia the 'God-given' right to cast off a wife without formalities is somewhat restricted by the required mediation of the court or the mediation council, by compulsory attempts at reconciliation, by the duty to register and/or by alimony requirements. In Turkey, casting off a wife is forbidden. Only in Saudi Arabia and Afghanistan do women have no broader divorce rights than those accorded by classical Sharia; in the remaining ten countries the possibilities have been considerably expanded, even in Iran (Otto 2006: 99-201).

The reforms are not limited to the three themes of polygamy, casting off of the wife, and divorce rights for women. There are still many other controversial issues, such as age at marriage, freedom of choice of marriage partners, freedom of movement for women and inter-faith marriage. In the revised family legislation there also is movement in these areas, with the exception of the right to enter an inter-faith marriage (of a woman with a non-Islamic man).

All in all, it appears that in a number of Muslim countries where family law is strongly determined by Sharia (something which was ended completely in Turkey in 1924), innovation is not ruled out. With the exception of Iran, Afghanistan during the Taliban government, and a period in Sudan, the rising Islamic movements have not succeeded in bending the family law that they considered as too liberal, in an orthodox direction; the divorce legislation for women, relatively liberal in countries such as Egypt, Morocco, Pakistan, Indonesia and Malaysia, has not been reversed. Nor has important new legislation, as in Egypt in 2000 (likely to have great influence on surrounding countries) and Morocco (2004) been blocked. The reforms were not without controversy; the 'great leap forward,' for example, of Morocco in 2004, which broke with the patriarchal family model and granted equal responsibility to men and women, provoked heavy resistance. Indonesia, which has had a relatively liberal legislation in regard to marriage since 1974, has further liberalized its laws. Polygamy and casting off of a wife have been radically restricted. An exception concerns inter-faith marriage in Indonesia; since the 1990s in this multi-religious country such marriages have been made more difficult. As mentioned earlier, in Malaysia, too, there has been a regression, namely in regard to polygamy.

133

Conclusion

In a great part of the Muslim world, Islamic family and inheritance law form the areas of law par excellence that are seen as something authentically Islamic, as symbolizing genuine Muslim identity. In almost all Muslim countries the law in these areas is founded on interpretation of the Sharia. Yet this does not exclude changes, especially with regard to family law. And in so far as changes occur, they move for the most part in the direction of the principle of equality, which is an important basic assumption in the constitutional state and in international law. What is involved here, however, is not so much external pressure from human rights organizations as an endogenous dynamism that partly comes from pressure from the women's movement. The discourse about (changes in) the rights of women in these countries remains cast in Islamic jargon and makes use of mechanisms of change acceptable in Islam, but nevertheless the trend in most countries is one of strengthening the position of women. Concerning Morocco, Buskens – in his country report – concludes that the role of Islamic law in the area of women's rights is decreasing, but as result of, in fact, a political idiom of Islamization, which serves all the participants (Buskens in Otto et al. 2006). The long-run trend in the improvement of the position of women also holds where Sharia is introduced instead of customary law or even secular law. In the first case, Sharia represents a step forward compared to the informal law in place, for example in Aceh; in the second case, the step is also forward when, as for example in Malaysia, the existing secular legal institutions are difficult to reach or function poorly (corrupt judges, etc.) Although hesitatingly (but much too fast for the orthodox parts of the society), family law is distancing itself from classical Sharia and, along with this, modern interpretations have made their entrance.

4.3   ISLAMIC AND UNIVERSAL HUMAN RIGHTS

4.3.1   UNIVERSAL AND ISLAMIC DECLARATION

The universality of the human rights concept is strongly disputed in the Muslim world as well as in the West. Thus the former Malaysia prime-minister Mahathir, in the face of Western criticism of his human rights policy, regularly attacked this universality as a display of Western imperialism and called for Asian or Islamic values (Noor 2000). On the Western side, the criticism of universality is insistently represented by Huntington. In his view, the constitutional state, human rights, and democracy not only arose in the West, but also are bound to the unique configuration of characteristics upon which Western culture is founded. He mentions characteristics such as the classical Greek heritage, Catholicism and Protestantism, separation of secular and religious authority, social pluralism, representation and individualism. His view is that the non-Western world, including, certainly the Muslim world, increasinly wants to base itself on its own Islamic civilization and will reject Western innovations, such as democracy and human rights (Huntington 1996).

The attraction of these Western innovations for many in non-Western countries is certainly greater than Mahathir and Huntington suppose. Opinion polls regularly show that democracy stands high on the wish list of populations in Muslim countries (Hofmann 2004; Inglehart and Norris 2004; Pew Global Attitudes Project 2003). Bielefeldt contests the idea that the principles named here inevitably flow from Western history and are exclusive to it. Retrospectively, humanitarian motives behind what now is understood by universal human rights can be traced to the Greek philosophers, the Church fathers, and the Reformation. But the present-day result was not pre-determined by these and is at the very least the result of an organic development; the contingency of history might well have led to another outcome. Fear of moral decline, of losing positions of power and of the undermining of the hierarchical order of church and society provoked increasing resistance to the notion of rights for all on the part of church and non-Christian conservatives. Human rights are therefore better seen as the outcome of lengthy and very fierce conflicts than as something deeply rooted in the cultural and religious traditions of Europe. Europe, then, has little reason to regard human rights as in essence a Western concept to be exported to the developing world from a position of moral superiority. Instead, the West itself should be more self-critical, and realize that its own rise and fall in overcoming the structural injustices which culminated in barbarity, can contain important lessons for others (Bielefeldt 2000).

This more modest proposition does not deny the universal value of human rights but strips the human rights concept from Western imperialist connotations. Respect for human rights is also for Western countries a task requiring continuous vigilance; thus, the situation is not: 'we in the West have them and they don't'. This position also sharpens the focus on the historical dynamics; in the West, there was little talk of formal – let alone actual – equal rights for men and women until a long time after 1948. The Western experience teaches also that striving toward human rights can provoke conflicts with the elites in authoritarian societies and protracted resistance from religious organizations. Only with the Second Vatican Council in 1965-1967 was the concept accepted by the Roman Catholic Church.

Recent Islamic activism arose in precisely the same period as 'human rights activism.' In Chapter 2 we sketched the negative attitude of Khomeini toward the concept of universal human rights. The views of Pakistan's Mawdudi were similar. He rejected the Universal Declaration of Human Rights (UDHR) because of its Western bias and the arrogance with which the West imposed these rights on others (Mawdudi 1976 in Bielefeldt 2000). Just as there could be no democracy based on the sovereignty of the people – sovereignty belongs only to God – the same idea applies to the *rights* of people: Islamic law is about *obligations* toward God and fellow believers. Furthermore, the duty of one does not imply the right of the other: men are responsible for supporting their wife or wives, but she or they do not automatically have the right to be supported by their husband. Also, if obligations are owed only to fellow believers that means that we cannot speak of *universality*, at least as long as the *Ummah* is not equivalent to humanity (Trautner 1999a: 3). On a conceptual level universal human rights here stand diametrically opposed to conservative and puritanical interpretations of classical Sharia. By founding human rights on human dignity we are indeed looking at a universal concept that abstracts from religions and religious grounds. With its ascribed rights, the Universal Declaration aims to protect the individual from the state; reciprocity of the rights of the individual and the duties of the state is therefore the core.

Given the orthodox Islamic view of an inherent conceptual antithesis of human rights and Islamic law, it is all the more remarkable that the formal discourse shows all the signs of appropriating the human rights concept (Halliday 2003). The Organization of the Islamic Conference, at its found-

135

ing, referred in the preamble of its charter of 1972 without religious reservations to international law and fundamental human rights and declared
that these are compatible with Islamic values (Mayer 1999). This reflects
the initial secular-nationalist orientation of many Muslim countries. For
the conference in 1981, however, two years after the Islamic revolution in
Iran, a first concept was formulated of the Declaration on Human Rights in
Islam, which was not yet accepted. In 1990 a new version was indeed
accepted, the already mentioned Cairo Declaration of Human Rights in
Islam. The course of development after 1972 thus reflects the influence of
rising Islamic, as well as human rights activism. The concept of human
rights as such remained accepted, but in 1981 and 1990 only in so far as it
agreed with Islam or Sharia. Given the conceptual differences cited above,
which were much played up by Islamic movements after 1980, this is an
important fact. In the Declaration of 1981 the rights of the individual
person were actually discussed, although they were still derived from religious duties. This recognition of *rights* as such was a major innovation
compared to the orthodoxy. The changes in the period 1981-1990 go even
further. The Declaration of 1981 still contained all sorts of quotations from
texts out of the Quran and words of the Prophet; yet in tone and style the

declaration of 1991 resembles much more strongly that of the UDHR.
Instead of on all kinds of Quranic stipulations based on religious groups,
the focus in 1990 is on the *individual as such*. This is an important innovation and a rapprochement on the level of principle with the secular concept
of human rights (Trautner 1999a).

The Cairo Declaration has, therefore, much more than its predecessor a
hybrid character, and is not recognizable as a classical Sharia text. This also
can be read from the role that the Declaration grants to the state; the state,
in conformity with the Universal Declaration, is charged with the duty of
guaranteeing the rights of the individual. But the Cairo Declaration is
indeed a hybrid: fundamental rights and universal freedoms are presented
as an integral part of Islam. The hybrid character manifests itself also in
referring not only to the state but also to society and the individual as
bearer of duties. Furthermore, Sharia is indicated as the source for the
interpretation of the cited rights, duties, and freedoms. What is understood by Sharia here is not further specified and leaves, therefore, much
room for interpretation. Sometimes the Declaration is more specific, such
as on the right to life and respect of the person, which the state should
protect and which can be violated only by "a reason prescribed by Sharia"
(art. 2). The text, however, is perfectly clear regarding one central point: in
spite of a ban on discrimination on the ground of religion, Muslims are
forbidden to convert to another religion or to become atheists; Islam is seen
as the religion of "unspoiled nature" (art. 10). In this, we can recognize the
notion that Islam represents the ultimate revelation.

In conclusion, one could posit that the human rights concept is gradually being adopted, but specifically by 'Islamizing' it and by giving it a Sharia seal of approval. Stated a different way: precisely by fitting it to Islam's own discourse is this concept legitimized and appropriated (Halliday 2003). This does not exclude further dynamism; perhaps such a translation of the concept into Islamic terms is exactly what is needed as a condition for further dynamism (Coleman 2006). The development from 1981 to 1990, in any case, reveals that the terminology displays rapprochement with that of the Universal Declaration, without coinciding with it. Traut-ner judges the Cairo Declaration to be an enormous step forward. That the duties, rights and freedoms are founded upon Islam and subject to Sharia, he considers logical. Such documents always involve stating the philo-sophical basis for positive law; as in the Universal Declaration, the stipu-lated rights and freedoms in the Cairo Declaration in themselves do not make up positive law. For that, one must refer to the binding laws that are based on the Declarations (Trautner 1999a).

4.3.2   MUSLIM STATES AND CONVENTIONS: RATIFICATION AND RESERVATIONS

The way in which many Muslim states have bound themselves to the important human rights conventions also displays a hybridness. Table 4.3 gives an overview of the ratification by the twelve countries researched of three conventions that are very important for human rights, and also of the reservations they have expressed on grounds of Sharia. This concerns the following three elaborations of the Universal Declaration of 1948:

- the International Covenant on Civil and Political Rights (ICCPR) of 1966, that went into effect in 1976;
- the Convention on the Elimination of All Forms of Discrimination Against Women (CEDAW) of 1979, that went into effect in 1981;
- the Convention against Torture, and other Cruel, Inhuman and Degrad-ing Treatment or Punishment (CAT) of 1984, that went into effect in 1987.

The three conventions cover important dimensions of the rule of law, namely, basic political rights (ICCPR), the principle of equality (CEDAW), and the integrity of the human body (CAT). They all came into effect in the recent period of Islamic activism and concern very sensitive subjects, certainly according to the classical interpretation of Sharia. The table thus could have been empty, but it is not. All twelve countries have joined at least one of the three treaties. Even Saudi Arabia, the only Muslim country which has not committed itself to the Universal Declaration, is party to two conventions. The CEDAW, the subject matter of which was the focus of section 4.2.5, and which forbids discrimination between men and women, is the only convention that runs up against reservations on the ground of Sharia; this is the case in four countries. Of the four countries which have taken up the hadd punishments in their national criminal law (Iran, Sudan, Pakistan, Saudi Arabia), two (Iran and Pakistan) are not party to the CAT; Sudan has not yet proceeded to ratification.

The conventions contain many points of tension with classical Sharia. Those concerning the equality of men and women and criminal law have been discussed in the preceding sections. Along with many other freedoms, the ICCPR deals with freedom of religion. According to classical Sharia, freedom of religion is formally not problematic for 'people of the Book', that is, Christians and Jews, no matter how many obstacles can be raised to the actual practicing of their religions. Depending on the ethnic and pre-Islamic situation, the constitutions of the various countries also recognize other religions, such as Zoroastrianism in Iran, and Hinduism in Indonesia which became a monotheistic religion under the Pancasila principle. But, as the Cairo Declaration demonstrates, Islam is certainly seen as the ultimate revelation and is formally accorded preferential treatment on many fronts (for example, in the marriage and inheritance laws, religious education, access to high state functions). It is sometimes also expressed in the severe sanctioning of apostasy or atheism. This formal position has, of course, drastic practical consequences. The appreciation for pluralism is limited; as Tibi argues, in the orthodox vision there is no

Table 4.3   Signatories to three human rights treaties

	ICCPR	CEDAW	CAT
Egypt	x ¹)	x ¹) ²)	x ¹)
Morocco	x ¹)	x ¹) ²)	x ¹)
Turkey	x ¹)	x ¹)	x ¹)
Afghanistan	x ¹)	x ¹)	x ¹)
Mali	x ¹)	x ¹)	x ¹)
Nigeria	x ¹)	x ¹)	x ¹)
Sudan	x ¹)		x
Saudi Arabia		x ¹) ²)	x ¹)
Indonesia		x ¹)	x ¹)
Pakistan		x ¹)	
Iran	x ¹)		
Malaysia		x ¹) ²)	

¹) Ratified

²) With reservations, based on Sharia

Source: Otto 2006: 165.

modern understanding of tolerance (Tibi 2004). In section 4.2.4 we saw
that in some countries apostasy is a grave offense. Yet discrimination is
directed not only against other religions; Islamic doctrines other than those
recognized by the state in coalition with the orthodoxy or with Islamic
movements, also can become victims of discrimination. Thus in Pakistan
the Ahmadis were declared to be apostates, as were the Baha'i in Iran, and
the Alewites in Turkey are not recognized as a religious minority. Thus, the
definition of apostasy can be drawn very broadly.

Against this background, one could be cynical about the meaning of joining
and ratifying human rights treaties. A right on paper is not yet a right in
practice. The human rights situation in many Muslim countries is not rosy.
But the goal of this chapter is not to make a survey of the current human
rights records of Muslim countries, but to assess to what extent Islamization of the law blocks the development toward accepting universal human
rights. That is a question about dynamics. If and when this rapprochement
presents itself, it represents an important reference point for the intensification of relations directed toward further rapprochement with the countries concerned.

139

At least on paper, there is acceptance of important human rights. Some
countries have expressed reservations on the grounds of Sharia. In itself,
that is not surprising for countries which, during their entire political
history, have viewed maintenance of Sharia as being an important source of
legitimation. Mayer notes in this regard that, in the last decade, Muslim
countries increasingly less often advance the position that the human
rights laid down in international treaties are in conflict with their Islamic
law. Unlike in the past, their standpoint is now that both are indeed
compatible; reservations are no longer motivated by Islamic law but by the
position that one should stand by the principles of one's own national law
(Mayer 1998). Otto comes to the same conclusion on the basis of the
records of discussions held with the representatives of these countries in
the treaty commissions dealing with national reports on treaty countries.
In these commissions, there is widespread criticism of the laws and practices of the Muslim countries researched. But the discussions are now less
about the general opposition between 'Islam' or 'Sharia' and the conventions than they used to be. Instead, they are more concrete and constructive, and progress is observed. Where Muslims also sit in these expert
commissions, claims in terms of 'Islam' are no longer automatically
accepted, and attention can be paid to national legal developments in relation to legal developments in other Muslim countries (Otto 2006).
Being party to a human rights treaty does not guarantee a spotless human
rights situation. However, against the background of classical Islamic
doctrine which rejects the concept of human rights as such, the situation

has fundamentally changed. One now encounters many more opinions to the effect that Islam or Sharia is reconcilable with human rights, or even that human rights were actually invented by Islam and all already present in the Quran (see Chapter 2). Be that as it may, annexation of the concept by translating it into one's own ideas is a very important reference point for the further development toward a constitutional state. It creates a basis on which the national and international discussion can further build without there being immediately polarized positions. That Muslim countries are exposed to world mechanisms of social control by becoming parties to international treaties, and – as it appears – now take a learning rather than a confrontational stance on the findings and recommendations that issue from these mechanisms, confirms that previous conflicts are losing force not only conceptually but also practically. In this regard, Nobel Prize winner Shirin Ebadi's call upon the West to no longer continually ascribe factual violations of human rights to Islam is important. Attributing human rights violations to Islam not only ignores this rapprochement, but also stirs up past conflicts and undermines practical progress (Ebadi 2004).

Baderin tries to further an objective discussion by systematically comparing the articles of two human rights conventions and their explanations with the pronouncements of Islamic legal scholars about these subjects. He also looks at the opinions of the Islamic schools of law. One of the two conventions he analyzes is the ICCPR, discussed above. This convention also contains many subjects that are further elaborated in the CEDAW and the CAT. On the grounds of his extensive research, Baderin concludes that for the overwhelming part of the very detailed ICCPR, there is no difference with Islamic law. The areas of conflict concern the scope of equality between men and women and between Muslims and non-Muslims, the ban on inhuman and humiliating punishments, freedom of religion and freedom of expression, and some crimes for which the death penalty is a possibility. But even in these cases, the differences can, in his view, be reduced , because in the various law schools one can almost always find interpretations that – while not in their outcomes than still in their reasoning – come close to those of international law (Baderin 2003). Berger reports that, unlike what formerly was customary, legislators meanwhile have given themselves the right to make a choice from among the legal rulings of all the schools of law (Berger 2006: 72). This flexibility, therefore, makes it possible to interpret the Sharia in as humane a manner as possible. The Sharia can – provided indeed that it is humanely interpreted – serve as an engine for the realization in Muslim countries of rights such as those laid down in the ICCPR, (Baderin 2003).

4.3.3 CONCLUSION

The human rights situation in Muslim countries does not meet international standards, but this situation in Muslim countries is no less favorable
than in other developing countries. The various indices in the *Human
Development Report 2004*, that measure the position of women, show a
great spread. Several Muslim countries score better than non-Muslim
countries in Africa, Asia, and Latin America (UNDP 2004). It is a hopeful
development that the concept of human rights as such has gained entry
into Islamic juridical thinking. Given the nature of classical Islamic thinking, that is an important innovation. It does not, however, for the most
part, represent a full acceptance of that concept; rights and freedoms are
still filtered through an Islamic lens. But that does not exclude further
rapprochement, and signs of such developments can in fact be observed.
This represents an important reference point for reducing the tensions
between Sharia and international law.

At present the ideas of the modernizers of the end of the nineteenth and
the beginning of the twentieth centuries mentioned in Chapter 2, such as
those of Mohammed Abdu, are being implemented in various countries,
despite attempts by the orthodox and fundamentalist sides to bring the law
more into agreement with the fiqh or so-called 'true' Islam, respectively.
At the same time, the current hybrid situation creates a great deal of uncertainty. Law on paper, with its often differing constitutional basic norms,
does not have to be in agreement with law in practice, and this discrepancy
can just as well fall to the advantage as to the disadvantage of actual human
rights. Law on paper can fulfill the function of pure symbolism or window
dressing (Aubert 1971). It can, however, be intended as much to satisfy the
national and international guardians of human rights as the guardians of
'true' Islam. An indication of the first is the constitutional right to freedom
of religion, while apostasy is made punishable in criminal law. An indication of the second is that in some countries the hadd punishments are
indeed formally introduced, but are not carried out due to buffers built into
the legal system. This hybrid situation raises questions about future developments.

4.4 INTERPRETATION OF THE LEGAL DYNAMISM

This chapter illustrates that one cannot make generalizations about Islamic
law in Muslim countries. Great differences are hidden by the banner of
Sharia, and Muslim countries are also very diverse in the ways their
systems of law fit an Islamic template. This holds as much for constitutional aspects as for important areas of law, such as family law and criminal
law. There is only one country that is governed by classical Sharia, namely

Saudi Arabia, and even here, not fully. All the other countries defined as Islamic in their constitutions, namely Iran, Pakistan, Sudan and the present Afghanistan, have not only Sharia as a constitutional basic norm, but the constitution itself, which also includes references to concepts other than religious norms (rule of law, rights and freedoms). The comparative study of legal systems for this report shows that all other countries exhibit a large measure of variation in the relationship between religious and non-religious basic norms. Even where the areas of law most influenced by Islamization are concerned, variety is the most striking characteristic. Otto proposes, on the basis of research in twelve countries, three categories: classical Sharia (Saudia Arabia and Iran), secular systems (Turkey), and mixed systems. The last, and largest, category can in turn be divided into three sub-categories on the basis of the role of Islamic precepts in some areas of law. This role is the greatest in three countries, that is in Sudan, Pakistan, and Afghanistan, though less explicitly than in Saudi Arabia or Iran. Indonesia and Mali comprise the most 'secular' of the three subgroups. The group in between consists of Egypt, Morocco, Nigeria, and Mali (Otto 2006: 37-39 and 128-132). This large spread regarding the role of Sharia in the legal system would not be less for the legal systems of the whole population of 48 Muslim countries.

Against the background of the historically given need for political legitimacy, it is not surprising that the Sharia or Islam, however further interpreted, have gained a place in the law of a number of countries. In the past decades, the card played by movements based on the Islamization of the law also therefore could not simply be ignored. Recently, as in Afghanistan, Nigeria, and Sudan, this has led to fierce and sometimes very bloody confrontations about 'Islam' and 'Sharia'. But rather than between 'civilizations,' *clashes* (Huntington 1996) have occurred, and continue to occur, *within* the Muslim world. As far as law goes, the question here is whether or not the confrontations lead to an 'Islamization of the law' or indeed a 'nationalization of Sharia into an all-encompassing national legal system. Put another way: what will be the outcome of the struggle for the monopoly of national law? In Muslim societies with heterogeneous views on legal systems, different 'masters of the law' are involved in this struggle: traditional tribal leaders, religious scholars, political rulers, elected representatives, professional national and international jurists. The coalitions that form among these 'masters' are important for the development of law (Otto 2006: 136-138).

A definitive answer to the question posed cannot be given, for neither the process of state formation nor the striving toward 'Islamization' constitutes a closed chapter. There are also great internal and external uncertainties: how stable are the peace accords in Afghanistan and Sudan, and what is the chance that their constitutions are going to function? What is going to happen in Iraq, Iran, Lebanon, Syria and with the peace process between Palestine and Israel? How stable is the situation in countries such as Egypt, Iran, Morocco, Algeria, Pakistan, and Malaysia? What will be the political and military position of Western countries? Everywhere the contingencies are great and events have consequences that reach beyond the countries directly involved. With the exception of Iran, Muslim movements have not yet succeeded in bringing about a national revolution. Other than was feared, they have not fallen like dominos before classical Sharia either. Although the system of law in Iran is indeed formally 'Islamized,' according to the classical model, this 'Islamization' itself is not complete and has partly been tempered again. The double constitutional basic norm – Islam as well as *raison d'etat* – which also became translated institutionally, has brought about a permanent struggle. This led to the creation of a new institution with the authority to define the 'common good,' which also formally prevails above Sharia. But in Iran, even this Sharia itself is not unambiguous; although the reform movement has temporarily come off the worst politically, it has contributed to the concept that Islam permits multiple interpretations. Thus, in this theocracy, a 'hermeneutical pluralism' has been introduced (Arjomand 2004: 22). Chapter 2 shows that this plurality also includes opinions that set themselves against the theocracy precisely on Islamic grounds. Here, too, we cannot speak of an unequivocal Islamization in the classical style; and furthermore there is rather a considerable measure of nationalization and encapsulating of Sharia in national legal systems.

143

The process in which Muslim countries are involved exhibits a certain analogy to the process of secularization of canonical law in Europe (Berman 1983). Just as in Europe, the nationalization of religious law in the Muslim world is not a process that takes place quickly and smoothly but one that comes about over a very long period and through great controversies and confrontations between the religious and state authorities and their followers. Even so, as Otto describes, the main line in Muslim states is still one of incorporating the legal system into the state and its constitution, and thus of nationalizing Sharia. This nationalization is paralleled by large changes in the sense that the formal and substantive characteristics of Sharia law increasingly differ from those of the classical fiqh.

For most countries, the answer to the question of who will be the winner of the struggle for the legal monopoly has until now come down in favor of the state. The codification that parallels state formation simultaneously leads toward a substantive change in the tenets of belief. The definition of national law is increasingly taken out of the hands of the ulama and is placed under the jurisdiction of state actors, in regard not only to legislation but also to judicial intervention. In Muslim states, the customary model is that of a Ministry of Religious Affairs controlling religious developments. Its jurisdictions is often considerable, including the design and execution of Sharia-related legislation, the management of religious courts, the control over religious education, the construction and administration of mosques, the distribution of religious information, the collection and distribution of religious taxes, and supervision in matters of marriage and divorce. These ministries form a buffer between the state and the ulama, and may thus offer a counterweight against radicalization. However, it is also possible that radicalization is strengthened, for example if regimes feel they can benefit from taking over parts of the Islamization agenda or if their efforts to propagate a 'moderate' Islam has the unintended consequence of playing into the hands of radical Islamic movements. Furthermore, such forms of state Islam will not easily encourage 'free thinking' , since this is seen as a threat by the vested (state) interests (see also Chapter 3). Thus, in these cases, too, it is the state that defines the space for religion, and not the reverse (Otto 2006: 189).

The role of the judiciary is striking. Where there exists a constitutional double basic norm, higher law institutions such as the High Council, the Constitutional Court or the Sharia Court of Appeal, in various countries (such as Egypt, Malaysia, Indonesia, and Pakistan) have limited the reach of classical Islamic norms in favor of more modern interpretations or existing secular norms. Thus in Egypt, the scope of the 1980 constitutional amendment that Sharia is the source of legislation has been severely curtailed by the Constitutional Court. It has thus also declared the development of secular law in many areas not to be in conflict with Sharia. Furthermore, the Court claims the exclusive right to interpret the principles of Sharia, without following the rules of Islamic jurisprudence (Arjomand 2004: 20). In Pakistan the high law colleges play a comparable role. The High Council has come down decidedly in favor of secular articles of the constitution a number of times in legal cases where conflicts between the two constitutional basic norms were in play. The Federal Sharia Court, given authority in, among other matters, hadd punishment cases, has time after time annulled decisions of lower courts that had imposed the highest hadd punishments. Both bodies are mainly composed of professional jurists. Just as in Egypt, it is therefore now the non-religious scholars who judge in matters of religious law (ijtihad). From Lau's research it appears in fact that also these non-religious judges nevertheless employ religious arguments for judgments that deviate from those of the ulama judges. Just as in countries like Egypt, Indonesia, Malaysia and Nigeria, the higher law colleges in Pakistan thus erect a barrier against Islamization of the law in a classical direction. This battle over the right to judge is intertwined with another similar struggle, namely that against the instrumentalization of the law and the judges by the executive. Where the Pakistani government has tried to meet radical groups with radical laws (rule by law), the higher law colleges have resisted this by calling upon fundamental principles of law on behalf of the public interest. Thus, they try to affirm their own formally independent position and also to underline the principle that the executive is also subject to the rule of law (Lau 2003). Independence of the judiciary is not yet self-evident in most Muslim countries. Rosefsky Wickham shows that for Egypt the 'victories' of the Constitutional Court over the ruling power can partly be traced to the willingness of the government to respect the Court's decisions (Rosefsky Wickham 2002: 224).

The comparative law analysis also shows that the re-introduction of Islamic law mainly occurred in the period 1965-1985. After that, it lost force, despite the growing tensions between Western and Muslim countries. This confirms Roy's view that the Islamic revolution has passed its zenith (Roy 1994 and 2004). Measured against the 'fervor' and the claims of Islamic activist movements described in the preceding chapter, the Islamization of law has actually remained limited. Except in Iran and for a time in Afghanistan (Taliban), and in Sudan and Pakistan, Islamic forces and the people in power could not 'hijack' the state and formal law; rather, the reverse has been the case. Islamization sometimes seems to be more of a symbolic exercise (such as, for example, in the case of introducing general references to Sharia in the constitution) than a major influence on positive law. In the preceding section, furthermore, mention was made of the rise of the concept of *Islamic* human rights, as a reaction against the universal concept of human rights. Nevertheless, in practice there seems to be rapprochement between both concepts. Also, it appears that more and more Muslim countries – even Saudi Arabia – want to become party to human rights conventions, and ever less resort to reservations based on Islamic argumentation. Even in the heavily Quranic field of family law, Sharia does not block the modernization of law in several countries.

This raises the question of whether modernization of law may actually become easier precisely because it takes place under the banner of Sharia and through reasoning based on Islam. If that were the case, then the adoption of Sharia as a basic norm in a constitution would not be an empty or purely tactical gesture but an important condition for further development towards a democratic constitutional state. In postmodern jargon: if changes can be legitimated from one's own frame, they are more easily acceptable than if they are supported by arguments that are foreign to that frame or even – for the time being – seem to be conflicting. Proof of this possibility cannot of course be given, but it seems quite plausible.

The adoption of Sharia in the constitution as *a* or *the* source of legislation does not – functionally – have to do with the level of binding law itself but rather with its *legitimation*. In this logic, it would facilitate the legitimation of law if legal subjects can experience it as their own. Thus, the framing of law becomes essential. While acknowledging all the cynical reasons for rulers to use Sharia as an instrument to maintain their position (for example as the result of a deal with the Islamic opposition), it must still be remembered that in recent decades, large sections of the Muslim world have been very receptive to a discourse in an Islamic key; rulers know what chord to strike. The slogan 'Islam is the solution' found and continues to find considerable resonance among the population. If the development of law follows an Islamic template it would be able to give modernization a less threatening face than is currently the case. In his study on the development of law in Morocco, Buskens shows that with the new openness in that country since the 1990s, two discourses have started to dominate politics, namely Islam and human rights. In part these go together: Islamic movements combine Islamic discourse with the idiom of human rights. As we have seen, in Morocco this has culminated in an important innovation in the area of family law (Buskens in Otto et al. 2006).

Trautner considers developments toward democratic constitutional states in the Muslim world as likely options, but he also sees it as essential that this takes place in an Islamic frame. He urges the West to pay more attention to the ideas of contemporary Islamic reformers, such as those discussed in section 2.3. Thinkers like Soroush (Iran), An Na'im (Sudan) and also al-Ghanushi (Tunisia) fit in with the need for authenticity and thus lay the theoretical basis for the Islamization of democracy, rule of law, human rights, plurality, etc. At present, various parties with essentialist motives still often claim a monopoly on the interpretation of Sharia. According to Trautner, it is precisely through a reconceptualization of traditional Islamic concepts that they can contribute to a gradual 'democratization' of interpretation (Trauner 1999b).

If the universal and the Islamic human rights declarations or the constitutions of some Muslim countries are compared with those of Western countries, we find evident differences alongside rapprochement. If on the basis of these differences we would conclude that these differences are fundamentally irreconcilable, then we would assume that legal systems cannot change. Such an assumption would ignore the dynamism that the law experiences everywhere as a result of changed circumstances, both – and perhaps first and foremost – in the *application* and in the substance of the positive law. Thus we are confronted with the question of whether the modernization of Sharia interpretations will not ultimately converge toward international law. This may occur not because of the hegemonic influence of international law but because countries simply want to catch up. 'Catching up' – in all imaginable variations – ultimately suggests a certain 'equality'. This argument will be illustrated by looking at the position of women.

Legal rules to a certain extent and at the risk of becoming dictatorial or irrelevant, reflect social norms. The qualification 'to a certain extent' is deliberate because a complete reflection of 'lived' norms is of course neither possible nor desirable. Certainly in countries with large inequalities, such norms vary greatly, for example between the elite and the masses, between traditional and modern, and among ethnic communities. This also means that formal law is connected to the stage of development of a country. From a Western point of view, the legal position of women in many Muslim countries is seen as 'strange or 'different', as characteristically belonging to 'Islamic' and thus foreign norms and values. Yet it must be remembered that many of the (sacred) beliefs about marriage, the family and the role of women in Muslim countries were not so long ago also generally accepted in the Netherlands, and are still harbored by some. In Christian circles – and not only there – the family was and is seen as the cornerstone of society. Dissolving marriages made in church through divorce was not possible in many congregations. Sex outside of marriage was also taboo for a very long time, and homosexual behavior is still taboo for many Christian denominations. The recent letter from the Vatican to the bishops on the cooperation between men and women in and outside the church still exudes the atmosphere of a 'natural' division of roles between men and women and of the special responsibility of the woman for the family, which is seen as "the primordial and, in a certain sense sovereign society" (Congregation for the Doctrine of the Faith 2004). The idea of complementarity, in which there was no equality of rights and obligations and women were seen as the weaker party deserving of protection, also prevailed in the Netherlands until the 1970s. Until 1957 married women in the Netherlands did not have full legal capacity, and until 1971 the man was the head of the family (In't Veld-Langeveld and Schoonenboom 1976).

147

In many Muslim countries there are large inequalities in levels of development: apart from a prosperous, well-educated elite there is also much poverty and illiteracy, especially among women. These differences manifest themselves in many other qualities such as the number of children, knowledge of the world, and religious views. Unlike the elites, the masses still hold very traditional norms with regard to the position of women. These societies live, as it were, simultaneously in different times: one layer lives in the highly modern era, the other still in the premodern era. Yet the developments in the coming decades will not leave the masses undisturbed. Further urbanization, rising levels of education for women, smaller families, participation in the workforce, increasing wealth and media consumption are changing the position of women, their self-perception and independence. In Iran, which has seen a rapid improvement in women's levels of education in recent decades, it is precisely women that have voted in favour of a deradicalization. Their 'subversive' actions against classical Islamic prescriptions also found other means of expression. In the heavily Islamic-ideological period immediately after the revolution, the regime lowered the minimum age of marriage from 15 to 9 and later raised it again to 13. However, the actual average age at marriage has now increased to above the age of 24. With the rise in the age of marriage, the number of children per woman declines. The ideologically sacrosanct vocation of women in marriage and family is thus refuted by actual behavior; the best possible education and a fitting job have become a normal part of the life of many young women, and the Iranian economy also needs them badly. Sooner or later the legal norms will follow the direction of social changes, be applied differently or become a dead letter. The recent expansion of divorce opportunities for Egyptian women, which were thought to be chiefly for the benefit of affluent women, illustrates this kind of different application of the law. This so-called *khul* divorce through which women who waive their financial rights are able to divorce in court without the agreement of their husbands, actually turns out to be used mainly by poor women (Berger and Sonneveld in Otto et al. 2006). Comparative legal research shows that in other Muslim countries such as Pakistan, Indonesia, and even Saudi Arabia, the juridical norms are also adapting to changes (Otto et al. 2006). Roy, too, observes that actual developments in the Muslim world in the areas of marriage, family, and divorce, among other things, correspond – with a delay – to those in the West and that even behind an ostensible return to tradition, like the return to the headscarf, modernization is hiding (Roy 2004: 140-141).

As lost ground is made up and this is translated into changes in family law, one can expect convergence. However, given the arrears of many countries in, for instance, education levels and the distribution of wealth (see Chapter 2), this is likely to be a long-term project that may take generations, even though this will differ among Muslim countries. At the same time, it must be remembered that adapting formal law to actual developments can be speeded up by the activities of social movements. Arjomand points out that, at present, women's movements are one of the most dynamic factors in Muslim countries (Arjomand 2004: 25). Even in Saudi Arabia women's NGOs are making themselves heard. Under their influence, one of the legal pillars of Wahhabism is now under fire, namely the principle of 'blocking of the means'. This principle forbids acts that can lead to sin; on this basis, women are forbidden from driving a car (Meijer 2005). Just as women's movements in the West in the 1960s and 1970s had a major influence on legislation, that may now be the case in the Muslim world. This may be all the more true once democratic openings are also available to women.

No matter how plausible continued convergence may be, there will remain differences or 'multiple modernities'. Eisenstadt uses this concept to oppose the idea, still present in the West, that modernization is a uniform and linear process leading to a situation in which the West – as forerunner – is still the model. Following Max Weber, Eisenstadt sees modernization as the gradual rooting of the idea that the universe does not represent an unchangeable, Divine order but one that can be changed by conscious human action. Through this insight, man becomes an autonomous factor who can free himself from traditional political and religious authority. The reactions to this process are not identical within and outside the West; they are context-dependent and continually evolving. History, social and economic dynamism, and institutional structure are all relevant. This does not exclude similarities in trajectories and/or results, nor does it exclude differences and hybrid forms (Eisenstadt 2000).

Eisenstadt's concept of 'multiple modernities' raises the question of what the 'multiple' will refer to in the area of family law. One can only speculate about this, but it does not seem plausible that religion and Sharia will disappear as sources of inspiration for law in the foreseeable future. In Western Europe, the development of secular law was to a great degree the result of its separation from canon law during the eleventh century. This created distance between religious and worldly law, but also created room for the development of secular law. Concepts like the rule of law, to which the king was also subject, could emerge because the resulting distance allowed the kingship to be stripped of its religious legitimacy (Berman 1983). This fundamental division of the two domains could occur because the church was an institution with decision-making power. This institutional condition is lacking in the Muslim world; certainly in the Sunni world institutional structures more resemble those of Protestantism than of Roman Catholicism. That does not mean that a separation of the religious community and the state or a secularization of law cannot occur; *de facto* this is going on everywhere. But the path of development is not identical.

'Sharia' in itself is plurifom and flexible enough to adapt to all sorts of circumstances; whether this will actually occur is of course dependent on, among other things, the development process and power relationships. It seems plausible that in the longer term, Sharia will, even more than now, function in the more abstract meaning of God's way and social justice than now is the case. In the discourse relevant for the legitimacy of the law,

Sharia will remain an important source of inspiration. Positive law, however, will increasingly be imbued with the values behind the letter of the commandments and the prohibitions. It will result in the implementation of all sorts of procedures that further soften the commandments and prohibitions, thus moving further away from classical Sharia. But this development will continue to take place in a *religious* discourse. And although the outcomes in many areas of law will appear normal to Western eyes, such a discourse will presumably lead to other restrictions on behavior than are drawn in parts of the West. For the time being, controversial issues will remain, from the acceptance of religious plurality to related issues of minority rights, of apostasy and unbelief, freedom of expression, the privileged position of men, and a complex of moral questions like sex outside marriage and homosexuality (Takeyh 2001/2002). There is also dynamism in all of these areas, although the situation differs from country to country. This dynamism expresses itself more in the shelter of the private sphere than in the public space. The heavy punishments for apostasy in some countries will discourage many from explicitly abandoning their religion; however, that does not rule out departing from the faith in less conspicuous ways, such as gradually complying less with religious prescriptions. Discrepancies between public prescriptions and privately exercised behavior creates tensions which sooner or later induce adaptation. In Malaysia, for example, in the relative anonymity of the Internet, a prison sentence for apostasy for the first time provoked a semi-public discussion over this taboo, in which Muslims spoke out in favor of the right to abandon one's religion as a part of religious freedom (Internet Malaysia 2005). Religion and morality will retain importance in legal thinking, but it is difficult to predict in what ways and how compellingly they will set the norms for social development.

4.5   CONCLUSION

The concept of Sharia has many meanings. It can be an indication of the abstract plan of God for the community of believers, it can refer to the elaboration of this plan in a set of rules of behavior by the early religious scholars, or it can involve contemporary interpretations by states, institutions, and groups. If we examine current law based on Sharia, we are especially struck by its great diversity. There are great differences among Muslim countries in the Sharia-based legal rules themselves and in their application. Furthermore, the Islamization of law since the 1970s has had a limited scope in most countries. The development of national law that meets modern social-economic needs and cannot be based on Sharia, also proceeds normally. The first wave of Islamization has not (yet) been followed by a second; rather there has been a decline in the influence of classical Sharia on national law in the part fifteen years (Otto 2006:

189).

In the overwhelming majority of Muslim countries we cannot speak of an effective constitutional state or a fully fledged rule of law. Instead, these states are marked by great heterogeneity in the field of law. However, the uncertainties and tensions resulting from legal plurality in these countries is similar to that of (other) developing countries. On balance, the confrontations over law following the wave of Islamization have resulted rather more in a 'nationalization of Sharia' than an 'Islamization of the law' according to the classical model. In only a limited number of countries have the form of government and the law (for a while) been Islamized in a classical direction under the influence of the Islamic activism of the past decades. Islamic law as a source of legislation plays a role in many countries, but this certainly does not always result in changes in positive law. The infamous Islamic criminal laws also only prevail in a small number of countries and moreover not always implemented. The recent Islamization of law and the long-standing national family laws based on Sharia have not blocked reforms. They do not seem to pose a hindrance on principle to further dynamism in the direction of international standards.

The West can contribute constructively to this process. Not only indirectly because it plays a role in the political contingencies mentioned above, but also because it meets with the Muslim world in many committees which are important for the development of law. It is of great importance that the West no longer characterize Sharia as self-evidently in conflict with universal human rights (Aliboni 2004). To this end, it must take into account the diverse meanings of Sharia: what is true about one country does not apply in another, and that also holds for the content and role of Sharia. One local version of Sharia is close to international human rights standards, while elsewhere the worst violations of human rights are committed under the banner of Sharia. The West does not have to shy away from criticizing such practices simply because they use religion as a justification for power considerations. Criticism does actually have an impact. Conversely, however, the West must also appreciate the positive meanings of religion and religiously-inspired law for large segments of the Muslim populations. Islam-based reforms of Sharia and islamic reforms in the direction of international human rights standards often appear to Western eyes either as going too slowly or even as a step backward. However, one should not exclude the possibility that it is precisely these kinds of reforms that have a better chance of taking root than large or Western-imposed steps. The following chapter will explore this theme further.

151

5   POLICY PERSPECTIVE

5.1   INTRODUCTION

The efforts by Islamic-inspired activists to take part in political power and to put law into an Islamic framework have caused considerable tension in the Muslim world. In addition, international Islamic terrorism in recent years has also led to fear of Islamic activism and Islamization in the West. This report focuses on the emotionally charged relationship between the Islamization of politics, the state, and law, on the one hand, and democracy and human rights, on the other, within the Muslim world. It examines the development of Islamic activism in Muslim countries and the possible starting points this offers for a rapprochement with the concepts of democratization and human rights. The central questions read as follows:

- *What insights can be derived from the development of Islamic activism since the 1970s in relation to democratization and the advancement of human rights?*
- *What reference points does Islamic activism offer for rapprochement with the concepts of democracy and human rights?*
- *What policy perspective for the Netherlands and Europe can, in the long run, reduce the tensions related to Islamic activism within the Muslim world and also support the processes of democratization and the advancement of human rights?*

In the preceding chapters, we examined the development of Islamic activism in Muslim countries and the reference points for a policy perspective along three dimensions, namely, the development of Islamic political thought, of Islamic political movements, and of Islamic law within the Sunni and Shiite mainstream. These chapters revealed a varied picture of the degree of Islamization of politics, the state, and law in different Muslim countries. The efforts toward Islamization seem to create no permanent impediments to democratization and the advancement of human rights; on various levels there is even rapprochement. These findings offer reference points for a policy perspective, in the sense of a vision and guiding framework with general policy principles that can contribute to reducing the tensions between Islamic activism, on the one hand, and democratization and respect for human rights, on the other. In this concluding chapter the WRR presents the main outlines of such a policy perspective.

Unfortunately, the current relationship between the Muslim world and the West does not offer a favorable context for reconciling the potential antagonism between Islamic activism and democracy and human rights. A nega-

153

tive spiral has arisen that has left deep marks both nationally and internationally (sec. 5.2). At the same time this increases the urgency of a constructive approach to supporting democratization and the promotion of human rights. The empirical analyses of Chapters 2, 3, and 4 indicate what points for policy action can be derived from the development of Islamic activism (sec. 5.3). The general policy principles are explored in section 5.4. This report is, of course, directed to the Dutch government. Nevertheless, a number of policy proposals concern cooperation on the European level because through that larger framework the Netherlands can exercise a much larger influence. Which specific European and Dutch policy options are available to give concrete shape to this engagement, is described in section 5.5. Although the WRR has not conducted any empirical research on the development of Islamic activism in the Netherlands, the policy vision developed here also has implications for domestic relations with Islamic activism within the Netherlands, also given the interrelatedness of domestic and foreign policy. These implications are discussed in section 5.6.

5.2   THE WORLD POLITICAL SITUATION

5.2.1   CONFLICTS

Recent developments in world politics make a constructive approach toward the Muslim world to promote democratization and human rights both more complicated and more urgent. The context within which these efforts must take place, have already been damaged by, among other events, the Islamic revolution in Iran, the first Gulf War, the war in Afghanistan, and the long drawn-out Middle East conflict. However, since '9/11' there has been an escalation of conflicts. The 'wars' against terrorism in Afghanistan and Iraq have provoked discussion of a *clash* between Islam and the West. Whether it indeed is primarily this clash, is disputed. Reza Aslan emphasizes that what is taking place now in the Muslim world as well as what took place after the attacks of 2001 is a purely internal conflict between Muslims and not a struggle between Islam and the West (Aslan 2005). In his view, clashes with the West are instrumental for conflicts *within* the Muslim world on the role and interpretation of Islam. Kepel supports this view; he sees terrorist acts in Western countries or elsewhere against Western targets as ultimately aimed at the mobilization of Muslims against the corrupt, apostate regimes in Muslim countries (Kepel 2004). Others, like Buruma and Margalit, believe that the West as the 'hotbed of idolatry,' arrogance, domination, and moral degeneration does indeed represents for radical Islamic movements the principal target for a violent 'jihad' in the name of Islam (Buruma and Margalit 2004: 126). Hans Jansen believes that both of these views can be true. He suggests that in today's radical ideology different motives have gradually come into play: resistance against apostate rulers of Muslim countries and apostate Muslims, as well as resistance against the West and, especially, the US (Jansen 2004).

Whether the earlier attacks on Western targets were aimed at punishing the West for acts of war against Muslims or Islam, at forcing Western countries to discontinue their support for authoritarian governments in Muslim countries, or primarily at impressing and mobilizing the Muslim population, one thing is clear. Since 9/11, the struggle against the West as the domain of 'Zionism, crusaders and unbelievers' has, in any case, become more explicit. Of course, that also has to do with the dynamics and characteristics of the conduct of the war itself. Earlier in this report we pointed to the increasing independence of violent transnational activism. It has separated itself from national agendas and is now directed at the international struggle against (alleged) injustice against Muslims anywhere in the world. The military intervention of the West in Afghanistan and Iraq strengthens the image of the West, or of the participating Western countries, as enemies of Islam. This also increases the willingness of the many thousand well-trained combatants from these conflicts to respond militarily elsewhere or in their own countries. Smaller units or 'cells' of these transnational networks have established themselves in many countries, thus creating a global battleground. If only because of the existence of this army of (ex-)combatants, it seems unlikely that the phenomenon of terrorist attacks against Western targets will disappear soon, even if the developments in Iraq and the Middle East proceed favorably.

The West itself has become a recruiting ground for this 'foreign legion.' Some Muslim youth feel themselves called to the defense of 'Islam under threat,' even though Western governments define their struggle as directed against terrorism and expressly not against Islam. Olivier Roy points out that a process of 'deculturalization' is taking place, particularly among the youth of the second and third generations. By abandoning the religious and cultural traditions of their parents, they become increasingly open to other influences, including those of a transnational religious nature. Under the influence of these new interpretations of religion, some become more susceptible to radicalization (Roy 2004). To them, 'Islam' and the *Ummah* are more important reference points than the country of their parents or the country where they live (Phalet et al. 2000/1). They view confrontations like those in Afghanistan and Iraq not as conflicts between states but as attacks on 'Islam'.

Some Salafist tendencies fit well with this process of deculturalization and identification with a collective Muslim identity. Through their emphasis on the 'true' Muslim and on personal piety, Salafist movements can assume extreme forms. The violent, jihadist tendencies within these movements are, of course, also suitable for transnational forms of violent activism (AIVD 2004a; IGC 2004 and 2005a). The requirement to conform to the example of the first followers of the Prophet can mean that these Salafists take the relevant Quran texts in such a literal and absolute fashion that no other interpretation is permitted. Because every reflection on the sacred texts is forbidden and because they consider all the interpretations of the text since the seventh century as deviations, Salafists are not very susceptible to politics or theological debate.

The obvious radicalness of these ideas means that it is precisely youth, who are in an impressionable phase of life, that have a greater chance of turning into radical *born agains*. The attractive power of these ideas is also great for some young people because they satisfy a need for a positive identity that neither their parents nor the society they live in can provide. The militant Islamic movements to which they feel called and the role models supplied by the *intifada*, Osama bin Laden, and other 'resistance heroes', do address that need. These youth are not only receptive to recruitment for participation in military operations far from home. They also turn their rage and feelings of victimization into religiously justified heroics by transferring the 'holy war,' through their own initiative, to the local context. Because they operate in "fluid, dynamic and often vaguely defined opportunity-structures," they especially contribute to fifth-column-like feelings among the population. This is the case even though in the Netherlands at least there are only an estimated ten to twenty such groups (Tweede Kamer 2005c: 29). From the research of Phalet et al. it also apparent that only a very small number of Dutch Muslim youth are prepared to adopt violence in the defense of religion (Phalet et al. 2001/1). But even if there are in fact very few youth who cross the threshold into active participation in terrorist activities in the countries where they live, the consequences of their actions can be completely out of proportion to their numbers. With only a few violent acts and threats of terrorist acts against public figures and vital objects, they succeed in creating an atmosphere of fear and mistrust between population groups.

5.2.2 CONSEQUENCES

Transnational and national terrorism and counterterrorism have, first and foremost, worsened the internal relations in many countries, both in the West and in the Muslim world. Pew Research Center reported that among the nine Western, non-Muslim countries surveyed, people in Germany and the Netherlands were the most negative towards Muslims: respectively 47 and 51 percent expressed a negative attitude (Pew Research Center 2005).[1] There is much fear in Western countries of fresh attacks, even though only a limited number of attacks have actually taken place. Because of the disproportional influence of small groups of extremists, an image has arisen of Islam as an inherently threatening religion which incites terrorism. Certainly in the Netherlands, a social and political division seems to have emerged between 'Muslims' and 'the autochtonous' population (Shadid 2005). This terminology has also penetrated policy papers (Minister van Vreemdelingenzaken en Integratie 2005). Such a divide is not only dangerous because it suggests conflict where none exists, but it also gives short shrift to the enormous plurality in the Netherlands in the sphere of religion, philosophy of life, country of origin, etc.

In some countries, the fight against terrorism has been seized upon for domestic political goals, namely the increased repression of unacceptable persons and groups. In Israel, the last few years have witnessed intensive anti-terrorist actions with American support and, again under the banner of combating terrorism, a wall has been erected that takes up a large space on Palestinian territory. The International Court of Justice termed the building of the wall contrary to international law (ICJ 2004). In their RAND study *The Muslim World after 9/11*, Rabasa et al. list several Muslim countries, for example Malaysia and Saudi Arabia, where the fight against terrorism has led to increased government repression (Rabasa et al. 2005: 50-52). According to the International Crisis Group (ICG), the fight against terrorism in a country like Somalia is so far off the mark that it causes the jihad movements to gain rather than lose sympathy among the population (ICG 2005b).

157

International relations have also been deeply influenced by the war in Iraq. It has damaged the Atlantic alliance and has brought about disunity within the EU. From the perspective of the subject of this report, however, perhaps the most negative aspect has been that 'the West' has lost moral authority and has thus sustained damage as the champion of democracy and respect for international law and human rights (UNDP 2005: 67). The 'war' against terrorism has strengthened relations with the governments of countries like Egypt, Libya, and Pakistan, which are not very particular about democracy and human rights. The American government justified the invasion of Iraq primarily on the grounds of the supposed presence of weapons of mass destruction and (later) the possible links of the Iraqi regime with al-Qaeda. When these motives could not be substantiated, the justification for the invasion was shifted to humanitarian goals and the establishment of a democratic regime. Although the weapons inspections indicated otherwise, the 'coalition of the willing', which initially consisted of more than thirty countries (including the Netherlands), persisted in defending the correctness of the invasion. This has not only damaged the international standing in the rest of the world of these countries involved, it has also fed the anger of many Muslims (Pew Research Center 2004). Along with this came the treatment of the prisoners in Guantanamo Bay (Cuba) and the Abu Ghraib prison in Iraq. Not only was this particularly offensive to Muslims, but it was certainly also a violation of the spirit of human rights incorporated in international treaties. All of this has further increased the cynicism among Muslims about how seriously the West itself treats democracy and human rights. It does appear, however, that the political damage on this score will be greater for the US than for the European Union. The division among European member states over whether to participate in the invasion of Iraq has also had as a partial consequence that 'the' West is now seen less as a unified quantity in the Muslim world (Joffé 2005).

All these events underscore the extent to which the world finds itself in a negative spiral. 'Security' has become a top priority in the international and national politics of many countries. In the West suspicion against Muslims has grown. It would, however, be incorrect to define this escalation exclusively in terms of the 'West' versus 'Muslims' or 'Islam'. The war in Iraq has the characteristics of – again cast in religious terms – a civil war between Sunnis and Shiites. But there are also tensions within these Islamic religious denominations; indeed there is a 'clash within' (Aslan 2005). As Chapter 3 revealed, the radical Islamic movements also put pressure on Muslims themselves – inside and outside Muslim countries – to conform to the norms of 'true' Islam. Some radical movements are just as violent towards what they consider to be apostasy among Muslims (*takfir*) as they are towards Western non-believers (Jansen 2004). Terrorist attacks occur regularly in Muslim countries; and attacks against Western targets also result in many Muslim victims.

In *The Future of Political Islam* – a book published before the invasion of Iraq – Graham Fuller described what a worst-case scenario would look like. It would include a difficult to settle war against terrorism led by the US, regular fresh attacks, growing animosity between and within population groups, restrictions on civil liberties, the creation of a 'bunker America,' and authoritarian states which would use the war on terrorism as an excuse to intensify domestic repression. Actual developments in world politics, to a large degree, match this scenario. The spiral effect predicted by Fuller has had disastrous consequences not only for open Western societies. The confrontations appeal above all to the violent and dogmatic side of Islamic activism. This has condemned itself to a permanently joyless and negative stance against the West and also against the mainstream of the Muslim population, with an obsession about everything that is forbidden and wrong ('The Islam that says no'). With this nihilistic role it has deprived itself of the chance to play a constructive and future-directed role with

regard to the moral, social, and economic problems which confront many
Muslim countries (Fuller 2003: 194 and 211-2).

5.3   REFERENCE POINTS

5.3.1   INTRODUCTION

The world political situation outlined here offers little to indicate a quick,
substantial improvement. The existing spiral of action and reaction cannot
easily be reversed, either with respect to the international political or local
motives behind terrorism. The reconstruction of Afghanistan and Iraq is
encountering great resistance, and an end to the violence appears to be still
a long way off. The chronic Middle East conflict also remains for the time
being an important breeding-ground for extremism on both sides and a
divisive issue for relations between the Muslim world and the West.
Nevertheless, the characteristics and dynamics of Islamic activism itself
over the past thirty years that were analyzed in this report, show that there
are also positive developments. There exists a great diversity of activist
orientations, not only in the field of Islamic political thought but also of
Islamic political activism and Islamic law. Furthermore, developments in
the past decades reveal reference points for a gradual rapprochement with
concepts of democracy and human rights. The findings for each of the three
areas will be briefly elucidated below.

5.3.2   ISLAMIC POLITICAL THOUGHT

In Chapter 2 it was found that many of the current militant Islamic movements derive their substantive inspiration from thinkers from the first half
of the previous century. They advocated new power of expression for Islam
in public life. In addition, they strongly opposed religious traditionalism,
the passive submission to God (quietism) and the dominance of the West
or Western ideas in the Muslim world. They also turned against the
monopoly of religions scholars over the interpretation of the Quran and
the Sunna. The utopia of Islam's founding years served as the principal
source of inspiration for their vision of the role of Islam in public life. The
literal text of the Quran and Sunna served as their guideline for pursuing
an Islamization of society and/or the state, from below or above, by evolution or revolution. They rejected concepts developed in the West that were
important in state-formation, such as the separation of church and state,
democracy, the rule of law, and human rights, as conflicting with Islamic
principles and the supremacy of Islamic law. The mobilization these
thinkers had envisioned, has materialized; their beliefs have determined
the image of Islamic activism in the West.

This explains in part why little attention is paid to other reform thinkers who, also since early in the previous century, opposed the reigning dogmatic traditionalism and also those who wanted to strictly comply with the letter of the Quran and the Sunna. These other reform thinkers are looking rather to connect Islam with modernity. They also want to come to new interpretations, but, unlike the above-mentioned category of reformers, they do not leave the texts of the Quran and the Sunna undisturbed in this effort. They believe that the meaning of the texts can only be understood from the context in which they were produced. Accordingly, these thinkers are concerned not with the letter of the text but with its spirit and its expressive force for conditions other than those of its conception. By recognizing the particular meaning of the historical context, a mental space is developed for appreciating human innovations like democracy and human rights. Some of the thinkers accept such innovations by grounding them in Islamic concepts, such as *shura* (consultation). Others see democracy and human rights as valuable products of human reason in themselves that favorably relate to the intentions of the Quran; Bayat identifies this tendency as post-Islamism (Bayat forthcoming). These two positions can be designated as the 'Islamizing of modernity' and the 'modernizing of Islamic thinking,' respectively. No matter how the relationship between Islam and the principles of democracy and human rights is precisely drawn, both positions imply a mutual rapprochement.

In Chapter 2 only a limited selection of these reformist thinkers was presented. Nowadays thinkers with similar views can be found in many Muslim countries. Their views are often controversial not only because they are at odds with Islamic orthodoxy and the views of extremist movements, but also because their advocacy of democracy and human rights is seen as threatening by the mainly authoritarian regimes in the Muslim world. Some of the thinkers discussed have had to flee their homeland. It is noteworthy that this line of thinking has expanded greatly in Iran, the cradle of the Islamic revolution. The quarter-century of experience with theocracy has led many, including philosophers who previously supported the Islamic revolution, to the conclusion that combining Islam with political power has led not only to great oppression but also to corruption of the religion itself. While these religious philosophers still try to reason out democracy and human rights from Islam, there is meanwhile also a category of secular intellectuals who base the desirability of these concepts on purely humanistic grounds (Jahanbegloo 2006).

In most Muslim countries the actual political effect of these views is unclear because this often occurs underground. But this is not to say that they have no influence. Abdurrahman Wahid, a prominent representative, even occupied the presidency of Indonesia for a time. In Iran these ideas resonate well among the large group of middle-class youth who are mostly well-educated and collect and exchange reform ideas, in part thanks to the Internet (Jahanbegloo 2005; *Financial Times* 2005).

What is clear is that the sacred sources of Islam – the Quran and the Sunna – can be read and interpreted in many ways. With the rise of Islamic activism the conflict over the correct interpretation – that is, over 'pure Islam' – has intensified significantly. In Muslim countries as well as among Muslims in the West, the influence of ideas that tolerate no deviation from a literal interpretation of the texts remains considerable, especially also because militant means of pressure are brought to bear. But although it is now not easy to concretely indicate the influence 'aboveground' of intellectuals who wish to interpret the sacred texts in context, their ideas do indeed have great *potential* relevance. It is true that changes in the religious views of believers are not exclusively based on intellectual insights, but also – and perhaps rather – are driven by actual changes in behavior (van Bruinessen 2004). However, then, too, a need can arise at some point for interpretations of Islam that are, for example, less rule-bound and more spiritual in nature. So, too, where the establishment of a state and law are concerned, changes in structure may precede changes in culture. The contrasting examples of Turkey and Iran show that many different developments, for example in the areas of demography, education, and politics, can bring about a situation where the relationship between Islam and democracy and human rights quickly becomes relevant. This can also mean that more and more groups will absorb themselves into alternative theological ideas and interpretations that see no barrier (any more) between Islam and democracy and human rights. In short: changes in the context often lead to a need for different interpretations of the text. These other interpretations are already available in many countries.

5.3.3 ISLAMIC POLITICAL MOVEMENTS

Chapter 3 presented the dynamics of Islamic political movements since the 1970s. In many Muslim countries, Islam has functioned for a considerable time as a vehicle for the just demands of segments of the population. Islamic political movements therefore form a potential political force with considerable grassroots support. At the same time, we saw that '*the*' Islamic political movement does not exist. Unlike what many in the West suppose and also what many authoritarian regimes in the Muslim world still want us to believe, political movements do not constitute a homogeneous, immutably fundamentalist and/or violent threat. A threat does, of course, arise from transnational terrorism that in various established and casual groupings concentrates on jihadist actions. In addition, however, there exist within Muslim countries countless movements and coalitions, with as many aspirations, that are influenced by the local political context and the local options available. Those movements most oriented to the *political arena* have shifted furthest in the direction of democratic principles and norms. They also usually declare themselves in favor of versions of Islamic legislation that are more suited to modern society (ICG 2005: 7).

Since the end of the 1990s, many of the leading early revolutionary activists have opted for a more constructive political position within the constitutional limits of the national state. Instead of striving to replace the often secular national state, violently if necessary, with an (*Ummah*-wide) Islamic state, they now aim at reform through participation in the regular political system and take part in elections. They have not undergone any fundamental process of enlightenment or reformation, nor do they generally have any well-thought-out theological or ideological foundation for a reconciliation of Islam, with democracy and human rights. Above all, they draw on a sizeable stock of political pragmatism (Nasr 2005: 15). To acquire functional political influence and to operate effectively, they have to be undogmatic, adapt themselves to the political rules, form coalitions and also formulate political programs. By doing so, they distance themselves from absolute truths and undefined forms of 'opposition Islam' that appeal mainly to radicals and extremists. Moreover, they become acquainted with the positive effects of democratic principles and human rights in the fight against state oppression, arbitrariness, lawlessness, and marginalization. Precisely because they are so close to the ordinary people, they employ a religious, often conservative, discourse. But that also gives them a legitimate basis to be able to hammer away at justice, economic development, fighting corruption, protecting ordinary people, and social emancipation within the political arena.

In this rapprochement with concepts of democracy and human rights lie favorable reference points for practical application. Thus Turkey, for example, thanks in part to the ambitions of the Islamic-inspired AKP, has started down the path of further democratization, strengthening the constitutional state, and EU-membership (see box 5.1).

Box 5.1   The Turkish AKP

In 2001 the Turkish AKP was founded by a newer guard of Islamic activists who, for pragmatic and ideological reasons, had resigned from a previous religious party that had been banned by the Turkish Constitutional Court. Unlike their predecessors, they presented themselves from an electoral standpoint as leaders of a broad conservative party that combined respect for Islamic norms and values with an agenda promoting further democratization and the advancement of human rights. But few at that time would have suspected that precisely an AKP-government would so energetically act to strengthen Turkish democracy and human rights and, partly thanks to the leverage of EU conditionality, would be in a position to gradually weaken the dominant role of the military in politics. The Turkish example also shows that despite many external pressure, incentives, and rewards, it was ultimately the *endogenous* political and social forces behind democratization that were decisive. However, it also reveals that the EU, thanks to its constructive engagement, can sometimes in a pragmatic and flexible way, take advantage of development opportunities that arise in this internal field of influence (WRR 2004).

Other countries exhibit similar endogenous reform processes. Successive rounds of elections in Indonesia, Malaysia, and Bangladesh have prompted religious political parties to adopt less exclusive and more pragmatic positions. Similar developments can be observed in Jordan, Morocco, Kuwait, and Yemen, where Islamic parties can take part in politics under certain conditions. Consequently, non-religious parties in turn have taken more heed of the voters' wishes to see political programs reflect religious values. The result of these shifts is increasing competition for the large group of voters in the middle of the political spectrum, which leads to further moderation and readiness to compromise. The political agenda and political behavior of Islamic parties in these countries also serve as examples for movements in neighboring countries and other regions of the Muslim world. Even in countries like Egypt and Tunisia where religious political parties and movements have no access to the political arena, the example of the Turkish AKP also serves as a source of inspiration for pragmatism, moderation, and the gradual appropriation of democratic and constitutional concepts (see Chapter 3).

163

5.3.4   ISLAMIC LAW

In Chapter 4 it emerged first and foremost that the concept of Sharia has different meanings. It can be an indication of the abstract Plan of God for the community of believers; it can refer to the elaboration of this plan by the early religious scholars in a corpus of rules of behavior (classical Sharia), or it can concern current interpretations of Sharia by states, institutions, and groups. Also when we look at current formal law based on Sharia, it appears that we cannot speak of a fixed body of rules that are valid for all Muslims. There are great differences between countries regarding both Sharia-based legal rules in themselves and in their practical application. Moreover, in most Muslim countries the Islamization of law since the 1970s has had a limited scope. In many of these, Sharia plays little or no role in the majority of legal areas, and there is thus a *de facto* separation of religion and state. In addition, the first wave of Islamization has not (yet) been followed by a second; rather, the last fifteen years have witnessed a decline in the influence of, at least, *classical* Sharia on national law. Extreme Islamization, that is, the introduction of this classical Sharia, including Islamic criminal law, has taken place in only a limited number of countries such as Iran, Afghanistan under the Taliban, for a time in Pakistan and Sudan, and in a number of Nigerian states. Classical Sharia has always been the law of Saudi Arabia. Even in some of these countries, the more severe aspects of Sharia seem to have gradually made way for more pragmatic applications.

In most other Muslim countries, such as Egypt, Morocco, Indonesia, Malaysia, Nigeria, and Mali, the Islamization of law has a more moderate character (see Chapter 4). In these countries Sharia has received constitutional recognition as 'source of legislation' and/or serves as codified law in a few specific legal areas. Where Sharia has acquired a place in the constitution, there is often a situation of constitutional dualism or mixed legal systems in which secular law is also valid as a source of law. Otherwise, the countries in this category also show among themselves great variation in their degree of orientation towards classical Sharia. In present-day Pakistan and Afghanistan, the orientation is much stronger than in countries like Egypt, Morocco, and Malaysia, where the constitutional role of Sharia is more abstract and symbolic, not to mention in the secular republic of Mali. Finally, in Turkey, Sharia long ago been completely removed from the legal system. Also where Sharia functions constitutionally as a source of legislation or is applied in concrete areas of law, it appears that this does not block modern interpretations as such. This applies, for example, in the area of family law. Although this concerns a key area of Islamic law, in most countries there is nonetheless a gradual improvement of the legal position of women. For most of the countries researched here, it holds that, over the long term, a progressive incorporation into the state and a professionalization of national law have occurred, even in those areas of law which are based on Sharia. The process of incorporation into the state can work in two ways, though. It can serve as a counterweight against extreme Shariaization, as in Egypt, for example, thanks to the complementary legislation and buffers in the legal system. However, it can also mean that Sharia is hijacked by the ruling powers for their own say, nationalistic, purposes, as was the case in Sudan and also in Pakistan for a time. Even if the state sets itself up as guardian of Islam 'to prevent worse', this often implies preferential treatment for orthodox views and forces. State Islam then forms a buffer not only against extreme Sharia but also against modernizing, pro-democratic ideas.

Chapter 4 also showed that a process of reconciliation is taking place between the concept of *universal* human rights and that of *Islamic* human rights. After an initially theologically motivated rejection of the concept of human rights as such, the Organization of the Islamic Conference (OIC) developed the concept of Islamic human rights. The idea of human rights to be respected by governments has thus been accepted and is usually constitutionally entrenched. But this Islamic conception of human rights is certainly not identical to the universal version. On the level of several individual human rights there sometimes exist significant differences, on paper as well as in actual practice. There are important hindrances to further reconciliation, such as discrimination against women and non-Muslims, absence of freedom of religion, and inhumane punishments. Many Muslim countries are signatories to the UN human rights treaties and have sometimes stipulated reservations to these treaties on the grounds of Sharia. In the treaty bodies, the areas of conflict are regularly reviewed critically with regard to each country. It is striking that since the 1990s Muslim countries are increasingly abandoning their objections of principle towards the human rights standards of these treaties. Unmistakably, then, there is a gradual movement toward legal recognition and implementation, even if this happens by way of appropriation, namely through placing the relevant laws or their interpretation in an Islamic framework (Halliday 2003). It seems, in fact, as if the acceptance of human rights is promoted precisely when they are placed under the banner of Sharia (Roy 2005).

In short, rapprochement is taking place, but it is a 'contingent' process. In addition, its course is sensitive to external and internal events and developments in power relations, as the recent elections in Iran again demonstrate. Whether in the long run rapprochement will result in convergence is therefore difficult to predict; nor can it be excluded that over some issues differences based on principle will continue to exist. However, when and where concrete windows of opportunity arise, the Netherlands and Europe should have a strategic policy at their disposal that could capitalize on them. That requires a pro-active approach that not only looks at the status quo and short-term problems and risks, but also searches for long-term opportunities.

5.4 CONSTRUCTIVE ENGAGEMENT WITH THE MUSLIM WORLD

5.4.1 THE NEED FOR NEW INITIATIVES

The tensions between the West and the Muslim world should not distract us from hopeful developments. In several countries of the Middle East, like Lebanon and Egypt, the people themselves have taken public actions aimed at democratization. Many even observe a new democratizing momentum that also puts pressure on heavily authoritarian regimes

(Emerson et al. 2005: 2; Rabasa et al. 2005; Roy 2005c). Terrorist attacks in the name of Islam also lead to increasingly stronger condemnation by Muslims themselves; to the extent that the objective of such attacks has been to mobilize Muslims en masse, they have been anything but a great success (Kepel 2004). Attacks by or in the spirit of Al-Qaeda can only flourish in the longer run if they can count on the sympathy of a substantial segment of the Muslim population. However, according to a study by the Pew Research Center, support for Al-Qaeda is declining among Muslims, especially in countries where attacks have been carried out (Pew Research Center 2005). Leading Muslims in the West are publicly distancing themselves from Al-Qaeda in increasingly unambiguous terms. To the extent that the means – attacks on the innocent – are more emphatically rejected by the major part of the Muslim population, terrorism becomes more isolated and thus ultimately could dry up. Mirrorwise, something similar applies. Among the population in the West, recognition has grown that democracy and human rights cannot be exported to the rest of the world by military means. Certainly many citizens in Western Europe opposed the invasion of Iraq, and – just as in the US – they were ashamed of the disgraceful treatment of prisoners in Iraq and other places. This suggests there may emerge a climate of receptivity for initiatives that in the longer run can break the spiral of violence.

For the time being, there are no political windows of opportunity for resolving current large-scale conflicts. But certainly the member states of the EU, with Muslim states in their immediate vicinity and many Muslims among their own populations, cannot permit a continuation or intensification of the violence and persist in standing aloof. Relations with and within the Muslim world have become a crucial factor for international stability and the rule of law as well as for the internal stability and rule of law within EU member states (Otto 2006). The open nature of European societies makes them vulnerable to new terrorist activities, which will further heighten the already tense relations between population groups. Thus, maintaining the status quo with regard to relations with the Muslim world is not an option. The stage for this has passed, not only because this situation itself has already created too much tension, but also because the internal dynamics will further increase domestic tensions within Muslim countries. In almost all of these countries at least 40 per cent of the population is under the age of 25; by 2025, the size of their populations will have increased by about 30 per cent. For these reasons alone, there will be more pressure in the coming years on the existing economic, social, and educational services, which are already partly supplied by Islamic organizations (Rabasa et al. 2005: 63).

It would be equally ill-adviced, therefore, to bring relations with these countries to a lower level of involvement. A Union turned in on itself that abandons external ambitions creates only an illusion of security ('Fortress Europe') that does not remove its existing vulnerability. The web of mutually dependent relationships can no longer be denied or averted. Moreover, remaining aloof means that the EU leaves opportunities unused that do actually exist for supporting promising developments in the Muslim world. In short, the WRR advocates an active and, above all, constructive stance by the Netherlands and the EU member states towards the reduction of tensions with and within the Muslim world concerning issues of Islamic activism, and towards improving the relations between Muslims and non-Muslims within Europe.

5.4.2 PRINCIPLES FOR CONSTRUCTIVE ENGAGEMENT

The WRR believes that the diversity and dynamism of Islamic political thinking, Islamic political movements, and Islamic law discussed above provide important reference points for a European and Dutch policy of constructive engagement. That policy should be based on a set of coherent general principles that will be discussed below:

167

- taking into account the diversity of Islamic activism;
- recognizing Islamic activism as a *potentially* constructive political and legal factor in the development of Muslim countries;
- engaging with endogenous development processes and trajectories that promote democracy and human rights;
- investing in an informed public opinion in Europe on Islamic activism and on the main European and Dutch policies in this area.

Taking into account the diversity of Islamic activism
One of the observations of this report is that generalizations about Islamic activism have very limited value. Both within and between Muslim countries, there are great differences in views on what a state and society based on Islamic principles should look like, just as there are also many different interpretations of how Islam relates to politics, democracy, and human rights. The Islamization of recent decades *in itself* does not present any definitive obstacle to democratization and respect for human rights. Moreover, in a number of countries it is precisely under the banner of Islam that space has been created for rapprochement with these principles. What is at issue, is the *nature and the direction* of Islamization. To the familiar question of whether Islam and democracy are compatible or not, one cannot simply answer that Islam in and of itself is either for or against democracy or that Islamic legislation in and of itself is at odds with human rights. The answer is: according to some ideas and/or practices of Islam or Sharia, it is not, and according to others, it is. Furthermore, there is not only a great

variation according to interpretation and place but also according to time. Today's Islamic activism has different characteristics than that of the 1970s and 1980s; in many countries Islamic movements that initially took a position against democracy and human rights now have many fewer objections. Perceptions about 'Islam' as a monolithic and static concept thus deny the great variety and dynamism of opinions and practices; they directly contribute to a socially distorted image of 'the' Muslim. Therefore it is essential in relations with Muslim countries to exercise subtlety and distinction with respect to Islamic activism.

Recognizing Islamic activism as a potentially constructive political and legal factor in the development of Muslim countries

Paradoxically, this need for subtlety also means that we should be aware that a purely religious perspective can also distort our view of Muslim countries and Muslims in general. Too often reprehensible phenomena involving Muslim countries or Muslims are automatically attributed to religion. The casual use of the adjective 'Islamic' also invites inaccurate generalizations in terms of characteristics *inherent* to Islam. The diversity and dynamism within the Muslim world mean that 'Islam' cannot be qualified or disqualified in general terms. Thanks to this recognition, space can emerge for the development of constructive relations directed at the promotion of democracy and human rights. Conceptually as well as in practice, rapprochement with democratic principles and norms and with international human rights standards is occurring in many places. That in many Muslim countries Islam serves as the vehicle for such reforms is not remarkable in itself, it had been (and in some countries remains) excluded from political and public life. In autocratically ruled Muslim countries, it is precisely Islamic political movements that represent important oppositional forces that expose abuses and advocate reform.

Democracy and law need to emerge primarily from within and cannot permanently be imposed from outside. If *constructive* Islamic forces present themselves in Muslim countries, taking democracy seriously demands that these forces be permitted political articulation. In the past, the EU's advocacy of democratization in Muslim countries had mostly secular movements and parties in mind. There was considerable fear that the admission of Islamic forces into the political system would open the door for parties that, once elected, would subsequently destroy the existing democratic system (the scenario of one man, one vote, one time). Given the absolutist claims of many Islamic movements in the early period of Islamic activism, there was every reason for this caution. The EU's fear was also fed by authoritarian regimes in Muslim countries that saw Islamic activism as a direct threat to their own positions of power. However, the WRR believes that the ensuing developments described in this report both illustrate the possibility and the desirability to employ an *inclusive* understanding of democracy that no longer automatically excludes Islamic movements from the political system. These developments also showed that calls for implementing Sharia are by no means always at odds with human rights, and are not seldom a reaction against extreme arbitrariness, corruption, etc.

Engaging with endogenous development processes and trajectories that promote democracy and human rights

The previous position of the EU on Islamic movements illustrates the tendency in the West to assume the 'power of definition' when it comes to democracy and human rights. However, the desire to model Muslim countries to fit a Western template is counterproductive. First, it ignores the many contextually determined differences among Western countries themselves in the manner in which they have implemented democracy and human rights, and thus also the importance of context and dynamics in the Muslim countries concerned. Second, it shows insufficient sensitivity for the enormous aversion that these countries have built up against external interference by the West. If one takes the right of self-determination of Muslim countries seriously, therefore, one has to influence without preaching or domination. Yet this does not require Western countries to to belittle their own values. It means that endogenous steps towards democracy and human rights should be encouraged, whereas steps away from these aims should be discouraged. The EU will have to accept in principle that within an Islamic frame of reference democracy and human rights will sometimes or temporarily come in different shapes and forms than are customary in Western countries. This implies a constant navigation between influencing and interfering and between endogenous frames of references and those considered to be universal or Western. What consequences this has for relationships with the EU (or its member states) is still uncertain. It definitely cannot be excluded that subtle advocacy for a process of inclusive democratization that extends to Islamic parties will meet with great resistance on the part of the governments concerned and will initially also harm European prestige. However, the reverse is also possible. In the case of Turkey, European pressure in favor of democratization and respect for religious freedom ultimately in the longer term surely contributed to a pro-accession sentiment among Islamic movements and parties (WRR 2004).

169

The topic of human rights is the prime example of a subject full of pitfalls and traps; human rights are, after all, in a UN connection defined as *universal* rights and freedoms. But even though they are established in international treaties, they must primarily be brought into application in *national* law and by *national* judges. Despite all the incentives and control mechanisms, they can only go beyond the level of rights on paper when they can boast internal legitimacy, in other words, when they are viewed as 'one's own law.' As was shown in Chapter 4, in a number of countries, however, this 'own law' is based on Sharia, and it is precisely because of its highly symbolic value that it is not realistic to expect religiously based human rights soon to be replaced by *secular* human rights. Therefore the EU cannot avoid taking a stand on Islamic human rights.

The dilemmas involved are well illustrated by a 2002 conversation between the German philosopher of law Heiner Bielefeldt and the Iranian scholar of Islam Mohammed Saeed Bahmanpour. Bielefeldt asked what precisely was meant by 'Islamic' human rights and all the reservations placed on international human rights treaties on the basis of Sharia. Does it involve a construct to undermine UN standards, or is it actually an attempt to come to a reconciliation with universal human rights from an Islamic perspective? In short: does it involve an undermining or a confirmation of the *universality* of human rights? Bahmanpour endorsed the latter in principle but did not exclude endogenous interpretations. In his view, the Western world must abandon the presumption of being able to control the pace of change in the Muslim world. Muslim countries must be allowed to resolve these issues themselves and be given time to do so. If changes are imposed from outside, there is a great chance of window dressing or a strengthening of dogmatic positions. After all, today, many Muslims simply want to live according to Islamic values; this reality cannot be denied, according to Bahmanpour (Bielefeldt and Bahmanpour 2002).

Bahmanpour emphasizes an aspect that is also crucial for the position of EU member states confronting Muslim countries on the issue of human rights, namely to pay attention to the endogenous *dynamics* within these countries. Muslim countries in many respects fail to satisfy the current international standards with regard to human rights. In this respect they are not all that different from many (other) developing countries. But then it becomes all the more important whether they want to try to improve these standards. Serious reforms in the direction of international standards thus deserve support, even if they occur under the banner of Sharia and in the terms of an Islamic discourse. Concepts such as 'inclusive universality' and 'universalizing universal human rights' express this effort (Brems 2003; Otto 2006; Baderin 2003). They convey that human rights are not the privilege of a limited number of countries but affect the dignity and welfare of everyone. These rights must therefore also be realized for everyone. Precisely because international law primarily acquires its force through national law, the EU must recognize that the legitimizing power of Sharia in Muslim countries can be used to realize international human rights. A universalism that denies that Islamic principles represent a normative value in the debate on human rights, would be dubious (Baderin 2003).

In most Muslim countries, progressive realization of human rights, for example in the areas of the position of women, freedom of religion, and criminal law, is simply easier to accept if these laws can be seen as parts of or related to their own traditions and cultures. From the perspective of a constructive engagement, it is therefore all the more important that the EU recognize and support a positive, development-directed application of Sharia (Otto 2006).

The engagement advocated here must thus take into account the local context and the fact that permanent improvements cannot be imposed and sometimes take a long time. This should not, however, result in downplaying one's own values or in the rejecting every critical judgment of other values. It does imply that instead of always judging Muslim countries on their 'shortcomings,' more attention needs to be paid to the *direction* of the changes in these countries. If this direction becomes the subject of judgment, then the discussion is about something other than the actual, suboptimal situation at a particular moment. What then stands to be judged is the demonstrated seriousness of a country's dedication, the degree to which it invests in the advancement of human rights and informs its population on this issue, the durability of its efforts over time, etc. In this respect, the EU member states must be prepared to address the shortcomings in these countries, such as in the case of changes that amount to nothing more than window dressing. Thus, such an approach does not relieve member states from the obligation to expose serious human rights violations committed in the name of Sharia. Otto uses the term 'destructive Sharia politics' for politics that uses the symbols and values of Sharia primarily directed to exercise of power and repression rather than to promote development and tolerance (Otto 2006). Many rulers would all too happily be inclined to legitimize their repression by calling upon Islam or Sharia. There is, however, no reason for the EU not to judge human rights violations justified on the grounds of religion any less harshly than other violations.

Does the goal of 'universalizing universal human rights' mean that eventually Islamic human rights will completely correspond with universal human rights? It is difficult to assess the practical possibilities for convergence; time will tell. In the current situation, an answer is of little practical importance because the area of common ground is sufficiently large to formulate common tasks for improvement. Some even argue that there exists overwhelming agreement with respect to human rights norms as such (AIV 1998). This is also underscored by the fact that most of the Muslim countries are party to the various human rights treaties.

Whereas human rights norms are thus broadly shared, their concrete *implementation* is a different case. Here the local context becomes a factor

171

which has also provided a reason for granting states a certain policy freedom. The jurisprudence of the European Court of Human Rights has developed a so-called doctrine of 'margin of appreciation' as a frame for judicial review. This allows the Court to do justice to the different ideas among state-parties on the definitions, for example, of a concept like 'good moral standards'. This doctrine may also have significance for the global political arena, given that some human rights do not allow for any policy freedom and that, where they do so, the final judgment does not belong to the state concerned but to an international forum (AIV 1998). In the case of human rights, the authorized UN committees fulfill this function. It is partly through their influence that reservations to the implementation of human rights laws that are made on the grounds of Sharia, have become less important.

Nevertheless, important areas of conflict between Islamic and universal human rights remain; these issues provoke much discussion in Muslim countries as well. In Chapter 4 we mentioned Baderin's research on jurisprudence in those areas of law in which at present the greatest differences exist between universal and Islamic human rights. It appeared that Islamic jurisprudence displays great differences among schools of law, but also that – even when it concerns precepts from the Quran – rulings are possible that, not in their reasoning but in their outcome, are close to the intention or implementation in the framework of the international treaties (Baderin 2003). This also offers the possibility that in Muslim countries where Sharia operates to any extent, Islamic jurisprudence in highly controversial areas can shift towards international standards. The EU obviously has no authority to judge interpretations of Sharia; this is pre-eminently a matter for the Muslim world itself. As Baderin suggests, the moral and religious principles in Muslim countries where Sharia serves as state law, will remain recognizable.

Given these diverse interpretations, the question arises whether it is possible to promote a *mutual* endogenous dynamic towards legal implementations that will be closer to international standards. Legal development is not only the result of internal pressure within Muslim countries and external pressure from multilateral institutions like the UN, but also of mutual discussions and comparison among Muslim countries themselves. It is particularly over such charged issues as gender relations, freedom of religion, and cruel punishments that mutual learning processes can often be more effective than external pressure that can be interpreted as paternalistic, uninformed, or even inimical to 'Islam'.

The implication of a policy that takes into account the diversity, dynamism, and local context of Islamic activism is that one cannot provide an unambiguous sequence or general policy prescription for such a transformation process, as for example, Fareed Zakaria does. Zakaria opposes the tendency to give priority to democratization. In his view, analogous to the path of development in Europe, economic liberalism supported by the rule of law should come as a necessary first. In the long run, this may result in a democratization process supported by the middle class (Zakaria 2003). The analyses in this report, however, point rather in the direction of a combination of democratic, constitutional, and economic reforms that is sensitive to contexts and fits in with the endogenous development opportunities of individual countries. In countries under autocratic rule it is conceivable that the restoration of human rights and constitutionalism deserve priority, but also that first a gradual expansion of political participation is sought. Often, completely postponing political reforms for the sake of economic growth is no longer a realistic option. Thanks to the media, migration, and higher education, more and more groups have become acquainted with democratic ideals. They are demanding a voice in politics and government now, even if the economic conditions for lasting democracy are far from favorable (Carothers 2003). In the Arab context, for example, the anger over earlier failed economic experiments and the Middle East conflict are already too great to legitimize further postponement of political change (UNDP 2005: 162). In this region, authoritarian rule not only accompanies human rights violations but also economic failures by an entrenched, corrupt elite. It is thus no accident that of all the regions researched in the world, it is precisely the populations of the Arab countries that give the most support to the proposition that 'democracy is better than any other form of government' (UNDP 2005: 68). This explains why the authors of the *Arab Human Development Report 2004* reject attempts to maintain the political status quo and regard the postponement of democratization as a 'disaster scenario' (UNDP 2005: 164). It means that general prescriptions, while normally attractive for policy-makers, do not suffice. Instead, there is a need for a more complex policy that differentiates according to place and time.

Investing in an informed public opinion in Europe on Islamic activism and on the main European and Dutch policies in this area

In line with the theme of this report, the discussion below explores policies towards Muslim countries. Such external policies, however, are also connected to Europe's internal affairs. If Europe tries to take account of constructive forces within Islamic activism in its external relations, then this should also be made visible within Europe itself, on the level of member states. Recent experiences with the Constitutional Treaty have shown that foreign policy cannot neglect domestic opinion with impunity. Moreover, a better insight among the public into developments and external policies concerning Islamic activism can also lessen the tensions

173

between Muslims and non-Muslims within EU member states. Therefore it is important that member states also invest in making their own societies aware of the diversity and dynamism of Islamic activism and of the main policy principles underlying this. Given that this is primarily a national and local task, the WRR returns to this theme in section 5.6, which focuses on Islamic activism in the Netherlands.

The general policy perspective formulated here will certainly not remove all the causes for the existing resentments that Muslims feel towards the West. As it was explained in Chapter 1, these resentments have many dimensions, including the colonial past, the recent armed conflicts, and the stagnating economic and political development in many Muslim states. These facts obviously cannot be reversed. Now the effort must be to start a process of constructive mutual engagement by which hostile images will gradually lose force and positive developments will be promoted. If the EU in its relations with Muslim countries follows the reference points outlined here, it will also meet with resistance. The exclusion of Islamic movements has already caused considerable tensions in these countries themselves. The changes advocated here require, by their nature, much time and patience and, of course, must be brought about by the countries concerned (Haass 2005). They are, however, certainly not unresponsive to the position that the EU adopts in this regard.

5.5 EUROPEAN AND BILATERAL POLICY OPTIONS FOR CONSTRUCTIVE ENGAGEMENT

5.5.1 INTRODUCTION

The Netherlands has at its disposal various European and bilateral channels through which it can shape a policy of constructive engagement. This section explores the most important of these. On a European level these concern proposals dealing, firstly, with Europe's direct relations with Muslim countries in its immediate neighborhood, i.e. through its Mediterranean partner countries of the Euro-Mediterranean policy (EMP), Turkey, the Gulf States, and Iran. Second, it involves proposals in which the EU plays an active role in the framework of the UN and the OIC. Third, it concerns the discussion on the development of a European Islam. With this theme we examine the recent debate on the possibility and desirability of a specific European variant of Islam. According to many, this could exert a moderating influence on those Muslim countries where the supposed opposition between 'Islam' and democracy is at stake.

5.5.2 THE EURO-MEDITERRANEAN POLICY AND THE EUROPEAN NEIGHBORHOOD POLICY

By far the most important EU policy instrument to shape relations with Muslim countries concerns the EMP, also known in bureaucratic jargon as the Barcelona process (see appendix 4). Therefore we will go into this in some detail. This policy, which began about ten years ago, is, however, very technocratic in nature. It meets with little interest on the higher political levels and is thus little-known among the populations of the member states. What possibilities do the EMP and the connected, more recent, European Neighborhood Policy (ENP) offer for greater constructive engagement? Before we answer this question, it is worthwhile to first look at the principal assumptions that form the basis for the original EMP. These still continue to work in dealings with Islamic activism and the discourse on Islamic democracy and human rights.

The EMP was created in a burst of optimism in the wake of the 1993 Oslo accords on the Israeli-Palestinian issue. The intention of the EMP's charter on political and security cooperation was to settle the peace relations among the Arab world, Israel, and the EU. But there was also worry about Islamic activism. With the rise of the FIS and the civil war in Algeria still fresh in memory, the framers of the Barcelona declaration (1995) associated Islamic activism chiefly with fundamentalist, violent movements that would seriously undermine stability in the region (Euromesco 2005a). The scenario of one man, one vote, one time dominated the risk analyses of the policy-makers concerned. By the time the Barcelona declaration was finally ratified, the political landscape had radically changed once again.[2] The desire to use the EMP in part to contain Islamic activism, however, remained (Aliboni 2004a).

In its original form the EMP rested on the assumption that mutually improved market access in combination with foreign direct investment and EU contributions to good government could set in motion a process of economic growth that ultimately would also lead to a stronger rule of law, political liberalization, democratization, and improved human rights. This would involve processes that must get their impulse from the bottom up via technical support, education and, last but not least, via contact with civil society organizations (Youngs 2004c). The idea behind the support for these organizations is that, in the course of time, they are going to form an important democratic force against the state and spur democratic reforms (NIMD 2005: 18; Roy 2005; Ottoway and Carothers 2005).

In practice, however, these starting points were reduced to an extremely cautious agenda. Southern members of the EU, such as Spain, Portugal,

Italy, and Greece, and recently also the Netherlands, are seeking to control immigration and to strengthen the security and stability of Europe's southern border. Others, especially West European and northern member states, emphasize that economic concessions from the Union must ultimately result in concrete improvements of human rights, while the partner countries themselves seem almost exclusively interested in Barcelona's economic agenda. They consider more intensive economic ties with the EU a useful buffer against the pressures of international competition. Moreover, they hope that economic reforms will ultimately take the wind out of the sails of Islamic activists. In the meantime, mutual irritations have arisen. The partner countries reproach the EU member states for an overly passive and sympathetic attitude toward Israel. External pressure from the EU aimed at improving democracy and human rights meets with resistance and drives the domestic political opposition again into the arms of the governing elites (Aliboni 2004a). On the other hand, the EU suspects that the regimes in these countries take advantage of the Middle East conflict and the widespread fear of religious terrorism to legitimize their own authoritarian behavior (Biscop 2005: 11).

Evaluations of the first ten years of the EMP endorse the view that the policy has contributed too little to economic reforms, democratization, and human rights in the region (Euromesco 2005a; Youngs 2004c; Joffé 2005; Ministerie van Buitenlandse Zaken 2004 and 2005a).[3] Mutual understanding and contacts have increased, and the notion of a 'dialogue among cultures' is eagerly embraced, but the policy to date lacks effectiveness and credibility. Where openings for political or economic reforms already existed, as in Lebanon, Morocco, Jordan, and Tunisia, the contribution of the Barcelona process was limited. Furthermore, in the aftermath of 9/11, the intervention in Iraq, and the recent bombings, the EU has placed increasing attention on combating terrorism. As a result, conducting a balanced policy which fights against terrorism and promotes human rights is becoming ever more difficult (Youngs 2005: 8-9; Joffé 2005: 17).[4] The conservatism and survival instinct of political elites in the partner countries and the understandable European preference for gradual, endogenously induced reforms and for positive incentives instead of sanctions, have led to support for the political status quo in the region.[5] Contacts with partner countries, apart from those with the governing elites, take place chiefly with secular opposition groups, Western-oriented NGOs, and so-called civil society organizations that are officially approved and financed by the state. But these are precisely the groups that usually turn out to play a marginal role in political and social relations (Perthes 2004: 27; Hamzawy 2005; Menendez Gonzalez 2005). By a clever combination of repression, patronage, and co-optation the political opposition is sidelined or 'bought off' (see Chapter 3). Many 'official' NGOs, such as community service organizations, unions, and chambers of commerce have close economic and personal ties with policy-makers, which they do not wish to jeopardize. Arab regimes, especially, have become masters in 'playing' with civil society organizations. They themselves finance NGOs that regularly organize large, much-discussed, international and national conferences with intellectuals from civil society, with themes like women's rights and democratization. But the invited people do not speak in the name of any grassroots support worth mentioning (Ottaway and Carothers 2005: 257; NHC 2005: 35-36). Islamic inspired political movements, parties, and organizations, which do mobilize the great mass of ordinary citizens (including also women), have thus far not been involved in the Barcelona process (Menendez Gonzalez 2005: 10; Emerson, Aydin et al. 2005: 21).

By now, there exists within the European Commission and among the member states support for a renewed EMP that introduces a link to the bilateral policy of the ENP. This means that the partnership (in an analogy with the national adjustment programs in the former EU candidate member states from Central and Eastern Europe) will also include specific national obligations. Most of the partner countries are not negative at this prospect of a new approach. After all, reform-oriented countries like Morocco and Lebanon look with some jealousy at the impressive transformation process that the new member states from Central and Eastern Europe have undergone, partly through EU support. Although both the global strategy and the set of instruments of the action plans still need further adaptation and precision, the foundations for the new process, formalized in November 2005, are in any case sound.[6] 'Barcelona new style' has dissociated itself from the old assumption that economic reforms supply the key to democratization (Euromesco 2005b).[7] There is recognition that economic reforms do demand political changes and yet do not necessarily lead to democratization. Thus democracy and human rights have acquired higher political priority along with economic reforms and education.

At the same time, the ENP system of bilateral Action plans offers greater chance of achieving concrete results. The system offers the opportunity to introduce a more forceful linking between political reform efforts and positive incentives, such as improved access to the internal EU market, financial aid, and loans. In this manner a better balance can be achieved between multilateral cooperation and individual reform trajectories. The range, the emphases, and the tempo of reforms no longer need to depend on the least enthusiastic reformers among the partner countries. Moreover, annual progress reports based on the specific benchmarks in the Action plans can offer a better view of actual reforms being carried out. This process can also stimulate mutual peer pressure and learning effects. Thus it appeared that, during the parallel bilateral negotiation processes of the

EU with Tunisia and Morocco in the framework of the national Action plans, the two countries kept a close watch on each other; there arose a process of constructive competition in which Tunisia, with better economic accomplishments, and Morocco, more inclined to political reform, unintentionally spurred each other on to higher levels of ambition, including the institution of a national commission for human rights. In short, new chances for success are now possible through the linking of the new-style EMP with the bilateral approach of ENP.

What is undoubtedly the most remarkable development is that the new EMP has abandoned the premise that the secular forces in the region are the natural allies in the battle against Islamic activism and that NGOs outside the political arena always provide the most important impulses to democratization and the improvement of human rights. The European Commission now appears to be rallying around the advice of independent regional experts and EU bureaucrats directly involved to be open to ties with *all* the relevant democratic actors, including the Islamic political movements and parties (Euromesco 2005a and 2005b; El-Din Shahin 2005: 4; Jones and Emerson 2005: 21).[8] The Commission has urged the participants in the Barcelona process 'to strive towards a common view regarding the challenges for democratization, including the role of democratic Islamic political movements in national politics.' (European Commission 2005: 4). Apparently, the understanding has gradually come about that support for processes that systematically exclude religious political activists from the political system is at odds with a credible European role in the region. This change of course forms an important condition for the constructive engagement advocated in section 5.3.

Up until now it has not been clear, however, how fundamental this change of course has been. The recent call by the European Commission for defining a standpoint on democratic Islamic parties had found little resonance on the ministerial level of the EU member states themselves. Partner countries such as Egypt and Tunisia also fiercely resist the participation of religious parties in politics. Earlier official declarations on this subject have had little impact. There is no unity either to be found among the embassies of the EU member states in the region.[9] Many diplomats and political representatives of the member states still believe that allowing Islamic activists into politics would ultimately bring to power all those fundamentalists and extremists who want to put an end to political freedoms. In its recent call, the Commission circumvents this dilemma by referring only to *democratic* Islamic political movements and parties. But this, of course, does not resolve the problem. Despite the growing moderation of mainstream Islamic movements, there are also groups who eagerly want to compete for political power, without as yet recognizing elementary democratic principles. In addition, there are smaller, radicalized movements that do not shun violence. Reality demands recognition that these movements can exercise a disproportional influence and can obstruct the political system for a long time. There is the additional problem that often the governments in the partner countries do not look with favor on contacts with religious or other non-recognized interlocutors. Overtures can lead to an initial cooling of relations with these regimes. The EU must face up to such dilemma's if it wants to design a longer term strategy for the EMP region.

Although the recent EMP proposals thus place a high priority on democracy and human rights and – however hesitantly – no longer exclude Islamic parties, on the whole they do not refer to Islamic legislation and Islamic interpretations of human rights. As discussed in section 5.3, in many Muslim countries, however, there exists the desire to base (parts of) the state and society, in some form or other, on Islamic norms and (legal) foundations. Thus it is not in the least improbable that the political participation of Islamic parties – whether democratically disposed or not – will in some Muslim countries be accompanied by the (re)introduction or accentuation of Islamic law. That is a thorny problem for the EU. After all, the EU bases its strong emphasis on democracy, constitutionality, and human rights on the secular law of the European Convention on Human Rights and universal principles of human rights. In addition, it pays special attention to the rights of minorities and women, including the equality of men and women. How should the EU deal with Islamic political groups that distrust external meddling and are at the very least skeptical about Western or European ideas of democracy and human rights?[10] And what to do if a democratically elected Islamic government tries to introduce an 'Islamic' democracy, an Islamic state, or Sharia? Can the Union still contribute to a firmer rooting of international human rights treaties in such societies? The advocates of a renewed EMP/ENP need to recognize these dilemmas as well.

179

In the long run, ignoring the political and legal agenda of religious activism is no solution and can even be counterproductive. Olivier Roy is correct to state: "The role of Shari'a is a political issue: to oppose or ignore Shari'a from a purely technocratic point of view (it does not fit with human rights) leads automatically to a return of Shari'a by opponents of western encroachments" (Roy 2005: 1011). Not only does a negative attitude discourage Islamic groups with large followings among the population who are ready to work towards gradual change *within* the existing system. But such an attitude also contributes to the widespread feeling among ordinary citizens that secularism and (Western) democracy by definition represent antireligious interests. This will only increase the demand for Islamization, either because fundamentalists get more support from the people for their religious ideas or because political rulers themselves play the 'Islamization card' to maintain political legitimacy (Roy 2005: 1003). Many authoritarian regimes in the region cast themselves as buffers against the exploitation of Islam for party interests but do not shrink from manipulating official state Islam to maintain their own political power.[11] This is why sometimes the fundamentalist activists and at other times the conservative religious *ulama* are rewarded, without these groups ever having to take political responsibility for their standpoints. As a result, these societies lack social and political correction mechanisms to moderate these radical and conservative reflexes.

How should the EU participants of the EMP and ENP deal with these dilemmas? The WRR believes that the first step is to recognize that Islamic political and social groups can be *potentially* legitimate and credible political interlocutors, who, therefore, should not be excluded in advance from the EMP and ENP processes. This recognition must not only penetrate the bureaucratic and diplomatic circuits of 'Brussels'; EU governments need to disseminate this line at the highest political levels and, through (parliamentary) debates and discussions and other means, communicate this to their own populations. In the current polarized climate they will thus send an important signal to the Muslim world and to their own (Muslim) populations in Europe, namely that *all* political activists, including also religiously inspired democratic groups, will be taken seriously as potential allies in the pursuit of political participation, democratization, and improvement of human rights.

The European Commission's call to reconsider the role of *democratic* religious movements and parties in national politics deserves forceful support from the Dutch government and other member states. But such a reconsideration needs to go further than only these parties. No matter how understandable the fear of the scenario of once-only democratic elections may be, a reconsidered policy must not translate into the broadening of the political dialogue to include only those movements and parties who in advance pronounce themselves *democratic*. The process of democratization has little chance as long as the Union and the EMP partner countries demand from political groupings a democratic political disposition *as the primary condition* for constructive discussions or entrance into the political arena, while the (semi)authoritarian regimes in the partner countries themselves continue to manipulate in undemocratic ways the rules for admission into the political arena solely to maintain their own positions of power. It is a fact that most political movements and parties, Islamic or not, take on the 'color' of the environment in which they find themselves. Authoritarian, repressive regimes with a political culture of 'all or nothing' offer few guarantees that they will produce movements that not only in word, but also in deed, are democratic. In such an environment, then, there is also less chance that movements will propagate their democratic disposition out of political conviction rather than opportunism (Roy 2005: 1003; Fuller 2005: 45).

The debates on how the EU should deal with Hizbollah in Lebanon and Hamas in the Palestinian territories illustrate the dilemmas of political rapprochement. Both organizations have a political party with a military wing, and both consider attacks as justified as long as Israel remains in the occupied territories. Since the withdrawal of Israel from Lebanon, Hizbollah has applied itself increasingly to politics and has experienced a process of institutionalization (Alagha 2006). Hamas has also shifted more to the political arena, though without recognizing the state of Israel or foreswearing violence (ICG 2006). Three years ago, in part under American and Israeli pressure, the EU decided to put this movement on its list of terrorist organizations. However, it would be neither conducive to the peace process nor to the future development of the region to consider Hamas merely as a terrorist movement or, in the wake of the massive election victory of January 2006, to isolate its democratically chosen leaders for years to come, and thereby deny them responsibility for taking a constructive role in the Israeli-Palestinian conflict. Hamas has attained great legitimacy and popularity among the population, in large part due to its social services and its exposure of corruption. Moreover, in the current situation its party leaders have to attune their strategies to political reality to maintain sufficient influence and support. The EU correctly decided at the beginning of 2006 to temporarily continue economic aid to the Palestinians and to judge an eventual future Hamas government primarily on its concrete contributions to the building of a Palestinian state and to the peace process in the Middle East.

Experience teaches us that movements and actors who, originally out of purely opportunistic motives, align themselves with or turn away from democratic procedures *can* develop over time into driving forces behind gradual, internal democratization processes. But there are no guarantees. What is involved is to promote in each country the conditions under which such development processes get started and then continue, and to reduce the risks of violent eruptions.[12] The political opportunities for reforms in the region are now somewhat greater than before, but there is also more instability (Roy 2005: 1010; Jones and Emerson 2005: 6). Moreover, every country has its own political culture and path of development, including persistent hindrances that the elites concerned will only want to remove if they can preserve enough political stability (Hamzaway 2005: 3; Perthes ed. 2004). Thus, this calls for cautious policy that takes account of the many risks, but is also prepared for unexpected opportunities.

The development of a strategic vision on the reference points for reform in the EMP countries first demands a thorough exploration by the Union of developments in the political and legal environment within the partner countries and in the Middle East region, including the characteristics and dynamics of Islamic legislation and of (religious) opposition movements and parties. Now that accession negotiations have begun with Turkey and there is a real possibility of its accession to the Union in 10 to 15 years, the urgency increases to strategically explore the longer-term opportunities and dangers of entering into closer ties also with the Gulf States and Iran, by then the EU's close neighbors.[13] Given the mutual unfamiliarity and distorted image-formation on both sides, it is advisable to first intensify the EU's cultural relations with these countries, as has occurred in the past 10 years with the EMP partners. Developing of a vision and conducting strategic explorations is first and foremost an EU matter. At the same time, the Dutch government, of course, also bears some responsibility for raising this issue, as well as for the political dissemination of the insights derived from these explorations.

Earlier is this chapter it was already argued that the reform processes in Muslim countries must develop chiefly along an endogenous path. There is no paternalistic role reserved for the EU in the EMP countries, much less should it impose democratic norms through stringent conditions. That would inevitably result in strongly nationalistic and anti-Western reflexes that drive the reformers within the opposition into the arms of the ruling elites. Similarly, openly supporting truly independent NGOs and political groupings would compromise these organizations in the eyes of the population or brings them into problems with the regime. Moreover, the ENP operates on the basis of bilateral, *joint* Action plans agreed upon by the EU and the partner countries. In practice this manifests itself in the cited paradox between European efforts to promote democracy and human rights in the region and the aversion on the part of the partner countries to every form of uninvited European interference. This field of tensions compels a continual search for opportunities to exert influence that manage to avoid (the appearance of) meddling.

Clearly then, the Union does have some room for maneuver to promote political reforms, but this is mainly the case in the partner countries that, in principle, are ready and able to agree in their Action plans on a long-term strategic and realistic course of reforms. The EU should therefore initially limit itself to an 'exportable minimum' of basic democratic principles (Euromesco 2005a). Overly detailed definitions and elaborations of democracy and human rights, which are often also strongly colored by European experience, do not satisfactorily take into account the endogenous dynamics. They arouse too much resistance to be productive. Moreover, they ignore the great variety in historical democratization experiences and democratic systems in Europe. The EU should also develop more positive incentives to stimulate and reward reforms (Jones and Emerson 2005). Furthermore, it must be ready to (temporarily) suspend the partnership in the case of serious violations of human rights. In this way, the Union provides room for different paths to democratization and progressive realization of human rights, while at the same time maintaining its own values in this area, as advocated in section 5.4.2.

The politically relevant elites in the EMP countries are not always, by definition, *against* reform, but they usually demand gradual and, above all, controllable reform processes that have an eye for the complexity of political transformations. Conditionality directed at swift regime change is not only ineffective but potentially counterproductive. However, by accepting that the concept of democracy can be reduced to a number of basic principles, such as transparency, accountability, free and fair elections, constitutionalism, and the independence of the judiciary, the EU can provide positive incentives and support. In turn, the political elites can forge coalitions that are able to support concrete, step-by-step reforms. Sometimes this takes place primarily in the area of political participation or party formation, sometimes chiefly in the area of constitutionalism, or on both fronts.[14]

183

Through setting concrete targets in the annual Action plans, the EU can entice countries to gradually introduce elementary rules that apply to *all* political parties and movements, such as the endorsement of non-violence, electoral participation on the basis of assessable political starting points, coalition forming, and democratic alternation of power. Political parties, whether religious or not, would have to accept these rules in exchange for formal recognition as regular political parties in elections. They should be required to contest elections on the basis of political programs that explain their goals and (religious) aspirations. What kind of (Islamic) society do they have in mind? What role do they reserve for Sharia in legislation, the constitution, and politics? It seems anything but clear where the political leaders themselves stand on these questions. If they are challenged to put their claims and slogans into assessable programs, this can create openings for coalitions and compromises. Programmatic politics reduces the risk of 'secret' agendas and increases the chance that the voters will have a real choice. As in many authoritarian political systems, many political actors in the EMP partner countries lack political experience and skills, including the skill to write party programs. In addition, their financial resources are sometimes limited. Financial and substantive support from the EU for strengthening political parties (whether or not through organizations such as the United Nations Development Program (UNPD), the International

Institute for Democracy and Electoral Assistance (IDEA) or the Netherlands Institute for Multiparty Democracy (NIMD) should partly help to
solve these problems.

5.5.3   THE RELATIONSHIP WITH TURKEY

Above we outlined in what ways a renewed EMP could contribute to
democratization and the improvement of human rights in the partner
countries. There is, however, still another strategy available to the EU: its
special relationship with Turkey. The European Council opened formal
membership negotiations in October 2005. This represents a historic decision, by which the EU member states declared they envisaged full Turkish
membership as a real perspective. In its 2004 report *The European Union,
Turkey, and Islam*, the WRR concluded that a process of consistently
pursued negotiations with Turkey would sends positive signals to the
Muslim world and to European Muslims (WRR 2004). It underscored that
there is no inevitable clash of cultures or civilizations, that Muslim populations can be fully part of the Union, and also that 'Islam' and Islam-
inspired politics do not in the least exclude a process of democratization
and the promotion of human rights. Recent and future Turkish experiences
with this process offers not so much a model or an instant solution as a
potential source of inspiration for experiments with democratization in
other Muslim countries.

Referring to its earlier report, the WRR re-emphasizes the importance that
Turkey represents for the EU in maintaining constructive relations with the
Muslim world. The continuing hesitations on the part of some member
states about possible Turkish membership accentuate the need for trans-
parent decision-making and a timely and informed debate on the opportunities and threats posed by Turkish membership. The WRR fully endorses
the European Commission's call on the member states to get this debate
going. Governments, parliaments, political parties, and civic organizations
must take the initiative. It is obvious that this should not be a one-time
effort, but should span the entire negotiation period.

The member states have for a long time been aware that Turkey can also
play an active role in EU foreign policy. Turkey was a participant in the
Barcelona process from the beginning, and has in the meantime, thanks to
the pre-accession process for EU candidate member states, attained the
political position of 'northern' rather than 'southern' partner in the EMP. In
addition, a treaty has been signed extending the customs union between
Turkey and the EU to the ten new member states, whereas security cooperation with Turkey was intensified in 2002, with the decision to allow
NATO allies from outside the EU to participate in the European Security

and Defense Policy (ESDP). Since then Turkey has already taken part in EU-led missions. There are many geopolitical, logistical, and cultural arguments for immediately intensifying foreign policy cooperation with Turkey rather than to wait until the final moment of accession in 2015 or even later. Turkey can to an increasing extent play an active role in the EMP/ENP and the OIC (see box 5.2) and can thus also contribute to a constructive EU position towards the Muslim world. This requires from Turkey a continuation, during the long process of negotiations, of the course of reforms already set into motion. For their part, the EU member states must consistently and credibly deal with the accession demands imposed on Turkey and be ready to convince their electorates of the importance of a future Turkish membership.

Until relatively recently, Turkey was certainly not an active and enthusiastic member of the EMP because it was disappointed over the stalled Middle East peace process and its position as a 'southern' partner in the Barcelona process (Emerson and Tocci 2004: 19). Now that the accession negotiations have begun, the Turkish attitude has changed, however. As was argued above, a renewed EMP/ENP that provides concrete incentives for political and economic reforms must offer the southern partners more in the area of trade. Access to the Turkish market and also agreements over the delivery of water from the Turkish-controlled parts of the Euphrates and Tigris and the Mediterranean Sea, can be attractive inducements for several partner countries.

185

Turkey's membership of the OIC is an additional asset in the EU's relations with the Muslim world. As a 'seasoned' secular Muslim state, Turkey was until recently an outsider, and felt rather uncomfortable in the OIC (Emerson and Tocci 2004: 26). But since it has headed in the direction of a more relaxed approach to Islam on its own soil and has experienced a process of deepening of democracy, matters have changed. The election of Ekmeleddin Ihsanoglu as secretary-general of the OIC underscores the rising prestige of Turkey within this organization. In December 2005 he declared that [we] Muslims "do not have the luxury to blame others for our own problems. It is high time that we faced our national and regional problems with courage, candor, and openness" (de Volkskrant, December 8, 2005). The current Turkish government has also shown itself to be a forceful advocate within the OIC for more self-criticism in the Muslim world and for democratization and human rights. Turkey's leaders are familiar with the political sensitivities in the region, know just the right tone to strike, and are therefore in a position to communicate with greater authority and conviction than most other European countries the necessity for reform. In the coming years, Turkey will thus find itself in a favorable position to maintain constructive relations with the Muslim states in the region and to put the efforts of the EU toward political reforms higher on the political agenda.

5.5.4 INITIATIVES IN THE OIC AND THE UN

In section 5.4.2 it was proposed that dealing with Islamic legislation on the basis of progressive realization means that the EU can do more justice to the context and dynamism of the development of law in Muslim countries. At the same time the relationship model discussed in section 5.5.2 remains that of an asking party (the EU) and a responding party (the Muslim country). This raises the question of whether further improvement of the human rights situation could be served by putting a greater emphasis on the endogenous dynamics of mutual learning processes among Muslim countries. It is after all a fact that most Muslim countries – whether with reservations or not – have already become signatories to the international human rights treaties. Can one imagine a complementary approach that promotes mutual learning capabilities and social control over the improvement and observance of human rights? If so, then the current discussions on human rights can become less charged with arguments about Western conceptual and actual domination. It would mean that the Muslim world, in its relationship with the West, could become more of an asking party regarding the contents and background of international human rights.

Provided that their jurisdiction is recognized, separate international human rights courts can exert an important stimulating influence on these endogenous dynamics towards greater authority of universal human rights principles in like-minded Muslim states. There are in principle two different ways to shape this, namely through the institution of regional courts and the institution of a court of Islamic law for the entire Muslim world. The first option involves human rights courts with their own separate, territorially limited jurisdictions, analogous to the European Court of Human Rights. These territorial courts can formulate their own human rights conventions that completely endorse universal human rights but at the same time take into account the specific regional (Islamic) heritages, cultures, and legal practices. By using the experience of the European Court, among others, and of the various human rights commissions of the UN, effective collective supervision of the interpretations and compliance with universal human rights can take place within such regional cultural and Islamic frames of reference (AIV 1998). And although these courts do not thus refer to *Islamic* legal norms, in practice, naturally, they may indeed when the occasion arises, deal with conflicts between Islamic law and international treaties, as well as think about solutions.

The power of this regional option is especially visible in Europe, where the Council of Europe adopted the European Convention on Human Rights in 1950 and created the European Court in 1959. The original group of ten member states has greatly expanded since the 1980s, primarily due to the relaxation of tensions between East and West. The current 46 participating countries (a total of 800 million inhabitants) all come under the compulsory jurisdiction of the Court. The European human rights regime employs the principle of *margin of appreciation*, but represents no deviation from the standards of the UN. Its different organs work explicitly within that framework and strengthen its effect by limiting the kind of cultural differences and problems between and within countries which can sometimes hamper actual legal implementation. The UN itself has brought about the creation of similar institutions in regions where they do not yet exist. In this spirit the *Arab Human Development Report 2004* advocated a regional strategy for the Arab world. Up until now, the report argues, 'specifically Arab' was too often used as an argument for undermining international human rights. Precisely to strengthen the effective power of international human rights conventions, the report proposes that the Arab world formulate its own Arab Human Rights Convention. This must completely conform to the Universal Declaration but at the same time also take into account Arab-Islamic culture (UNDP 2005: 71-77).

187

If this suggestion for an Arab Human Rights Convention with its own court will indeed elicite a positive response from Arab governments, the Netherlands, in its role as center of expertise in international law, should offer opportunities for its further examination. The Council of Europe and the EU can assist these governments with their own learning processes, including the expansion of knowledge of human rights among Islamic judges. Just as in the case of the European human rights regime, it is obvious that the number of parties to the convention will initially be small. In the long run, however, this number will grow if the court obtains demonstrable successes and increasing prestige.

A second approach has been proposed with the same goal of reconciling Islamic law and universal human rights (Baderin 2003). This option involves the institution of a separate, *global* human rights regime with a *court specialized in Islamic legislation* composed of leading judges who are qualified in Islamic as well as international human rights. This court would be able to issue binding rulings over the reach and interpretation of Sharia in relation to complaints about human rights violations in the member states. It can eventually be made part of the OIC, the organization to which a great portion of the Muslim world is already affiliated and which earlier took the initiative to formulate the Cairo Declaration on Human Rights in Islam (see box 5.2). The advantage of such a global Islamic human rights court, according to Baderin, is that it expressly works on constructive ways to create as much harmonization as possible between Islamic and international human rights. It can also refer to diverse Islamic legal theories, schools, and practices in a large number of different Muslim cultures in such a way that a broad range of doctrines is available for maximal rapprochement with the universal norms.

Box 5.2   The Organization of the Islamic Conference (OIC)

The task of this organization, which was founded in 1969, is to promote cooperation among Muslim states in economic, social, cultural, scientific, and other vital areas. The OIC is the only organization that includes almost all the Muslim states; it has 57 member states, all of them also members of the UN. The Charter of the OIC is registered as an international agreement with the UN. Its preamble states that the member states consider themselves bound to the UN Charter and Fundamental Human Rights, and want to preserve Islamic spiritual, ethical, social, and economic values. The OIC even deems the 'right to human rights education' as a human right and has taken a series of initiatives to encourage Muslim states to an interpretation of Islamic values that contributes to a progressive realization of international human rights. The drafting of the Cairo Declaration on Human Rights in Islam is one of these initiatives. There is a formal cooperation agreement between the OIC and the UN.

Against these advantages there are, however, many disadvantages. The large mutual differences and political divisions among the member states would make an Islamic court of human rights under the OIC banner practically unfeasible. A principled objection is that the institution of an explicitly *Islamic* human rights court can be interpreted as reaching out to the conservative forces in the Muslim world, who, by appealing to Islamic interpretations of human rights, turn against the universal application of human rights treaties. If these forces succeed in naming their own Islamic judges to the court, this can result in an institutionalization of existing differences between Islamic and international interpretations of human rights. Instead of a progressive realization via constructive dialogue, there would even be the risk of a gradual undermining of much that the UN has accomplished in promoting a normative rapprochement with universal human rights in recent years (AIV 1998). And that much has been accomplished can be shown, among other things, from the fact that the UN committees that oversee the compliance with human rights standards carry out an almost permanent and constructive dialogue. Because of this, today it is no longer acceptable that governments 'explain' human rights violations by an appeal to religion. Thus, having weighed the advantages and disadvantages, the WRR believes that the first option, the territorial court, deserves preference.

Although a binding human rights regime in connection with the OIC is thus a bridge too far and would also meet with objections based on principle, the OIC does have concrete ambitions in the area of human rights education which are worth supporting (see box 5.2). For example, the EU can, through the OIC's Turkish secretary-general, offer help to set up a ten-year program for human rights education. Moreover, there can be support for a permanent training program in human rights, specially directed at the judiciary in Muslim countries. Even office holders are little acquainted with (Islamic) human rights; they need to have a knowledge of international jurisprudence. Furthermore, the EU can help Muslim countries institute independent human rights commissions, as is now occurring in the framework of the ENP. These commissions could also play a role in the education and training programs mentioned above. In addition, the OIC can be encouraged to mobilize the study of those areas of Islamic legislation that are very controversial from a human rights perspective. A moratorium on the harshest punishments for *hadd* crimes, as advocated by Tariq Ramadan, among others, could be one of the outcomes (Ramadan 2004). This can start a process of opinion-forming that ultimately results in an authoritative judgment more in agreement with international standards. But even if there is no readiness to introduce a moratorium, the very fact of studying this subject already has the important function of stimulating awareness and debate.

189

5.5.5   A EUROPEAN ISLAM?

There is regular debate on whether in Europe a particular European Islam or Euro-Islam can and should develop, in the sense of an Islam clearly recognizable as European. This debate often suffers from a confusion of concepts and wishful thinking. Many speculations are insufficiently specific on what elements such a European Islam would contain (Steinbach 2005). For example, Bassam Tibi, a professor of international relations in Germany, emphasizes the need for Muslims to completely accept the dominant European culture (or *Leitkultur*). In his view, this means that they not only must embrace democracy, human rights, and pluralism, but also must accept that religion is a private matter. Only in this way can it be prevented that Muslims create parallel societies that turn away from the principles of the democratic constitutional state. Tariq Ramadan, a Swiss philosopher popular among young European Muslims, also cherishes a hope for a future European Islam that embraces the democratic constitutional state. But unlike Tibi he stresses that Islam's common frame of reference can and should flourish in the European public space, provided that Muslims do indeed embrace democracy and constitutional principles (see box 5.3). And while Tibi primarily calls upon Muslims in Europe (and European governments) to adopt a strategy of assimilation, Ramadan urges participation and integration on the basis of a separate Muslim identity. Despite considerable substantive differences, there are also points of agreement between these two authors. Both attach great importance to overcoming the 'we and they' situation and to stimulating full citizenship for Muslims. Their objective goes well beyond the peaceful co-existence that some consider to be the most attainable outcome. They also keep hammering on the importance of learning how to deal with plurality through dialogue and discussion, within and between different strains of Islam as well as between Islam and other religions and philosophies of life. Both correctly state that plurality, in the sense of respect for those with different beliefs, must be learned, by Muslims as well as by non-Muslims.

Box 5.3   European Islam according to Tibi and Ramadan

Bassam Tibi sees no place in Europe for jihadism, orthodoxy, and fundamentalism. Of course, they are present there, and they constitute a major threat to an open society and to the integration of dissident Muslims. The Euro-Islam he advocates involves a cultural model that is adapted to the political culture of civil society and the separation of culture and politics. Cultural relativism and multiculturalism on the part of the receiving society are dangerous, since these shut Muslims out and promote the ghettoizing of communities and parallel societies. Tibi also strongly opposes any form of recognition of Sharia; the concept of citizenship demands that the same laws apply to everyone (Tibi 2001). Without becoming Eurocentric, Europe must reaffirm its own value(s), whereas Muslims in Europe must embrace 'the idea of Europe' to become citizens 'of the heart.' This European idea, the *Leitkultur*, concerns a system of norms, values and an associated world view. Liberal democracy, individual human rights, and the demands of civil society form its core. An open Islam based on these orientations is characterized by *laïcité*, cultural modernity, and an understanding of tolerance that goes beyond the Abrahamic religions. Euro-Islam recognizes religious and cultural pluralism and relinquishes any claim to Islamic domination. Under these conditions an Islam can develop in Europe that will also have great influence elsewhere (Tibi 2005).

Like Tibi, Tariq Ramadan sees developments among Muslims in Europe and the US as being of potentially great importance for the entire Muslim world. He observes that in the shelter of the overwhelming attention for radical Islam, a 'silent revolution' is taking place, especially among intellectual and younger Muslims. These Muslims shape a European and American Islam that is rooted in their respective European and American cultures, but at the same time remains faithful to universal Islamic principles, such as justice and human dignity. This grassroots movement will gain worldwide influence because it has developed under the conditions of modernity and globalization that will also increasingly affect Muslim countries. Ramadan wants to contribute to shaping this European 'Muslim personality' by supplying the theological tools that enable Muslims to participate fully in society. Many Muslims in Europe have isolated themselves in their own, seemingly secure, parallel communities, because they have a sometimes obsessive fear of losing their religious identity. They are supported in their reluctant accommodation to their immediate surroundings by existing Islamic doctrines on how to live as a minority in non-Muslim countries. Ramadan calls upon Muslims to abandon this self-definition as a minority and to give up their relative isolation from European society.

Instead of the dichotomy of *dar al-Islam* (house of Islam) and *dar al-harb* (house of the enemy), which he considers outdated, Ramadan proposes the new perspective of the *dar al-shahada* (house of testimony). The West is not an enemy, but a 'house' for Muslims, and that is what should direct their lives. The existing rule of law, freedoms of religion and of assembly, the right to knowledge, and other rights and freedoms all allow Muslims to live their religion fully and to develop it further in freedom. They should no longer attempt to reproduce Islam from their countries of origin, nor remain dependent for their choices on the religious authorities in Muslim countries. They should dare to follow their own paths and act as responsible, free, and loyal citizens who contribute to the society they live in, on the basis of the universal principles of their religion. Ramadan does not say that Muslims, acting in this way, must abandon Sharia. Sharia concerns primarily universal principles and a frame of reference to translate these into behavior, but the rules of conduct derived from Sharia are bound by time and place. As long as the existing laws of Western society do not explicitly conflict with the conscience of Muslims – and this will occur only in exceptional instances – Sharia dictates that these law be respected (Ramadan 2004).

191

Underlying speculations about a future European Islam is often the assumption that governments in Europe can and should give direction to the content of religious beliefs and their evolution. It also seem to be assumed that such an Islam will be both recognizably European and in the long run, as an 'enlightened' version, will be exportable to Muslim countries outside Europe that still play up the conflict between 'Islam,' and democracy and human rights. However, both of these assumptions require comment.

First, governments in Europe are committed to freedom of religion on the basis of international treaties like the ECHR and the Charter of Fundamental Rights. It is precisely in the area of religion that they must exercise caution and certainly not meddle in the *content and direction* of religious development. This also applies to EU institutions: the Union has expressly reserved legal authority over religious organizations to the member states. In the separate, legally non-binding Declaration nr. 11 of the Amsterdam Treaty, it is thus stated: 'The European Union respects and does not prejudice the status under national law of churches and religious associations or communities in the Member States. The European Union equally respects the status of philosophical and non-confessional organizations' (European Union 1997). To the extent that mechanisms to influence religions are available, therefore, these do not reside on the European but on the national level, in institutions and behavior that fall under state authority. Second, even were the EU to have such mechanisms available, their presence would not necessarily result in a recognizably *European* religious identity. This would, at the least, demand an approachable institutional form. Unlike for instance the Roman Catholic Church in Christianity, these institutional forms are absent in the Sunni variants of Islam. And even the transnational, strictly hierarchical organization of the Roman Catholic Church has not produced any typically *European* Catholicism; one can always easily distinguish a Dutch Catholic from, say, a Polish one. This underscores that it is mainly the national and local contexts that exercise influence on the direction of the faith and the characteristics of the religious perceptions of Muslims, alongside transnational influences on the level of the *Ummah* (such as Internet, television, etc.), which transcend the European level.

There is, however, no unambiguous, empirical proof of a religious current from below at the level of individual Muslims or stimulated by local governments and institutions that would results in a recognizably European Islam. If anything characterizes Islam in Europe today, it is its enormous variety. Muslims living in Europe reflect the worldwide variety of Islamic religious tendencies. Although almost every European country of immigration has an over-representation of certain groups of Muslims and tendencies, within most European countries there is a greater diversity than exists or is permitted in the countries of origin (Boutachekourt 2003). This holds not only for non-radical believers or Islamic free-thinkers who are persecuted in their countries of origin and who continue their scholarly work in Europe; it also includes spokesmen and their supporters in European countries who reject the democratic constitutional state and strive for an Islamic state. Levels of education and socio-economic background of Muslims differ considerably between and within European countries. Thanks to the greater diversity and greater freedom of religion and expression, the religious debate in Europe can thus be broader than in the countries of origin. Whether this debate is carried out to the full and leads to (religious) assimilation and modernization depends also, however, on the intellectual contribution, openness, critical position, and readiness for self-criticism of *all* those involved, irrespective of their (religious) conviction or origin.

At national and local levels, there are complex processes involved. Important Islamic movements that previously were strongly oriented towards their country of origin, are now taking more autonomous positions. Foreign governments in turn involve themselves less with these movements or, as in the case of imams posted abroad, increasingly recognize the importance of knowledge of the local context and language. And mosque leaders in many European countries are more appreciative of the impor- tance of connecting to the local situation and needs if they want to continue to attract youth. Muslim organizations are increasingly joining national and local institutions to have access to facilities for education and social and cultural activities. In addition to contacts on the European level, national and local inter-religious dialogues also take place. In various member states, such as Austria, Spain, Italy, Germany, Great Britain, France, Belgium, and the Netherlands, formal links have been created to make consultation possible between national governments and representa- tives of 'the' Muslim world, including in emergency situations. The form of representation that is created in each country between Muslims and the state is sometimes modeled on the national relationship between church and state (Shadid and Van Koningsveld 2002). In many municipalities, consultative bodies with the Muslim communities have recently been established (Koning Boudewijnstichting 2004). Also in some countries fatwa-centers have been established to find answers for the problems of Muslims living in Europe; for questions arising from living in a minority situation, many fatwas have been developed – also in dialogue with authoritative religious institutions in Muslim countries (Shadid and Van Koningsveld 2002). Thus in Europe 'Islam' takes on the color of its local environment. The agenda of Milli Görüs Nederland, for example, was until recently completely different from that of its original movement in Turkey or its sister organization in Germany. This adaptation is not only institu- tional, but also substantive. For example, Dutch Muslims show a lower acceptance of homosexuality than the average Dutch person, but this level of acceptance is much higher than usual stereotypes lead one to expect (Motivaction 2005), while Muslims in France score very high on the indi- cators for secularism (Müller 2005). All these trends contribute to the fact that Islam in Europe is developing more autonomously in relation to Muslim countries, engages in increasingly more institutional links with the receiving society, and therefore is acquiring its own national and local characteristics.

Most important, of course, is the evolution of religion among Muslims themselves. This is all the more crucial because (especially within the Sunni variant) Islam, despite the current trend of institutionalization, will not take on the shape of a church congregation. The emphasis is on the individual believer and the mosque; it is precisely on this individual level that similar developments are taking place among Muslims in the member states. In section 5.2 we referred to Olivier Roy's observation that a process of deculturalization is taking place among the second and third genera- tions. Young people distance themselves from the Islamic traditions of their parents' country of origin and identify increasingly with Islam as such.

How this new Islam is given content is now becoming a matter of individual choices; it is a quest that produces great uncertainty. Along with freeing themselves from traditional authority structures, young people are at the same time exposed to new influences both from the Muslim world and the society in which they live. In comparison with their parents, they are growing up in a situation with much greater diversity of Islamic religious views, including radical variants. The Internet and peer groups also play a very important role in the process of religious 'shopping'.

Roy points out that deculturalization can lead to radicalization (Roy 2004). But the vast majority is moving in a different direction. Dutch research confirms Roy's general observation on deculturalization. Islam and Muslim identity remain important, but are becoming dissociated from religious practice, especially through increased levels of education and command of the Dutch language. Moreover, some convergence of autochtonous and allochtonous values takes place among young people. This applies particularly to social equality and democratic values in the public sphere. Especially among the higher educated, there is also convergence in values concerning marriage and the family, even though the ideas of young Muslims are much more conservative than those of the average Dutch youth. There is only a marginal following for undemocratic ideas and actions in the name of Islam (Phalet and Ter Wal 2004; Phalet et al. 2000/1). Research by the German *Zentrum für Turkeistudien* shows a similar picture for Germany. This underscores that young people define themselves as Muslims, but fewer and fewer follow strict religious practices. Furthermore, the second and third generations more often than the first have a modern liberal orientation; what the first generation considers a religious obligation has become a matter of choice for subsequent generations. The outcome of this evolution could be an Islam in which the mainstream has clearly freed itself from a non-pluralistic traditional religion. This means that there is fertile ground for active stimulation of a pluralistic Islam, but this would require stronger theological guidance by Muslim organizations (Zentrum für Turkeistudien 2004).

This last point touches upon an important question. The first generation was very poorly educated, lived strongly turned in on itself, and 'survived' by preserving its own culture and religious customs as much as possible. The second and third generations have grown up in more open contact with the surrounding society. The democratic constitutional states as well as the advantages of education in Europe in principle provide substantially favorable conditions for the development of a similar Islam across European countries. But these new conditions also mean that the second and third generations are confronted with many competing 'Islams,' attacks on Islam itself, and with other religions and philosophies of life. If young

Muslims distance themselves from the traditional faith but also want to give meaning to their Muslim identity, they have to reinvent their faith and maintain it in the full wind of this plurality. That they grow up in the middle of plurality does not mean that they also experience this as inherently valuable. This is what Jonathan Sacks has in mind with his concept of 'the dignity of difference' (Sacks 2002). To find one's own way in this confusing and threatening plurality is a difficult process. This is also apparent from the questions and discussions on various Internet sites. Changes in behavior and religious interpretation often go hand in hand; people look for religious guidelines to determine behavior, as well as for religious justification for new behavior. In this process of interaction between practice and conviction, the availability of differing religious viewpoints is crucial. Providing this diversity is something that should best happen on the local and national levels. The WRR will return to this question in the conclusion of this report, when discussing Islamic activism in the Netherlands.

In conclusion, to the extent that European Islam is on the horizon, this does not offer the perspective of religious uniformity on a European scale. Instead of the Euro-Islam or European Islam that Tibi or Ramadan wish for, Islam in Europe will remain characterized by great diversity. We should be aware of the tenacity of religious differences that are central for those involved, even if these are barely observable to outsiders. Plurality itself is, after all, not the problem. What it is ultimately about is that all the nationally and locally colored variants of Islam are continuing to develop amidst acceptance of the principles of the democratic constitutional state. These same principles expressly exclude governmental steering of the content of religion or its development; the believers themselves must bring about any possible modernization, and this process is also well underway. It is, of course, the task of governments to guard the constitutional framework. In some cases that can mean that limits to acts and utterances are established or that governments make resources available that facilitate the free exercise of religion. The autonomy of religious communities does not after all mean a total *absence* of the state with regard to religion; that is also not the intent of the doctrine of the separation of church and state (WRR 2004).

195

The great diversity of Muslim communities in Europe, their position as a minority in European countries (with the exception of Albania, Bosnia, Kosovo, and Turkey) and the partially similar developments with which Muslims in Europe are confronted can, however, contribute to a certain uniformity among European Muslims. This also means that there are correspondences between Islamic activism with which each of the European countries has to deal on its own territory, and the social questions and policy issues with which they wrestle. For the WRR it seems obvious that EU member states should use European policy frameworks for the mutual exchange of best practices regarding Islamic activism. That Islam in Europe can eventually exercise influence on the developments within the faith in Muslim countries is of course quite conceivable, given the current global means of communication. That it will be a decisive influence, as Tibi and Ramadan foresee, is less plausible. This idea rests too much on the assumption that Europe and the US are the seats of modernization. Local contexts differ from country to country and therefore will lead to individual responses to the relationship between religion, democracy, and human rights.

5.5.6   BILATERAL POLICY OPTIONS

Even if European countries or EU member states fail to develop a common strategic view on Islamic activism, that does not relieve the Dutch government of the obligation to give as much content as possible to constructive engagement. It has available additional *bilateral* channels through which it can influence directly or indirectly relations with parts of the Muslim world. First, there are the regular foreign policy instruments, including the extensive network of development-aid links with a number of Muslim countries and the political ties with countries like Morocco, Turkey, Indonesia, and Surinam, where many of the Muslims living in the Netherlands still have their roots. Second, there are NGOs, universities, the business world, and the media, which in indirect ways can become involved in Dutch foreign policy toward the Muslim world.

Taking into account the diversity and endogenous dynamism of Islamic activism requires a basic knowledge of current and future developments within the Muslim world, including the numerous different intellectual, political, cultural, and legal manifestations of Islamic activism. The Dutch government needs to stay informed about these developments and to nourish its policy, politics, and public opinion with its insights, based on the realization that domestic and foreign policy are closely intertwined (Otto 2006). But the level of knowledge in the Netherlands about Islam and the Muslim world is distressingly low. Transmission of factual information will contribute to the correction of inaccurate images and stereotypes on both sides and will stimulate critical awareness. This can be accomplished, for example, by structurally investing in relevant information and cultural centers, NGOs, and universities within and outside the Netherlands. It can be done by contributing to making Western scholarly and cultural products more accessible in Muslim countries, by facilitating exchanges of teachers and students, and by promoting a situation in which leading thinkers, political activists, and legal scholars can inform policymakers and public opinion on both sides. Previously, we already mentioned that the Netherlands should use its worldwide reputation as a center for international law to offer help, if requested, in establishing an Arab court of human rights that conforms to UN principles (sec. 5.5.4).

In addition, the Dutch government must further investigate with what other instruments it can broaden its knowledge about and contacts with Muslim countries. It should also examine how it can disseminate its own policy abroad and at home, for example, by making optimal use of the expertise present in the Netherlands. Both its international and domestic policies should express that the Netherlands takes the principles of democracy and human rights as its reference points, that it takes account of the diversity of Islamic activism and Islamic legislation, and that it applies an explicit distinction between constructive and destructive political forces (Otto 2006). Positive changes in Islamic legislation in the direction of international human rights norms deserve forceful support in Dutch foreign policy, while serious violations of human rights in the name of Islam must be sharply condemned.

5.6 ISLAMIC ACTIVISM IN THE DUTCH DEMOCRATIC CONSTITUTIONAL STATE

5.6.1 INTRODUCTION

Constructive *external* relations can only thrive in the long run if there are constructive *internal* relations between religious and non-religious citizens, Muslims and non-Muslims, and among believers of different Islamic denominations. In internal relations, too, it is important to take into account diversity, to recognize that Islamic activism can *potentially* be a constructive political and juridical factor, to associate with endogenous developments, and to invest in an informed public opinion. Political and public debate in the Netherlands certainly attests to the fact that there is insufficient knowledge of the many tendencies within Islamic political thought and that little attention is given to the diversity of Islamic political movements. The last few years have indeed witnessed "a new intellectual Islamophobia which is not being countered on the intellectual level" (Slomp 2003). The stigmatizing of Islam and Muslims is offensive to the vast majority of Muslims who accept Dutch democracy and human rights as self-evident. Only a more balanced and open position in the debate can produce a climate in which the parties concerned are not only self-aware, but also open to self-criticism. Such a climate would also allow for more uninhibited discussion about possible new arrangements for the relationship between the public domain and religion, a theme that will be addressed in a separate study by the WRR. It is partially also the government's task to facilitate this debate.

There are two sides to taking into account the diversity and potentially constructive character of Islamic activism within Dutch society. On one hand, more attention should be paid to concrete, existing Islamic religious beliefs and the *behavior* of Muslims who relate positively to the democratic constitutional state. On the other hand, behavior which appeals to 'Islam' but runs counter to prevailing constitutional principles is not acceptable. The principles of the constitutional state offer freedom but at the same time set limitations; these also apply to behavior based on religious beliefs. As long as behavior is primarily concerned with mutual relations among citizens, the role of the government is naturally limited to the safeguarding of general constitutional principles, particularly those of equality (art. 1 of the constitution), freedom of religion, and the separation of church and state.

At the moment, the emphasis is on closer monitoring of the boundaries of the rights and freedoms currently in force. While appeals to hate and violence in the name of Islam were previously tolerated or ignored, they are now punishable by law. Balancing these various rights and freedoms is a difficult task. The constitutional state shows its greatest powers of persuasion by maintaining its principles even under threat and by not employing double standards (Buijs 2002). However much repressive action is taken against terrorism or abuses of freedom of religion and expression, there must be no illusion that the *convictions* that result in hate and violence will also disappear under repression. Rather, they will 'go underground' and further withdraw from public contestation. In the longer term it is crucial that Muslims conform to the existing constitutional norms *on the basis of their own choice* and not because pure force restrains them from violating these norms. The overwhelming majority of Muslims, of course, fully comply to the rules of the democratic constitutional state. These rules offer both protection for existing views, opportunities for debate and ultimately – in the case of persisting differences of opinion – also workable compromises (WRR 2003: 153). Radical views that do not conform to these rules also deserve other than merely legal (criminal justice) responses. They call for a public debate that explores concrete alternatives and clarifies opinions, complaints, and mutual demands. In the current climate, sweeping but vague words like 'Islamic norms and values,' 'Muslim identity,' 'Dutch identity,' and *Leitkultur* often dominate. Dialogue and debate can bring greater precision to the diagnoses and remedies.

As stated earlier, the policy means examined here mainly concern the national and local levels. They will be further discussed below, where we explore general principles for dealing with the three dimensions of Islamic activism outlined in this report, i.e. Islamic political thought, Islamic political activism, and Islamic law. It emphasizes the role of the government as supplier of *general, structural* provisions for dealing with plurality via encounter, knowledge acquisition and debate, education and participation in politics and society of *all* segments of the population, irrespective of religion or origin.

5.6.2   ISLAMIC POLITICAL THOUGHT

In Chapter 2 we saw that the common denominator of Islamic activism is opposition to traditionalism. The quest for reform can take on many forms, from the literal following of texts considered sacred, to the multitude of interpretive approaches based on scholarly research. The much-advocated reform of Islam, via 'a new Luther' as it were, thus gradually takes shape, and its roots go far back. Usually, however, the literal approach is not recognized in the West as reform, while the second gets insufficient attention. It is precisely those thinkers of the second category who do away with the dogmatic religious obstacles to the appreciation of democracy and human rights. The Islam that they advocate is more spiritual in nature than directed at following prescribed prohibitions and commandments. It is also based on theological and scholarly research of various sorts, such as the theory of interpretation (hermeneutics), anthropology, linguistics, philology, and history.

199

Widening and deepening of knowledge; meeting and debate
This latter category of reformist thought is far removed from the dogmatic truths offered by 'cyber-imams' or poorly educated imams, or those depicted in the various fundamentalist, often violent video clips of 'web-Islam' (Safi 2003). These truths are more readily found among the 'seeking' youth of the second and third generations than the well-thought-out academic theology books that also exist. Other (mass)media besides the Internet reinforce the image among young people that there is only one, dogmatic interpretation possible of Islam, one that is primarily fundamentalist and violent. Ramadan (2004) points out, for example, that the 'pamphlet-Islam' of Muslim fundamentalists and the information from the bookstores in Muslim neighborhoods are alarmingly one-sided. Thus, the views of authors who construct a positive relationship between Islam, democracy, and human rights (also, for example, those of the prominent authors from Chapter 2) are little known. There is theological guidance, but it is often one-sided and sometimes steers in the wrong direction. It is therefore important to make the views of the many differing thinkers available in places where young people are looking for answers, and to foster deepening of knowledge, encounter and debate among Muslims and non-Muslims.

The government, of course, does not *itself* have the task of filling existing theological information gaps. It does, however, have an obligation to put into effect the freedom of religion and of philosophy of life (Tweede Kamer 2004: 8). This obligation, which has after all for ages been the justification for the Dutch government's interference with the broadcasting system and the arts, implies that it has the means to encourage that a broad range of sources of information – including also through translation – is opened for the (Muslim) public, so that views are made available that allow for more carefully considered personal choices.[15]

The Dutch Cabinet has presented plans for monitoring radicalization and strengthening preparedness and social cohesion. Among the goals are expanding and deepening knowledge about Islam itself, the role of women in Islam, modern forms of Islamic religious experience, Islam and modernity, etc. (Minister van Vreemdelingenzaken en Integratie 2005). At the same time, the Cabinet has conceived a plan to create a Center for Cultural Dialogue (Nicolaï 2005). There is also an initiative in Amsterdam to establish a center for Islamic culture and religion and in many cities and towns religious communities are also organizing inter-religious dialogues. It is important that the various local and national authorities facilitate active and structural initiatives that address the information needs of Muslims and non-Muslims, that contribute to broadening the supply of information about Islam and thus also promote identity formation among (Muslim) youth. Structural contributions directed at a mobilizing policy for the longer term can offer a counterweight to one-sided information and influence-mechanisms.

The effort to broaden the basis of knowledge, and therefore also to seek out the places where the youth most susceptible to radicalizing influences are to be found, deserves high priority and active (financial) support. Combating discrimination and countering exclusion, both important points of special interest in Cabinet policy, deserve the same priority. This WRR report is not directed at these last two issues; the Council will later return to them in a separate report on identity issues. But their importance for the subject of this report is evident. The exclusion of and discrimination against Muslims are leading contributors to a breeding-ground for radical-religious rancor against which the spread of knowledge ultimately is no match.

Educational institutions

The young need to obtain insight not only into their own world views or religious convictions but also into those of others in our society. Parents are, of course, the first to rely on to convey such knowledge to their children. But it is also a legal obligation of both public and private schools, in addition to imparting the basic skills, such as language, mathematics, and writing. Government funding of private, general, formative education has been at the heart of the political discussion of recent years: the discussion on article 23, section 7 of the Dutch constitution. Many people wondered whether (Islamic) private education and integration into Dutch society are, in fact, compatible. That subject lies beyond the scope of this report. This report emphasizes that in the Netherlands every citizen, whether religious or not, Muslim, Christian, Jewish, or Hindu, should be confronted with dissidents. It is pre-eminently public education, which historically is characterized as *neutral* with respect to religion or philosophy of life, which is formally charged with the duty of paying attention to the diversity of philosophical values. Research has shown that pupils and parents as well as teachers find this task important, but that it is often overlooked because of all the other educational goals and responsibilities (Veugelers and De Kat 2005).

It is, however, important that every pupil, *regardless of what kind of school he or she attends*, learns about the various spiritual movements and their backgrounds. This knowledge serves not only to put their own faith or philosophy of life into perspective, but also fulfills a necessary condition for the development of mutual tolerance and respect. From several recent policy papers it appears that the Dutch government and parliament endorse the importance of this aspect of education, as evidenced by the intention to adopt (in the framework of values and norms and citizenship-formation for primary education) the following compulsory core goal: "Pupils learn essentials about spiritual movements that play an important role in the Dutch multicultural society" (Tweede Kamer 2005a). This requirement takes effect in the 2006-2007 school year. While under the earlier 'Decree Core Goals Primary Education 1998' this learning goal concentrated on ways of life and holidays and memorial days, this general formulation offers an opportunity for a more penetrating approach to the subject. And because the learning goal is separate from religious education and philosophy of life, it does not create any strains with the constitutionally guaranteed freedom of religion. As it represents a very recent initiative, the translation of this new core goal into specific learning objectives and rules (as is customary with other core goals like Dutch language and mathematics) will still take some time. The WRR believes that energy is required here. Specific learning goals, teaching methods adapted to the experiences of young children, and adequate support from the teacher training colleges mean that the core goal will take a valued place in education, and that teachers themselves do not have to reinvent the wheel. In addition, specific goals enable the education inspectorate to test whether schools and teachers indeed fulfill their roles as conveyers of knowledge of the leading philosophies within society.

201

Although knowledge of life-philosophies is not a separate core goal *within the required curriculum* of secondary education (for pupils 12 years old and older), knowledge of the different philosophies and reflection on values and norms and citizenship-formation do deserve attention throughout the entire course of schooling. The memorandum *Basic rights in a plural society* points this out and proposes that, for example, school subjects like 'people and society' and, later, the compulsory subject social studies offer room for this teaching. The responsibility for the way in which this happens rests, however, with the school (Tweede Kamer 2004). The WRR believes that in secondary and (general and intermediate) higher education attention to this aspect of education must become more intense. It is precisely during this period that young people increasingly distance themselves from the views that they received at home, their own views have not yet crystallized, they come into contact with people of different views, and they experiment with behavior and may seek new religious footing. It is important that in this phase they have more information resources available than the one-sided supply of religious radicalism from the sources they heavily consult, such as the Internet.

Broadening the supply of alternative views must contain more than offering abstract material on 'the other religions,' including also the tendencies within Islam. Alternative information should relate to the existing prejudices, questions, and grapplings that young people in secondary education experience, precisely those subjects that they seek advice about from 'expert' peers and the Internet. Educational institutions should therefore not avoid conflict-ridden and taboo subjects but focus on them, using unorthodox methods specially addressed to the young. On the basis of discussions with, for example, well-educated imams, it can be made clear at school that Islam offers more answers than only those of cyber-imams. The individual responsibility of the educational institutions allows for experiments with this approach, for example, by throwing open seminars to interested outsiders, by inviting imams to class, etc. It goes without saying that these should not be one-time activities but structural tasks. The government should create the financial space for institutions to fulfill this role as required.

With regard to higher education much attention is given to the education of imams. Quite a few politicians have high hopes that a new kind of training, with Dutch as the language of instruction, will contribute to better integration of newcomers from Muslim countries in the future. But one should not count on it too much. A large portion of the Muslims in the Netherlands have no direct connection with a mosque (Shadid and Van Koningsveld 2004). The government is also not authorized to interfere in any way with the content of this spiritual education. It rightly places the responsibility with the Muslim communities themselves. The only demand government can make is that the religious authorities be more informed about Dutch language and culture, so that they can better understand and guide the Muslims living here. Also, it is up to the governors of the mosque themselves to select imams. Finally, for many, the designation 'approved by the Dutch government' would actually be a counter-indication of proven suitability.

The government is authorized to create the general preconditions for a high level of scientific education and research, including in the field of religion. There are professorial chairs in Dutch universities that deal with aspects of Islam, such as languages and cultures of the Middle East, social processes in modern Islam, Islam in Western Europe, and Islamic law. The only institute in the Netherlands that studies Islam in an interdisciplinary way is the International Institute for the Study of Islam in the Modern World (ISIM), which was established in Leiden in 1998. This institute is a collaborative effort of the universities of Leiden, Amsterdam, Utrecht, and Nijmegen. It employs a socio-scientific approach to expand the knowledge of and insight into the manifestations of contemporary Islam. That is an important contribution, but not identical with the general religious-scientific deepening of understanding that the WRR is advocating here. It is therefore advisable to create complementary possibilities at a general university for a fully-fledged study devoted to the scientific treatment of Islam. In the longer term this can bear fruit for religious development, including in Muslim countries. Through various kinds of exchanges, scholarship in Europe can benefit from the knowledge that exists in Muslim countries, while Muslim countries benefit from the fruits of the free and open research at European universities. Although the effect on society of such a program occurs outside the mosque, it can be considerable: through publications, appearances in the media, and scholarly discussions. It is even conceivable that the training of imams will in the long run take place in cooperation with academic education on Islam, allowing students to follow part of their training at universities. In this way, imams would also obtain a higher level of scholarly education.

5.6.3 ISLAMIC POLITICAL MOVEMENTS

Islamic movements have been active in the Netherlands and also in other member states of the EU for a considerable time. However, the formation of parties on an Islamic basis or according to the Muslim region of origin has taken place only on a limited scale and only very recently. Belgium is ahead of the Netherlands in this respect, with the Noor party, the *Parti de la Citoyenneté et de la Prospérité*, the Arab European League (AEL), and the Resist party, which was originally connected to the AEL and which consequently led to the Muslim Democratic Party (Koning Boudewijnstichting 2004). Some of the parties in Belgium have already participated in elections, however without winning any seats in representative bodies. The Dutch AEL tried to follow the Belgian example by setting up a Muslim Democratic Party; the intention was that this party take part in local elections in a number of large municipalities in 2006 (Douwes et al. 2005). This intention has since been abandoned. The aim of the AEL is now to find interest within the existing parties for its longer term goals, such as the recognition of a Muslim identity and cultural and economic integration (NRC *Handelsblad*, November 18, 2005).

It is important that existing parties pay more attention to issues that concern Muslims. But in addition, the formation of parties in whole or in part on the basis of Islam or Muslim identity should be considered as a potentially constructive contribution to politics. Analogous to our argument above regarding political activism in Muslim countries, our approach to such parties should proceed from an inclusive conception of democracy. Such parties can also give a voice to those who do not feel themselves represented in Muslim representative bodies. It appears from recent research that Muslims in the Netherlands also find it important that parties based on Islam or Muslim identity be formed, separate from the question of whether they themselves would vote for these parties (TNS NIPO 2005). The Dutch election system creates few obstacles to party formation: there is a relatively high degree of accessibility, with the only substantive demand being that the designation of the party not be in conflict with public order (art. G 1 Electoral Law). Participation in the democratic process implies that the grievances and aspirations of Muslims are articulated via existing rules and can be included in the political debate and decision-making. For even if a party is small, that does not mean its influence has to be. If a Muslim party should expose existing impediments to full participation in society (such as discrimination in the labor market), this can wake up the larger parties. Participating in parliament and in local councils increases the chance that the supporters will feel they are taken seriously, thus preventing frustrations from building up in the informal sphere.

In the Netherlands there has not yet been discussion of setting up a political party based on Islam that advocates the introduction of some form of Sharia. According to the Dutch intelligence service AIVD, this was one of the ambitions of the AEL, but the party itself expressly denied this in a newsletter in 2005 (AIVD 2004b: 40). As was shown in Chapter 4, this ambition in itself does not indicate very much. The party programs of many (religious) parties employ language and symbols which can seem abstract, vague, or even radical to non-party members. What this means for the position of the party in daily politics cannot be derived just like that. This is also true of parties that use the term 'Sharia.' Often it is only from political behavior itself that one can determine what the party members concretely intend and aspire to with reference to Sharia. Should it appear that the intention is to introduce an Islamic state by democratic means in the Netherlands, then that would require serious procedures that are connected to amending the constitution.[16] The political chance of realizing such an ambition is very small. But Sharia as a source of inspiration, for example, for striving for justice and an 'ethical politics' on the part of such a party could translate into planks of a social-conservative platform, which could find broader support beyond Muslims.

It is equally evident that an Islamic or Muslim party, no matter how small and whether or not referring to Sharia, would introduce points of views into the Dutch political debate that could deviate from the normal political discourse or even be taboo. This could for instance be the case of subjects like the Dutch attitude to the Middle East conflict, the participation in missions in Afghanistan and Iraq, and the support for autocratic regimes. As appeared with the establishment of the AEL in the Netherlands, some of these program points will provoke reactions of shock. However, it is time to recognize that through the immigration of the past decades, other ways of looking at the world have been simultaneously introduced into Dutch society. It is obvious that sooner or later these views will be translated into politics. There is no reason to avoid debate on these (sensitive) subjects. Whether this discourse and the concrete aspirations that arise from it are incompatible with current democratic and constitutional norms, can then become clear in the political arena.

In conclusion: on the basis of the points discussed above, the forming of political parties with an Islamic foundation or Muslim identity is considered as a constructive contribution to Dutch politics, which demonstrates the striving towards participation in existing institutions and democratic rules.

5.6.4 ISLAMIC LAW

Because of the large number of Muslims, the question of recognition of (elements of) Islamic legislation can at some moment become relevant in by means other than the formation of political parties. It is evident that some of the Muslims living in the Netherlands want to live according to what they understand to be Sharia. That does not have to be problematic if the norms of behavior concerned are not in conflict with the existing legal order. But given the many definitions of Sharia, problems could occur. How considerable such problems could be, was again shown by the lawsuits against Mohammed Bouyeri, the murderer of the Dutch filmmaker and playwright Theo van Gogh. Bouyeri repeatedly testified: 'Your constitutional state is not mine.' If Sharia is called upon to legitimize behavior that conflicts with existing legislation, the investigation and prosecution of such behavior are obviously required. However, alongside this, there exists a sliding scale of behavior that is not illegal but is at odds with prevailing social and moral norms (such as individual autonomy) and that is supported through group pressure. National and local governments must be alert to these phenomena and to the tensions they create. The government has a special responsibility to guarantee a social climate in which groups can peacefully live together. The WRR previously examined this subject in its publication *Waarden, normen en de last van het gedrag* (WRR 2003: 169-196).

In this report the Council is looking at a different issue, namely the *formal* recognition of (elements of) Islamic legislation in the prevailing legal system. This is a different subject from the regulation of the status of foreigners living in the EU member states or of persons with dual nationality where international private law or bilateral agreements with third countries are applicable. There is a real possibility that in the Netherlands an appeal will be made to freedom of religion to seek recognition the application in particular areas, like civil law, of law derived from religion. It would involve the formal right of using religious laws *exclusively for one's own group.* This can relate to a formal possibility for persons from this group to voluntarily opt for the application of either the laws that are generally in force or the laws in force for the group. In Muslim countries it is not uncommon that in areas where religious law is applicable, followers of other (large) religions can choose their own law and courts. There have been efforts to introduce such a system in Canada and Great Britain (see box 5.4).

Box 5.4   Sharia Jurisprudence in Canada and Great Britain

In Canada, an intense debate took place on the recognition of arbitration commissions, which issue binding judgements on conflicts in the area of family law on the basis of Sharia, with the possibility of appeal to a regular court. The possibility for this formal recognition was based on the Arbitration Law that is in force in the province of Ontario and is intended, through the new model of mediation and arbitration, to unburden the public legal system and to reduce its costs. After the Jewish community seized this opening, the Muslim community followed, in this case from a desire to apply Islamic legislation to family law, the core area of Sharia. However, the proposals for this group law led to a sharp rejection by, among other bodies, the Canadian Council of Muslim Women. It argued that it would be unclear which of the many interpretations of Sharia the relevant commissions would follow, thus creating great legal uncertainty as well as a convenient opportunity to apply orthodox interpretations. The Council feared, moreover, that the formal freedom of choice does not exist in practice and that arbitration would turn out to be to the disadvantage of women, because the social control in their own community would force them to follow the path of 'good' Muslims. The Council also thought that this opening would create a precedent that certainly Muslims in Europe would be encouraged to use to achieve similar provisions in their countries. But the Canadian Council also used an argument of principle for rejecting the proposal. According to its definition of Sharia, the Council saw no opposition between this Sharia and human rights as defined in the Universal Declaration. The Council saw the norms laid down there, along with the conventions based on them, as completely consistent with the ideals of Islam and the Quran. Because Canadian legislation and its legal system are based on these human rights, there is no reason to apply any other law. Recognition of Sharia would just mean a convenient opportunity to damage the position of women (Canadian Council of Women 2005). Because of the resulting commotion, the Prime Minister of Ontario in the meantime decided to forbid all religious arbitration. For the time being, it is not clear whether this decision will be upheld.

The desire to institute group law is in play not only in Canada but also in Great Britain. Since the 1970s there have been efforts to introduce a parallel system of family law, under which Islamic law would automatically apply to Muslims. Unlike in Canada, this would not involve recognition of a possibility offered by existing legislation, but new legislation. The Islamic Shari'a Council (UK), which informally settles conflicts related to family law, seeks formal recognition within the British legal system. Although a certain degree of *cultural* pluralism is permitted in Great Britain, a renewed request in 1996 for legislation to formally recognize Islamic family law was again rejected. The most important argument of the British government was that there was no certainty that the non-secular legal system would apply universally accepted human rights, particularly where equal rights for women were concerned. As the Canadian Council also argued, there is also the problem of the many differing interpretations of Islamic family law. Even apart from the practical problems of how to do these justice, this would certainly lead to great dissension within the Muslim world and to formal legal inequality among Muslims (Fournier 2004).

On the basis of the efforts towards the 'universalizing' of universal human rights that are advocated in this report (see sec. 5.4.2), the WRR considers it inadvisable to pursue the path of pluralizing national law or to abandon secular law that rests on the separation of church and state. The ambition expressed by the concept of the universalizing of human rights is precisely to lead to *extending* rather than *limiting* the reach of universal human rights. The law in force in the Netherlands is in part based on the ECHR; formal recognition of Islamic legal norms that do not comply with this standard would mean a setback. Such recognition would also be in conflict with the principles of equality established in the ECHR and the constitution.

In section 5.4 it was argued that in Muslim countries rapprochement with universal human rights can go through Islamic law. For the Netherlands, the reverse path is appropriate. Immigrants from Muslim countries other than Turkey are often socialized in legal systems that are in part based on a version of Sharia. The knowledge that Muslims have regarding the existing laws in the EU member states – including human rights – is sometimes very limited, which leads to a natural preference for the Sharia with which they are familiar. According to some, there is indeed a misunderstanding in principle among many Muslims regarding the existing relationship between religion and the state in Europe (Bielefeldt and Bahmanpour 2002). The frequent designation of the state as secular causes considerable misunderstanding. That secular character is now often understood by a number of Muslims to mean that the state is anti-religious or 'post-religious,' or that European countries are 'finished with religion.' This perception also explains in part their mistrust of the Western state. They do not understand that the non-religious state and secular law precisely serve as guarantors of the right of each person to equal respect for his or her religion. As the earlier resistance of Christian churches leads us to suppose, it will clearly take some time before believers realize that the state is not by definition secular in the sense of being anti-religious, but by being secular can actually safeguard religious freedom (Bielefeldt and Bahmanpour 2002). This perception has also gradually emerged among Islamic political movements in Turkey, and has even led to a reversal in attitudes there towards EU membership (WRR 2004).

As shown in section 5.4.5, both Tariq Ramadan and the Canadian Council of Muslim Women find that universal human rights and legislation derived from them in the EU member states are not in conflict with Sharia. As a consequence, Muslims in almost all cases can be loyal to the law that exists in the member states (Ramadan 2004). Islamic thinkers discussed in Chapter 2, like An Na'im and Soroush, hold the same opinions. This shows how important it is for the member states of the Union and for Muslim countries to make it their task to expand the understanding and knowledge among Muslims living in Europe about the principles of the prevailing law, human rights and their relationship with Islamic law. Once Muslims have a better knowledge of the principles of the prevailing law and their concrete rights, and once they recognize that they do not have to reject that law on Islamic grounds, this can also contribute to the development of Islam in Europe and the Netherlands.

In conclusion, the Council believes that the presence of Muslims cannot be the occasion for the formal incorporation of Islamic legislation into existing law, which is after all in part based on the ECHR. But it is of great

importance that Muslims in the member states be made more familiar with
the principles of law applied in EU member states.

5.7   CONCLUSION

With the policy perspective presented in this final chapter the Council
aims to contribute to stopping the downward spiral of action and reaction
that has come to characterize the relations among Muslim states as well as
those between Western states and Islamic activism in recent years. The
consequences of this spiral affect not only relations between countries but
also between segments of the population within countries. Fear of Muslims
and Islam has also emerged within the Netherlands, and in turn Muslims,
because of their religion, feel increasingly like unwelcome strangers.

A climate of confrontation is hardly conducive to the creation of lasting
conditions for security, democratization, and increasing respect for human
rights. Therefore, there is no desirable alternative to trying to find a way to
associate with the reference points for democracy and human rights present in Islamic activism itself. The analyses presented in this report unmistakably show that these in fact exist. Islamic activism cannot be identified
across the board with an antidemocratic disposition and a denial of the
value of human rights. Rather, there is great diversity in Islamic activism's
relationship with democracy and human rights and a gradual rapprochement with these concepts.

These empirical insights form an important correction to the image that
has established itself in Western countries, and certainly also in the
Netherlands, regarding Islamic activism. In the current atmosphere of
confrontation little attention is given to what is actually happening on the
other side; stereotypical thinking dominates. A policy of constructive
engagement with the Muslim world needs to take into account the diversity and dynamism of Islamic activism. Then can it also be recognized that
Islam in its political and legal aspects really can play an important role in
the development of Muslim countries. Supporting endogenous developments to promote democracy and human rights can lead to more lasting
results in the longer term than trying to impose these from outside. This
approach requires, however, a cultural shift, in the sense that it needs to be
acknowledged that Islam can be an important vehicle for the realization of
democracy and human rights. The cultural shift also involves acceptance of
the possibility that universal values can, in Muslim countries (for the time
being) assume different expression than is common in Western societies.
The West does not have a monopoly on the interpretation of universal
human rights nor on the behavior that is in agreement with them. Along
with the self-criticism to which Western countries regularly call the

Muslim world, it would not be amiss that they also search their own hearts. By admitting that the demand for universal human rights is also a permanent task for Western countries, the West gains credibility.

The policy options indicated here show that stimulating positive internal dynamics in Muslim countries is not easy. It means that one must simultaneously exercise influence and avoid meddling, and use windows of opportunity as they appear. In every case this demands a very substantial knowledge of the situation in different Muslim countries where the venture is undertaken. The cultural shift that this report also has in mind does not mean that the Netherlands and the EU must support developments that conflict with their own values. It does mean that Islamic-inspired forces are not to be excluded in advance from external contacts and that policy efforts should be directed toward the long term. Only when constructive forms of Islamic activism are accepted gradually into the existing democratic order do they have a chance to develop into an Islamic democratic movement. Western political history itself reveals examples of an analogous passage from diverse forms of broadly supported activism to democratic movements. There is no reason why an analogous development cannot occur with respect to Islamic activism. The empirical findings above illustrate that a similar process of normalization is actually in progress in several Muslim countries.

The Council realizes that the strategic perspective of rapprochement presented here requires sustained effort. Furthermore, it is a vulnerable perspective. Actual rapprochement can easily be frustrated by a flare-up of violence in running conflicts or by actions of individuals. The interdependencies in today's world are such that events elsewhere have consequences at home, and promising improvements in relations can be nipped in the bud. This means that the current accent on security will (have to) be maintained for yet a long time. But for longer term security it is of utmost importance to make the alternative proposed here the guideline for all levels on which the Netherlands can exercise influence.

NOTES

1   In comparison: in the other seven countries the percentage varies from 22 per cent (US) to 37 per cent (Spain).

2   The peace process became deadlocked after the assassination of Yitzhak Rabin and the election of Benjamin Netanyahu in Israel. During a subsequent discussion of a new charter, which lasted four years, it appeared that the Arab countries did not want to become involved in military cooperation with Israel before that country signed a peace treaty with Syria, Lebanon, and the Palestinians.

3   In the area of economics, it is not only the vested interests in the partner countries who are resisting; to date the EU itself has not been in the forefront of external liberalization; the free entry of agricultural products and textiles and the free movement of labor are especially sensitive points. Real free entry is applicable only to oil, gas, and industrial products. Since 2005 progress has been made in the negotiations over a free trade zone.

4   The Commission warns that the fight against terrorism causes tensions between internal security considerations, on the one hand, and the human rights and democratization agenda, on the other, that ultimately can be at the cost of human rights (Biscop 2005: 13).

5   Euromesco, the research group of the foreign policy institutes and think-tanks within the EMP, comes to the somber conclusion that 'the banalization and routine nature' of violence against citizens and political leaders of the opposition form the major impediment to peace, democracy, the rule of law, and human rights (Euromesco 2005a). 150,000 inhabitants of the southern flank of the region have already died as a result of political violence since 1995. But the EU in the ten years that the EMP has been in existence has not even once used the possibility of suspending the association treaties in response to serious human rights violations. Worse yet, the EU member states are reproached for applying double standards; when prominent secular human rights activists or political leaders are rounded up, European protests follow. When something similar happens to Islamic activists, they mostly remain silent (Joffé 2005: 17; Panebianco 2004: 154).

6   See among others Jones and Emerson (2005) for an extensive treatment of the reform process on the basis of the Action plans.

7   In development policy, this assumption has also recently come under fire. See among others UNDP 2002; Van Ardenne 2005.

8   As the NIMD also notes, in recent years the EU has invested in supporting elections, government reforms, civil society, and strengthening of the constitutional state, but it has largely ignored political life. The NIMD considers political parties as an important missing link in EU aid policy

directed to the promotion of democracy and human rights (NIMD 2005: 26).

9   As Youngs notes: "Despite the commitments made by countless ministe-rial statements and policy documents, in practice little new engagement with Islam has been forthcoming. Donors have proceeded no further than including general discussion on 'Islam and democracy' in some civil soci-ety forums. A plethora of initiatives aim at 'cultural understanding' between Islam and the West, but concrete political support is lacking for moderate Islamists concerned to widen political participation in their soci-eties. (…) The EU's new guidelines on democracy and human rights promotion in the Middle East fail even to mention the Islamist issue. The EU largely avoids working with Islamists even on fairly apolitical issues: for example, declining to work through professional syndicates captured by Islamists. In short, Islamists continue to be the apparent untouchables of the democracy assistance world" (Youngs 2004b: 12).

10   This special attention to the rights of women is emphasized by the Euro-pean Parliament. See, for example, the motion of the European Parliament regarding the revised EMP of the end of September 2005 (European Parlia-ment 2005).

11   The Egyptian NDP, the government party that has monopolized power for decades, is a textbook illustration of this intertwining of supervision of religion with political party control over Islam in Egypt. Before the May 25, 2005 referendum on the changing of constitutional article 76, the official *ulama* and the Minister of Religious Affairs called on all Egyptians to vote in favor of these changes, regarding it as their religious obligation to do so. All the major opposition parties were opposed to this proposition (ICG 2005c: 21-22).

12   The experience of organizations such as the International Institute for Democracy and Electoral Assistance (IDEA) underscores that assistance for democratization that takes into account the dynamics of political develop-ments and power relations of a country is more effective than assistance on the basis of static, normative standards that start from a 'deficit' with respect to established (Western) democracies. Precisely by taking the driv-ing forces behind political and social changes as the starting points, can a better understanding arise of the chances and limits of democratization initiatives (Tommasoli 2005). Today, Islamic political movements and the truly independent civil society organizations constitute the pre-eminent driving forces.

13   In June 2004 the EU member states adopted the initiative for a 'Strategic Partnership with the Mediterranean Region and the Middle East.' In addi-tion to the EMP Partners, the Gulf Cooperation Council (Saudi Arabia, the United Arab Emirates, Kuwait, Bahrain, Oman, Qatar), Iraq, Iran, and Yemen are also intended partners (European Commission 2003: 7). See also: NHC 2005 and Bertelsmann Stiftung 2005.

14   The examples of Egypt, Bahrain, and Jordan reveal that the courses indeed differ, while there is also great variety in the tempo of reform. In Egypt the reforms proceed extremely cautiously and in the main via the party elite of the NDP. The party congress of October 2004 implemented a number of reforms; it has, among other powers, control over the admission of formerly banned political parties to the political arena. Jordan's course has been one of gradual expansion of political participation under control of a special Ministry for Political Development that is also responsible for the modernization of the political landscape and the political parties. In 1991 that led to the lifting of the ban on leftist and Islamic political parties, after which they won seats in the parliament. In Bahrain the course of changes can be characterized as 'gradual constitutionalism' (Perthes 2004b). The introduction of a new constitution in 2002 means that this country is now formally a constitutional monarchy. This step has given more room for political debate and new forms of political participation. In addition, a number of steps have been taken towards the expansion of individual and political freedoms, women have for the first time obtained the active and passive right to vote, and the parliament has been reinstated after a suspension of 27 years.

15   The government itself does not have to allocate the available funds; that can be done by independent agencies.

16   Changes to the Dutch constitution require first that a law be adopted that rules that the constitutional change is considered. This consideration law must receive in both the First and Second Chambers half plus one of the votes cast. Then, during a second reading in both Chambers, a second majority is needed. Only after a new election for the Second Chamber has taken place, can discussion begin on the proposal to change the constitution.

BIBLIOGRAPHY

Abou El Fadl, K. (2003) 'The Ugly Modern and the Modern Ugly: Reclaiming the Beautiful in Islam', 33-77 in: O. Safi (2002) *Progressive Muslims. On Justice, Gender, and Pluralism*, Oxford: Oneworld.

Abu Zayd, N. (2004) *Rethinking the Qur'an: Towards a Humanistic Hermeneutics*, Amsterdam: SWP.

Abu Zayd, N. (2006) *Reformation of Islamic Thought. A Critical Historical Analysis*, WRR-Verkenning nr. 10, Amsterdam: Amsterdam University Press.

AIV (Adviesraad Internationale Vraagstukken) (1998) *Universaliteit van de rechten van de mens en culturele verscheidenheid*, AIV, no. 4.

Ahmad, I. (2005) *From Islamism to Post-Islamism. The Transformation of the Jamaat-i-Islami in North India*, Amsterdam: ASSR.

AIVD (Algemene Inlichtingen- en Veiligheidsdienst) (2004a) *Saoedische invloeden in Nederland. Verbanden tussen salafitische missie, radicaliseringsprocessen en isla-mitisch terrorisme*, nr. 0000000/01, 9 June, The Hague: Ministerie van Binnenlandse Zaken en Koninkrijksrelaties.

AIVD (2004b) *Van da'wa tot jihad. De diverse dreigingen van de radicale islam tegen de democratische rechtsorde*, 23 december, The Hague: Ministerie van Binnenlandse Zaken en Koninkrijksrelaties.

Alagha, J. (2006) *The Shifts in Hizbullah's Ideology: Religious Ideology, Political Ideology, and Political Program*, Amsterdam: Amsterdam University Press.

Aliboni, R. (2004a) *Promoting Democracy in the EMP. Which Political Strategy?* Euromescoreports, Working Group I Third Year Report, Lisbon.

Aliboni, R. (2004b) *Democracy promotion and democracy.* Paper voor het Internationale Symposium 'Civilization and Harmony: Values and Mechanisms of the Global Order', Istanbul, 2-3 October.

An-Na'im, A. (1990) *Towards an Islamic Reformation. Civil Liberties, Human Rights, and International Law*, Caïro: The American University in Caïro Press.

Ardenne, A. van (2005) 'The Ship and the Raft', Speech for the Netherlands Association for International Affairs, The Hague, 13 October, http://www.ngiz.nl/lectures/lecturesindex.htm

Arjomand, S.A. (2004) 'Islam, Political Change and Globalization', *Thesis Eleven*, 76, 9-28.

Arkoun, M. (1992) *Islam in discussie. 24 vragen over de islam*. Amsterdam: Contact.

Asadi, A. et al. (1976) *Culturele tendensen en publieke opinies in Iran. De nationale survey van 1974*, Teheran: Faculty of Communication, University of Tehran (translated from the Farsi).

Aubert, V. (1971) *Proeven van rechtssociologie*, Antwerpen: Wetenschappelijke Uitgeverij.

Azlan, R. (2005) *Geen God dan God. Oorsprong, ontwikkeling en toekomst van de islam*, Amsterdam: De Bezige Bij.

Baderin, M. (2003) *International Human Rights and Islamic Law*, New York: Oxford University Press.

Bälz, K. (1998) 'La réconstruction séculière du droit islamique: La Haut Cour constitutionnelle égyptienne et la bataille du voile dans les écoles publiques', *Droit et Société*, 39.

Baran, Z. (ed.) (2004) *The Challenge of Hizb ut-Tahrir. Deciphering and Combating Radical Islamist Ideology*, Washington D.C.: The Nixon Center.

Barends, M. and E. van Eijk (2006) 'Sharia en nationaal recht in Saoedi-Arabië' 85-111 in: J.M. Otto, A.J. Dekker, L.J. van Soest-Zuurdeeg (eds.) *Sharia en nationaal recht in twaalf moslimlanden*, WRR-Webpublicatie nr. 13, Amsterdam: Amsterdam University Press.

Bayat, A. (1997) 'Revolution Without Movement, Movement Without Revolution: Comparing Islamic Activism in Iran and Egypt', *Comparative Studies in Society and History*, 40, 1, 136-169.

Bayat, A. (forthcoming) *Post-islamism: Social Movements, Islam and the Challenge of Democracy*.

Bayat, A. and B. Baktiari (2002) 'Revolutionary Iran and Egypt: Exporting Inspirations and Anxiety', 305-326 in: N. Keddie and R. Mathee (2002) *Iran and the Surrounding World: Interactions in Culture and Cultural Politics*, Washington: University of Washington Press.

Baylouny, A. (2004) 'Emotions, Poverty, or Politics: Misconceptions about Islamic Movements', *Strategic Insights*, 3, 1, www.ccc.nps.navy.mil/si/2004/jan/baylounyJan04.asp

Beke, D. (1996) 'Islam-recht en geloofsafval: Leer en praktijk', in: F.A. van Bakelen (ed.) *Recht van de Islam*, Groningen: RIMO.

Berger, M.S. (2006) *Klassieke sharia en vernieuwing*, WRR-Webpublication no. 13, Amsterdam: Amsterdam University Press.

Berman, H.J. (1983) *Law and Revolution. The Formation of the Western Legal Tradition*, Cambridge: Harvard University Press.

Berman, S. (2003) 'Islamism, Revolution and Civil Society', *Perspectives on Politics*, 1, 2, 257-272.

Bertelsmann Stiftung (2005) *The EU and the GCC. A New Partnership.* Gulf Strategy Paper, februari, www.cap-lmu.de/publikationen/2005/eu-gcc.php

Bielefeldt, H. (2000) '"Western" versus "Islamic" Human Right Conceptions? A Critique of Cultural Essentialism in the Discussion on Human Rights', *Political Theory*, 28, 1, 90-121.

Bielefeldt, H. and M. Bahmanpour (2002) 'The Politics of Social Justice: Religion versus Human Rights?' *Open Democracy*, 7 November, www.openDemocracy.net

Biscop, S. (2005) 'The European Security Strategy and the Neighbourhood Policy: A New Starting Point for a Euro-Mediterranean Security Partnership?' *Paper voor de EUSA Ninth Biennial International Conference*, Austin, Texas, 31 March- 2 April.

Boutachekourt, K. (2003) *De verlichte islam in de praxis*, Working paper for WRR, The Hague.

Brems, E. (2003) 'Inclusieve universaliteit: een theoretisch en methodologisch kader om inzake mensenrechten universaliteit te verzoenen met diversiteit', *Tijdschrift voor rechtsfilosofie en rechtstheorie*, 2, 139-161.

Bruinessen, M. van (2004) *Production of Islamic Knowledge in Western Europe*, UNESCO Lecture, University of Birmingham, Faculty of Theology and Religion.

Buijs, F. (2002) *Democratie en terreur. De uitdaging van het islamitisch extremisme*, Amsterdam: SWP.

Buruma, I. and A. Margalit (2004) *Occidentalisme. Het Westen in de ogen van zijn vijanden*, Amsterdam: Atlas.

Canadian Council of Women (2005) *Position Statement on the Proposed Implementation of Sections of Muslim Law (Sharia) in Canada*, www.ccmw.com/Position%20Papers/Position_Sharia_Law.htm

Clark, J. (2004) 'Social Movement Theory and Patron-Clientelism. Islamic Social Institutions and the Middle Class in Egypt, Jordan and Yemen', *Comparative Political Studies*, 37, 8, 941-968.

Coleman, I. (2006) 'Women, Islam, and the New Irak', *Foreign Affairs*, 85, 1, 24-38.

Congregation for the Doctrine of the Faith (2004) *Letter to the Bishops of the Catholic Church on the collaboration of men and women in the Church and in the world*, 31 July.

Coolsaet, R. (2005) 'Het islamitische terrorisme. Percepties wieden en kweekvijvers dreggen', *Justitiële Verkenningen*, 31, 2, 9-27.

Dekker, A. and M. Barends (2006) 'Sharia en nationaal recht in Iran', 203-234 in: J.M. Otto, A.J. Dekker, L.J. van Soest-Zuurdeeg (eds.) *Sharia en nationaal recht in twaalf moslimlanden*, WRR-Webpublicatie nr. 13, Amsterdam: Amsterdam University Press.

Diamond, L. (2003) 'Universal Democracy?' *Policy Review*, 119, www.policyreview.org/jun03/diamond_print.html

Diamond, L. and L. Morino (2004) 'The Quality of Democracy. An Overview', *Journal of Democracy*, 15, 4, 20-31.

Douwes, D., M. de Koning and W. Boender (eds.) (2005) *Nederlandse moslims. Van migrant tot burger*, Amsterdam: AmsterdamUniversity Press/Salomé.

Ebadi, S. (2004) *Human Rights, Women and Islam*, ISIM-Lecture, The Hague, 16 April.

Economist, The (2006) 'Egypt: New Dawn of More of the Same?', 12 January.

Eisenstadt, S. (2000) 'Multiple Modernities', *Daedalus*, 132, 3, 14-31.

El-Din Shahin, E. (2005) *Political Islam: Ready for Engagement?* Fride Working Paper, February.

Emerson, M., S. Aydin and G. Noutcheva et al. (2005) *The Reluctant Debutante. The European Union as Promotor of Democracy in its Neighbourhood*, CEPS Working Document 223, July.

217

Emerson, M. and N. Tocci, *Turkey as a Bridgehead and Spearhead. Integrating EU and Turkish Foreign Policy*, EU-Turkey Working Papers 1, August.

Esposito, J. (2003) 'Islam and civil society', 69-100 in: J. Esposito and F. Burgat (eds.) *Modernizing Islam. Religion in the Public Sphere in the Middle East and Europe*, Londen: Hurst.

Esposito, J. and F. Burgat (eds.) (2003) *Modernizing Islam. Religion in the Public Sphere in the Middle East and Europe*, London: Hurst.

Euromesco (2005a) *Barcelona Plus. Towards a Euro-Mediterranean Community of Democratic States,* A Euromesco Report, Lisbon.

Euromesco (2005b) *Barcelona 2005: Fresh Endeavors to Promote Democracy in the Euro- Mediterranean Partnership*, www.euromesco.net/euromesco/print.asp?cod_artigo=122317

European Parliament (2005) *Report on the Barcelona Process Revisited (2005/2058(INI)*, Final A6-0280/2005, 30 September.

European Union (1997) *Declaration on the status of churches and non-confessional organisations*, http://europa.eu.int/eur-lex/en/treaties/dat/amsterdam/html # 0133040028.

European Commission (2003), *Communication from the Commission to the Council and the European Parliament. Reinvigorating EU actions on human rights and democratisation with Mediterranean partners. Strategic guidelines*, com(2003) 294 final.

European Commission (2005) *Communication from the Commission to the Council and the European Parliament. Tenth anniversary of the Euro-mediterranean partnership: a work program to meet the challengers of the next five years*, com (2005) 139 final.

Fair, C. (2005) 'Islam and Politics in Pakistan', 247-295 in: A. Rabasa, C. Benard and P. Chalk et al., *The Muslim World After 9/11*, Santa Monica: Rand.

Filali-Ansary, A. (2003) 'What Is Liberal Islam. The Sources of Enlightened Muslim Thought', *Journal of Democracy,* 14, 2, 19-33.

Financial Times (2005) 'On Line, Off Message', 16 december.

Fish, M. (2002) 'Islam and Authoritarianism', *World Politics*, 55, 4-37.

Fournier, P. (2004) *The Reception of Muslim Family Law in Western Liberal States,* Canadian Council of Muslim Women, Sharia/Muslim Law Project, 30 September.

Freedom House (1999) *Democracy's Century. A Survey of Global Political Changes in the 20th Century*, www.freedomhouse.org/reports/century.html

Freedom House (2004) *Freedom in the World Country Ratings 1972-73 to 2003-2004,* www.freedomhose.org

Freedom House (2003) *Combined Average Ratings: Independent Countries – 2003,* www.freedomhouse.org

Fuller, G. (2003) *The Future of Political Islam*, New York: Palgrave Macmillan.

Fuller, G. (2005) 'Political Islam in Action', 15-25 in: *What Future for Political Islam? Dilemmas and Opportunities for the Next Decade.* The Hague: WRR, www.wrr.nl/english/wrr/nieuwsdetail.php?id=61

Gambill, G. (2004) 'Democratization, the Peace Process, and Islamic Extremism', *Middle East Intelligence Bulletin*, 6, 6-7.

Goedarzi, M. et al. (2004) *Values and opinions of Iranians. The national survey of 2004, Tabels and trends*, Tehran: Ministry of Culture and Public Morality (translated from the Farsi).

Göle, N. (1996) *The Forbidden Modern: Civilization and Veiling*, Ann Arbor: University of Michigan Press.

Haass, R.N. (2005) 'Regime Change and Its Limits', *Foreign Affairs,* 84,4, 66-78.

Hafez, M. (2003) *Why Muslims Rebel. Repression and Resistance in the Islamic World*, London: Lynne Riener.

Hafez, M. (2004) 'From Marginalization to Massacres: A Political Process Explanation of gia Violece in Algeria', 37-60 in: Q. Wiktorowicz (ed.) *Islamic Activism. A Social Movement Theory Approach*, Bloomington: Indiana University Press.

Hafez, M. and Q. Wiktorowicz (2004) 'Violence as Contention in the Egyptian Islamic Movement', 61-88 in: Q. Wiktorowicz (ed.) *Islamic Activism. A Social Movement Theory Approach*, Bloomington: Indiana University Press.

Hajjar, L. (2000) 'Domestic Violence and *Shari'a*: A Comparative Study of Muslim Societies in the Middle East, Africa and Asia', http://www.law.emory.edu/IFL/thematic/Violence.htm

Halliday, F. (2003) *Islam and the Myth of Confrontation: Religion and Politics in the Middle East,* London: Taurus.

Hamzawy, A. (2005) 'The Key to Arab Reform: Moderate Islamists', *Carnegie Endowment Policy Brief*, 40, 1-7.

Harding, A. 'Sharia en national recht in Maleisië', 303-334 in: J.M. Otto, A.J. Dekker, L.J. van Soest-Zuurdeeg (eds.) *Sharia en nationaal recht in twaalf moslimlanden*, WRR-Webpublicatie nr. 13, Amsterdam: Amsterdam University Press.

Hart, H. (1997) *The Concept of Law*, Oxford: Oxford University Press.

Hassan, R. (1987) 'Equal before Allah? Woman-Man Equality in the Islamic Tradition', *Harvard Divinity Bulletin*, 17, 2, 2-14.

Hofmann, S. (2004) 'Islam and Democracy. Micro-Level Indications of Compatibility', *Comparative Political Studies*, 37, 6, 652-676.

Hourani, A. (1984) 'Conclusion', 226-234 in: J. Piscatori (ed.), *Islam in the Political Process*, Cambridge: Cambridge University Press.

Huntington, S. (1993) 'The Clash of Civilizations?', *Foreign Affairs,* 72, 3, 22-49.

Huntington, S. (1996) *The Clash of Civilizations and the Remaking of the World Order*, New York: Simon and Schuster.

ICG (International Crisis Group) (2003a) 'Pakistan: The Mullahs and the Military', *Asia Report*, 49, March.

ICG (2003b) 'Afghanistan: The Problem of Pashtun Alienation', *Asia Report*, 62, April.

ICG (2003c) 'Central Asia: Islam and the State' *Asia Report*, 59, July.

ICG (2004a) 'Islamism in North Africa I: The Legacies of History', *Middle East and North Africa Briefing*, April.

ICG (2004b) 'Islamism in North Africa II: Egypt's Opportunity', *Middle East and North Africa Briefing*, April.

ICG (2005a) 'Understanding Islamism', *Middle East/North Africa Report* 37, March.

ICG (2005b) 'Counter-Terrorism in Somalia: Losing Hearts and Minds?', *Africa Report*, 95, July.

ICG (2005c) 'Reforming Egypt: in Search of a Strategy', *Middle East/North Africa Report*, 46, October.

ICG (2005d) 'The State of Sectarianism in Pakistan', *Asia Report*, 95, April.

ICG (2006) 'Enter Hamas: The Challenges of Political Integration', *Middle East Report*, 49, January.

ICJ (International Court of Justice) (2004) *Legal Consequences of the Construction of a Wall in the Occupied Palestinian Territory*, Summary of the Advisory Opinion of 9 July.

IDEA (International Institute for Democracy and Electoral Assistance) *Democracy in the Arab world. Challenges, Achievements and Prospects*, Stockholm: idea.

IFES (International Foundation for Election Systems) (z.d.) *Arab Election Law Compendium: Sudan*, www.arabelectionlaw.net/search_eng.php

Inglehart, R. and P. Norris (2004) *Sacred and Secular: Religion and Politics Worldwide*, Cambridge: Cambridge University Press.

International Constitutional Law (z.d.) *Constitutional Documents*, www.oefre.unibe.ch/law/icl/index.html

Internet Malaysia (2005), *Talking Apostasy*, www.littlespeck.com/region/CForeign-My-041228.htm

Jahanbegloo, R. (2005) 'Iranian Intellectuals in Struggle for Democracy: The Past Strategies, the Future Choices', presentation in De Balie, Amsterdam, 15 November.

Jansen, J.J.G. (2004) *De radicaal-islamitische ideologie: van Ibn Taymiyya tot Osama ben Laden*, Inaugural lecture, University of Utrecht, www.arabistjansen.nl/tekstoratie.doc

Joffé, G. (2005) *The Status of the Euro-Mediterranean Partnership*, Euromesco, www.euromesco.net/euromesco/artigo.asp?cod_artigo=117802

Jones, S. and M. Emerson (2005) *European Neighbourhood Policy in the Mashreq Countries. Enhancing Prospects for Reform*, CEPS Working Document 229, September.

Jones Luong, P. and E. Lust-Okar (2002) *State Strategies Toward Islamic Mobilization: A Comparative Analysis of the Middle East and Central Asia,* Paper for 'The Silk Road in the 21st Century, Security and Insecurity in Central Asia and the Caucasus', Yale Center for the Study of Globalization, 19-21 September.

Kadhim, N. (2003) 'Introduction', www.islam21.net/pages/confrences/D13sep2003.htm

Karatnycky, A. (2002) 'Muslim Countries and the Democracy Gap', *Journal of Democracy*, 13, 1, 100-112.

220

Kepel, G. (2002) *Jihad. The Trail of Political Islam,* London: Tauris.

Kepel, G. (2004) *The War for Muslim Minds: Islam and the West,* Harvard: Harvard University Press.

Khan, M. (2003) 'Syed Qutb – John Locke of the Islamic World', *The Globalist,* 28 July.

Kodmani, B. (2005) *The Dangers of Political Exclusion: Egypt's Islamist Problem,* Carnegie Endowment for International Peace Working Paper 63.

Koning Boudewijnstichting (2004) *Islam en moslims in België. Lokale uitdagingen & algemeen denkkader,* Brussels.
www.kbs-frb.be/code/page.cfm?id_page=153&ID=274

Köndgen, O. (2006) 'Sharia en nationaal recht in Soedan', 113-144 in: J.M. Otto, A.J. Dekker, L.J. van Soest-Zuurdeeg (eds.) *Sharia en nationaal recht in twaalf moslimlanden,* WRR-Webpublicatie nr. 13, Amsterdam: Amsterdam University Press.

Kugle, S. (Sirai al-Haqq) (2003) 'Sexuality, Diversity and Ethics in the Agenda of Progressive Muslims', 190-235 in: O. Safi (2003) *Progressive Muslims. On Justice, Gender, and Pluralism,* Oxford: Oneworld.

Kurpershoek, M. (2004) 'The Catch 22 of Political Islam', 27-41 in: *What Future for Political Islam? Dilemmas and Opportunities for the Next Decade, The Hague:* WRR, www.wrr.nl/english/wrr/nieuwsdetail.php?id=61.

Lacroix, S. (2005) 'Post-Wahhabism in Saudi Arabia?' *ISIM Review,* 15, 17.

Lakoff, S. 'The Reality of Muslim Exceptionalism', *Journal of Democracy,* 15, 4, 133-139.

Lapidus, I. (2002) *A History of Islamic Societies,* Cambridge: Cambridge University Press.

Lau, M. (2003) 'Article 2a: The Objectives Resolution and the Islamisation of Pakistani Laws', 173-204, in: H.-G. Ebers and T. Hanstein (eds.) *Beiträge zum islamischen Recht* 3, Frankfurt am Main: Peter Lang.

Lerch, M. (2004) *What is the Content of a European Profile in Democracy Support? The Human Rights Dimension,* Paper for the European Conference 'Enhancing the European Profile in Democracy Assistance', 4 July.
www.democracyagenda.org

Lewis, B. (1990) 'The Roots of Muslim Rage', *Atlantic Monthly,* 266, 3, 47-60.

Mandaville, P. (2001) *Transnational Muslim Politics. Reimagining the Umma,* London: Routledge.

Mawdudi, A. (1980) *The Islamic Law and Constitution,* Lahore: Islamic Publications.

Mayer, A. (1998) 'Islamic Reservations to Human Rights Conventions', 25-46 in: S. Rutten (ed.) *Recht van de Islam,* 15.

Mayer, A. (1999) *Islam and Human Rights. Tradition and Politics,* Colorado: Westview Press.

Meijer, R. (2005) 'Jihadi Opposition in Saudi Arabia', *ISIM Review,* 15.

Menendez Gonzalez, I. (2005) *Arab Reform: What Role for the EU?* Egmont paper 8, Gent: Academia Press.

Minister van Vreemdelingenzaken en Integratie (2005) *Nota weerbaarheid en integratiebeleid,* 19 August 2005.

221

Ministerie van Buitenlandse Zaken (2004) *Kamerbrief inzake revitalisering Barcelonaproces*, 13 April.

Ministerie van Buitenlandse Zaken (2005a) *Mededeling over het 10-jarig bestaan van Euro- Mediterranean Partnerschap*, www.minbuza.nl/default.asp?CMS_ITEM=C7DE90CBE09947B4954A39 2BC39 AEDF7X3X39501X07&CMS_NOCOOKIES=YES

Ministerie van Buitenlandse Zaken (2005b) *Verslag Euromed top 27 en 28 november j.l.*, 14 December.

Motivaction (2005) *Factsheet maatschappelijke barometer: acceptatie van homoseksualiteit*, broadcast 4 July 2005.

Müller, C. (2005) *Is Allah a Frenchman? France and the Challenge posed by Islam*, www.qantara.de/webcom/show article.php/ c-476/ nr-298/i.html

Nasr, V. (2005) 'The Rise of "Muslim Democracy"', *Journal of Democracy*, 16, 1, 13-27.

NHC (Netherlands Helsinki Committee) (2005) *Bridging the Gulf. Elements of the Helsinki Process as Inspiration for the Gulf Region*, 29 November 2004, The Hague: NHC.

Nicolaï, A. (2005) 'Crossing Deserts, Crossing Oceans, Crossing Cultures. Or, the Story of the Merchant from Caïro' *Speech for Forum Amsterdam, Imagining Europe*, 11 December, Amsterdam, www.minbuza.nl/default.asp?CMS_ITEM=E24ABA677F7B49608B86476 F400F 0C99X3X53574X97

NIMD (Netherlands Institute for Multiparty Democracy) (2005) *No lasting Peace and Prosperity without Democracy & Human Rights. Harnessing Debates on the EU's Future Financial Instruments*, The Hague: NIMD.

Noor, F. (2002) *The Other Malaysia. Writings on Malaysia's Subaltern History*, Kuala Lumpur: Silverfish Books.

Noyon, J. (2003) *Islam, Politics and Pluralism. Theory and Practice in Turkey, Jordan, Tunisia and Algeria*, London: Royal Institute for International Affairs.

NRC *Handelsblad* (2005) 'Interview met ael-voorman Abou Jahjah', 18 November.

Okruhlik, G. (2004) 'Making Conversation Permissible: Islamism and Reform in Saudi Arabia', 250-269 in: Q. Wiktorowicz, (ed) *Islamic Activism. A Social Movement Theory Approach*, Bloomington: Indiana University Press.

Ottaway, M. and T. Carothers (2005) 'Getting to the Core', 251-267 in: T. Carothers and M. Ottaway (eds.) *Unchartered Journey: promoting democracy in the Middle East*, Washington D.C.: Carnegie Endowment for International Peace.

Otto, J.M. (2006) *Sharia en nationaal recht. Rechtssystemen in moslimlanden tussen traditie, politiek en rechtsstaat*, WRR-Verkenning no. 11, Amsterdam: Amsterdam University Press.

Otto, J.M., A.J. Dekker, L.J. van Soest-Zuurdeeg (eds.) *Sharia en nationaal recht in twaalf moslimlanden*, WRR-Webpublicatie nr. 13, Amsterdam: Amsterdam University Press.

Panebianco, S. (2004) *The constraints to EU actions as a 'norm exporter' in the Mediterranean*.
Paper voor de Europese Conferentie 'Enhancing the European Profile in Democracy Assistance', 4 July, www.democracyagenda.org

Perthes, V. (ed.) (2004a) *Arab elites. Negotiating the politics of change,* Boulder: Lynne Riener.

Perthes, V. (2004b) 'America's "Greater Middle East" and Europe: Key Issues for Dialogue', *Middle East Policy,* 11, 3, 85-97.

Perthes, V. (2004c) *Patterns of reform in the Arab East. Summary of presentation at International Symposium Civilization and Harmony: Values and Mechanisms of the Global Order,* Istanbul, 2-3 October.

Perthes, V. (2004d) *Bewegung im Mittleren Osten. Internationale Geopolitik und regionale Dynamiken nach dem Irak-Krieg,* Berlin: Stiftung Wissenschaft und Politik.

Pew Research Center for the People and the Press (2004) *A Year After Iraq War: Mistrust of America in Europe ever Higher, Muslim Anger Persist,* Washington: pew.

Pew Research Center (2005) *Islamic Extremism: Common Concern for Muslim and Western Publics,* 17-Nation Pew Global Attitudes Survey, 15 juli, Washington: pew.

Pew Global Attitudes project (2003) *Views of a Changing World. How Global Publics View: War in Iraq, Democracy, Islam and Governance, Globalization,* http://peoplepress. org/reports/display.php3? ReportID=185

Phalet, K., C. van Lotringen and H. Entzinger (2000) *Islam in de multiculturele samenleving,* Utrecht: Ercomer Report 2000/1, www.ercomer.org/publish/reports/Rot Islam.html

Phalet, K. and J. ter Wal (eds.) (2004) *Moslim in Nederland. Religie en migratie: sociaal-wetenschappelijke databronnen en literatuur,* scp-Werkdocument 106a, Den Haag: scp.

Piscatori, J. (1984) *Islam in the Political Process,* Cambridge: Cambridge University Press.

Piscatori, J. (2000) *Islam, Islamists and the Electoral Principle in the Middle East,* Leiden: isim.

Platti, E. (2004) 'De factor religie en de idealisering van de eigen groep. De eerste oorlog van de eeuw: West versus islam?', 199-207, B. Pattyn, and J. Wouters (2004) *Schokgolven. Terrorisme en fundamentalisme,* Louvain: Davidsfonds.

Polity iv Project, *Political Regime Characteristics and Transitions, 1800-2003,* www.cidcm.umd.edu/inscr/polity/

al-Qaradawi, Y. (z.d.) *The Status of Women in Islam,* Caïro: Islamic inc. Publishing & Distribution.

Rabasa, A. et al. (2005) *The Muslim World after 9/11,* Project Air Force, Santa Monica: Rand.

223

Ramadan, T. (2004) *Western Muslims and the Future of Islam*, New York: Oxford University Press.

Raphaeli, N. (2003) 'Saudi Arabia: A Brief Guide to its Politics and Problems', *Middle East Review of International Affairs*, 7, 3, 21-33.

Rosefsky Wickham, C. (2002) *Mobilizing Islam. Religion, Activism and Political Change in Egypt*, New York: Columbia University Press.

Rosefsky Wickham, C. (2004) 'Interests, Ideas, and Islamist Outreach in Egypt', 231-249 in: Q. Wiktorowicz (ed) *Islamic Activism. A Social Movement Theory Approach*, Bloomington: Indiana University Press.

Roy. O. (1994) *The Failure of Political Islam*, Cambridge: Harvard University Press.

Roy, O. (2004) *Globalized Islam. The Search for a New Ummah*, Londen: Hurst & Company.

Roy, O. (2005) 'The Predicament of "Civil Society" in Central Asia and the "Greater Middle East"', *International Affairs* 81, 5, 1001-1012.

Sacks, J. (2002) *The Dignity of Difference. How to Avoid the Clash of Civilizations*, London: Continuum.

Safi, O. (2003) *Progressive Muslims. On Justice, Gender, and Pluralism*, Oxford: Oneworld.

al-Sayyid, M. (2003) *The Other Face of the Islamist Movement.* Carnegie Endowment for International Peace Working Paper 33.

al-Sayyid, M. (2004) *Disaggregating the Islamist Movements.* Paper presented to the Conference on the Roots of Islamic Radicalism, Yale, New Haven, www.yale.edu/polisci/info/conferences/Islamic%20Radicalism/papers.htm

Scott, J. C. (1990) *Domination and the Arts of Resistance. Hidden Transcripts*, New Haven: Yale University Press.

Shadid, W. (2005) 'Beleidsmatige en wetenschappelijke aandacht voor de islam in Nederland: ontwikkelingen en maatschappelijke gevolgen' *Beleidswetenschap*, 1, 3-17.

Shadid, W. and S. van Koningsveld (2002) 'Religious Authorities of Muslims in the West: Their Views on Political Participation', 149-168 in: W. Shadid and S. van Koningsveld (eds.) (2002) *Intercultural Relations and Religious Authorities: Muslims in the European Union*, Louvain: Peeters.

Shadid, W. and S. van Koningsveld (2004) 'Een imamschool is een onzinnig idee', *Trouw*, 25 May.

Shah, A. (2003) 'Pakistan's "Armored" Democracy', *Journal of Democracy*, 14, 4, 26-40.

Singerman, D. (2004) 'The Networked World of Islamist Social Movements', 143-163 in: Q. Wiktorowicz (ed.) *Islamic Activism. A Social Movement Theory Approach*, Bloomington: Indiana University Press.

Slomp, J. (2003) 'Antwoord op Sajid', *Ander Nieuws*, March/April, www.initiativesofchange.nl/andernieuws/p4mrt03.html

Sonneveld, N. (2005) *Four Years of Khul in Egypt: The Practice of the Courts and Daily Life*, (forthcoming).

Steinbach, U. (2005) *Euro-Islam: One Word, Two Concepts, Lots of Problems,*
www.qantara.de/webcom/shoe_article.php/_c-478/_nr-278/i.html

Stepan, A. and G. Robertson (2003) 'An "Arab" more than "Muslim" Electoral
Gap', *Journal of Democracy*, 14, 3, 30-44.

Stepan, A. and G. Robertson (2004) 'Arab, not Muslim, Exceptionalism', *Journal
of Democracy* 15, 4, 140-146.

Takeyh, R. (2001/2002) 'The Lineaments of Islamic Democracy', *World Policy
Journal*, 18, 4, 59-67.

Tarzi, A. (2004) 'Hurdles in Implementing the New Afghan Constitution'
Eurasianet 2 februari,
www.eurasianet.org/departments/insight/articles/pp020804.shtml

Tibi, B. (2001) *Islam between Culture and Politics,* New York: Palgrave.

Tibi, B. (2004) 'Pleidooi voor een hervormingsgezinde islam', *Eutopia*, 7, May.

Tibi, B. (2005) 'Euro-islam, juridisch burgerschap en burgers van het hart',
NEXUS, 41, 173-203.

Tommasoli, M. (2005) 'Democracy Building and the Political Dimensions of
Development', 29-37 in: IDEA, *Ten Years of Supporting Democracy Worldwide*, Stockholm: IDEA.

TNS NIPO(2005) 'Islamitische partij in Nederland heeft weinig kans van slagen',
30 August, http://www.tns-nipo.com

Trautner, B. (1999a) *The Caïro Declaration on Human Rights in Islam: juridical,
political, and religious implications of the status of minorities*,
www-user.uni-bremen.de/~bjtraut/sofia.pdf

Trautner, B. (1999b) *The Clash* within *Civilizations: Islam and the Accomodation of
Plurality. Empirical Evidence and Contemporary Reformist Approaches*,
Institut für Interkulturelle und Internationale Studien, Working Paper 13,
University of Bremen.

Tweede Kamer (2004) *Grondrechten in een pluriforme samenleving,* vergaderjaar
2003- 2004, 29 614, no. 2.

Tweede Kamer (2005a) *Kerndoelen basisonderwijs. Brief van de Minister van Onderwijs, Cultuur en Wetenschap*, vergaderjaar 2004-2005, 29488, no. 1.

Tweede Kamer (2005b) *Vaststelling van de begrotingsstaten van het Ministerie van
Justitie (VI) voor het jaar 2005*, vergaderjaar 2004-2005, 29 800 vi, no. 123.

Tweede Kamer (2005c) *Terrorismebestrijding. Verslag van een notaoverleg*,
vergaderjaar 2005-2006, 29 754, no. 54.

UK (United Kingdom) HomeOffice (2004) *Country Report Afghanistan*,
www.unhcr.org/cgi-bin/texis/vtx/rsd?search=coi&source=INDUK.

UK Home Office (2005) *Country Report Sudan*, www.unhcr.org/cgi-
bin/texis/vtx/ rsd?search=coi&source=INDUK&skip=40

UN (United Nations) (2005) *Interdependence Between Democracy and Human
Rights. Expert Meeting on Democracy and the Rule of Law, Geneva, 28
February-2 March 2005. Conclusions and Recommendations*,
www.ohchr.org/english/issues/democracy/seminar2.htm

UNDP (United Nations Development Program) (2002) *Human Development Report*

2001. *Deepening Democracy in a Fragmented World*, New York: Oxford University Press.

UNDP (2003) *Arab Human Development Report 2002.Creating Opportunities for Future Generations,* New York: UNDP.

UNDP (2004) *Arab Human Development Report 2003. Building a Knowledge Society*, New York: UNDP.

UNDP (2005) *Arab Human Development Report 2004. Towards Freedom in the Arab World,* New York: UNDP.

United States Institute of Peace (2002) 'Islam and Democracy', *Special Report* 93, www.usip.org/pubs/specialreports/sr93.html

Utvik, B. (2003) 'The Modernizing Force of Islam', 43-67 in: J. Esposito and F. Burgat (eds.) *Modernizing Islam. Religion in the Public Sphere in the Middle East and Europe*, London: Hurst.

Vasconcelos, A. de (2005) 'Summit Drama and Beyond', *Euromesco e-News* no. 2, December.

Veugelers, W. and W. de Kat (2005) *Identiteitsontwikkeling in het openbaar onderwijs*, Antwerpen: Garant.

Volkskrant, de (2005) 'Saudische koning wil tolerante islam', 8 December.

Wessels, M. (2001) *De extremistische variant van de Islam. De opkomst van het eigentijdse moslim-extremisme*, The Hague: Teldersstichting.

White, J. (2002) *Islamist Mobilization in Turkey. A Study in Vernacular Politics*, Seattle: University of Washington Press.

Wiktorowicz, Q. (2004a) 'Conceptualizing Islamic Activism' *ISIM Newsletter* 14, 34-35.

Wiktorowicz, Q. (ed.) (2004b) *Islamic Activism. A Social Movement Theory Approach*, Bloomington: Indiana University Press.

WRR (Wetenschappelijke Raad voor het Regeringsbeleid, Netherlands Scientific Council for Government Policy) (2001) *Ontwikkelingsbeleid en goed bestuur*, Rapporten aan de Regering 58, The Hague: Sdu.

WRR (2003) *Waarden, normen en de last van het gedrag*, Rapporten aan de Regering nr. 68, Amsterdam: Amsterdam University Press.

WRR (2004) *The European Union, Turkey and Islam,* Reports to the Government no. 69, Amsterdam: Amsterdam University Press.

Yassari, N. and H. Saboory (2006) 'Sharia en nationaal recht in Afghanistan' 173-201 in: J.M. Otto, A.J. Dekker, L.J. van Soest-Zuurdeeg (eds.) *Sharia en nationaal recht in twaalf moslimlanden*, WRR-Webpublicatie no. 13, Amsterdam: Amsterdam University Press.

Yavuz, M. (2003) *Islamic Political Identity in Turkey*, Oxford: Oxford University Press.

Yavuz, M. (2004) 'Opportunity Spaces, Identity, and Islamic Meaning in Turkey', 270-288 in: Q. Wiktorowicz, (ed) *Islamic Activism. A Social Movement Theory Approach*, Bloomington: Indiana University Press.

Youngs, R. (2004a) *Trans-Atlantic Cooperation on Middle East Reform. A European Misjudgement?* London: Foreign Policy Centre.

Youngs, R. (2004b) *Europe's Uncertain Pursuit of Middle East Reform,* Carnegie
    Paper no. 45, June.
Youngs, R. (2004c) *Democracy as Product Versus Democracy as Process.* Paper voor
    de Europese Conferentie 'Enhancing the European Profile in Democracy
    Assistance', 4 juli. www.democracyagenda.org
Youngs, R. (2005) *Ten Years of the Barcelona Process: a Model for Supporting Arab
    reform?* FRIDE Working Paper, January.
Zakaria, F. (2003) *The Future of Freedom: Illiberal Democracy at Home and Abroad,*
    New York: W.W. Norton & Co.
Zentrum für Turkeistudien (2004) *Euro-Islam. Eine Religion etabliert sich,* ZvT
    Aktuell, November 2004.

APPENDIX 1

Comparison of the scores of Muslim countries with regard to political rights and civil liberties, early 1970s and 2003/2004

	Freedom House score (1972)			Polity IV score, 1971	Freedom House score (2004)			Polity IV score, 2003 and regime type[1]
	Political rights	Civil liberties	Status	–	Political rights	Civil liberties	Status: NF=not free; PF= partly free; F=free	
Middle East and North Africa								
Algeria	6	6	NF	-9	6	5	NF	-3
Bahrain	6	5	NF	-10	5	5	PF	-7
Chad	6	7	NF	-9	6	5	NF	-2
Egypt	6	6	NF	-7	6	5	NF	-6
Eritrea	-	-	-	-	7	6	NF	-7
Iran	5	6	NF	-10	6	6	NF	3
Iraq	7	7	NF	-7	7	5	NF	Itp.
Jordan	6	6	NF	-9	5	4	PF	-2
Kuwait	4	4	PF	-8	4	5	PF	-7
Lebanon	2	2	F	5	6	5	NF	Itp.
Libya	7	6	NF	-7	7	7	NF	-7
Mauritania	6	6	NF	-7	6	5	NF	-6
Morocco	5	4	PF	-9	5	4	PF	-6
Oman	7	6	NF	-10	6	5	NF	-8
Qatar	6	5	NF	-10	6	5	NF	-10
Saudi Arabia	6	6	NF	-10	7	7	NF	-10
Sudan	6	6	NF	-7	7	7	NF	-6
Syria	7	7	NF	-9	7	7	NF	-7
Tunisia	6	5	NF	-9	6	5	NF	-4
UAE	7	5	NF	-8	6	6	NF	-8
West Bank, Gaza	-	-	-	-	-	-	-	-
Yemen	-	-	-	-	5	5	PF	-2
Yemen, North	4	4	PF	-6	-	-	-	-
Yemen, South	7	7	NV	-3	-	-	-	-
Sub-Saharan Africa								
Burkina Faso	3	3	PF	-4	5	4	PF	Itp.
Comoros	-	-	-	5 (1975)	4	4	PF	4
Djibouti	-	-	-	-8 (1977)	5	5	PF	2
Gambia	2	2	F	8	4	4	PF	-5
Guinea	7	7	NF	-9	6	5	NF	-1
Mali	7	6	NF	-7	2	2	F	6
Niger	6	6	NF	-7	3	3	PF	4
Nigeria	6	4	PF	-7	4	4	PF	4
Senegal	6	6	NF	-7	2	3	F	8
Sierra Leone	4	5	PF	-6	4	3	PF	5
Somalia	7	6	NF	-7	6	7	NF	Itg.

229

APPENDIX 1 (continued)

Comparison of the scores of Muslim countries with regard to political rights and civil liberties, early 1970s and 2003/2004

	Freedom House score (1972)			Polity IV score, 1971	Freedom House score (2004)			Polity IV score, 2003 and regime type[1]
	Political rights	Civil liberties	Status	–	Political rights	Civil liberties	Status: NF=not free; PF= partly free; F=free	
Asia								
Afghanistan	4	5	PF	-8	5	6	NF	ltp.
Azerbaijan	-	-	-	-	6	5	NF	-7
Bangladesh	2	4	PF	8 (1972)	4	4	PF	6
Brunei	6	5	NF	-	6	5	NF	-
Indonesia	5	5	PF	-7	3	4	PF	7
Kazakhstan	-	-	-	-	6	5	NF	-6
Kyrgyzstan	-	-	-	-	6	5	NF	-3
Malaysia	2	3	F	4	4	4	PF	3
Maldives	3	2	F	-	6	5	NF	-
Pakistan	3	5	PF	Fall of regime	6	5	NF	-5
Tajikistan	-	-	-	-	6	5	NF	-3
Turkmenistan	-	-	-	-	7	7	NF	-9
Uzbekistan	-	-	-	-	7	6	NF	-9
Europe								
Albania	-	-	-	-9	3	3	PF	7
Turkey	3	4	PF	-1	3	3	PF	7

(1) ltp.= Interruption of the regime. ltg. = interregnum.

Notes Since 1972 the Freedom House indicators have measured (on a scale from 1 to 7) the degree of political rights and civil liberties in a country. A score of 1 is the most free, a score of 7, the least free. *The index of civil liberties* is compiled on the basis of indicators for: 1. the freedom of expression and religion; 2. the freedom of association and organization; 3. the rule of law and human rights; 4. personal autonomy and economic rights. From this is derived a general score to determine whether a country is Free (F, average score 1.0-2.5), Partly Free (PF, average score 3.0-5.0) or Not Free (NF, average score 5.5-7.0). The Freedom House indicators are, of course, not without controversy. There are doubts regarding their objectivity and cultural neutrality.

The Polity IV score measures the democratic quality of political systems on a scale from -10 (high autocracy) to 10 (high democracy). This score is based on the assumption that a democratic system must include three mutually connected elements: 1. the presence of institutions and processes through which citizens can express their will regarding which alternative policy and which alternative political leaders they prefer; 2. the presence of institutionalized limitations on the exercise of executive power; and 3. civil liberties in daily life and during moments of participation in the political process. All the other elements of democracy, such as the presence of a constitutional state, checks and balances, and press freedom are in this approach considered as deriving from or being expressions of these three basic elements. A completely 'mature' democracy, according to this classification, is a political system in which political participation by citizens leads to considerable opportunities for choice and competition, the executive power meets considerable countervailing forces and is chosen by elections.

APPENDIX 2

Classification of Muslim countries by regime type - 2002

	Regime type
Middle East and North Africa	
Algeria	Electoral, non-competitive, authoritarian
Bahrain	Electoral, non-competitive, authoritarian
Chad	Electoral, non-competitive, authoritarian
Egypt	Electoral, non-competitive, authoritarian
Eritrea	Electoral, non-competitive, authoritarian
Iran	Electoral, competitive, authoritarian
Iraq	Politically closed, authoritarian
Jordan	Electoral, non-competitive, authoritarian
Kuwait	Electoral, competitive, authoritarian
Lebanon	Electoral, competitive, authoritarian
Libya	Politically closed, authoritarian
Mauritania	Electoral, non-competitive, authoritarian
Morocco	Electoral, competitive, authoritarian
Oman	Politically closed, authoritarian
Qatar	Politically closed, authoritarian
Saudi Arabia	Politically closed, authoritarian
Sudan	Politically closed, authoritarian
Syria	Politically closed, authoritarian
Tunisia	Electoral, non-competitive, authoritarian
UAE	Politically closed, authoritarian
West Bank, Gaza	-
Yemen	Electoral, competitive, authoritarian
Sub-Saharan Africa	
Burkino Faso	Electoral, non-competitive, authoritarian
Comoros	Electoral, non-competitive, authoritarian
Djibouti	Electoral, competitive, authoritarian
Gambia	Electoral, competitive, authoritarian
Guinea	Electoral, non-competitive, authoritarian
Mali	Electoral democracy
Niger	Electoral democracy
Nigeria	Ambiguous regime
Senegal	Electoral democracy
Sierra Leone	Ambiguous regime
Somalia	Politically closed, authoritarian
Asia	
Afghanistan	Politically closed, authoritarian
Azerbaijan	Electoral, non-competitive, authoritarian
Bangladesh	Electoral democracy
Brunei	Politically closed, authoritarian
Indonesia	Ambiguous regime
Kazakhstan	Electoral, non-competitive, authoritarian
Kyrgyzstan	Electoral, non-competitive, authoritarian
Malaysia	Electoral, competitive, authoritarian
Maldives	Electoral, non-competitive, authoritarian
Pakistan	Electoral, non-competitive, authoritarian
Tajikistan	Electoral, non-competitive, authoritarian
Turkmenistan	Politically closed, authoritarian
Uzbekistan	Politically closed, authoritarian
Europe	
Albania	Electoral democracy
Turkey	Electoral democracy

Source: Polity IV index

231

APPENDIX 3

Status of Islam and Sharia as a legal source in the constitutions of Muslim countries

	Islam		Sharia			
	Islamic state	Islam as state religion	The source, of the main source	An important source	A source	Not a source[1]
Middle East and North Africa						
Algeria	Yes	Yes	Yes			
Bahrain	Yes	Yes		Yes		
Chad	No	No				Yes
Egypt	No	Yes	Yes			
Eritrea						
Iran	Yes	Yes	Yes			
Iraq			Yes			
Jordan	No	Yes				Yes
Kuwait	No	Yes		Yes		
Lebanon	No	No				Yes
Libya	No	Yes				Yes
Mauritania	Yes	Yes				Yes
Morocco	Yes	Yes				Yes
Oman	Yes	Yes	Yes			
Qatar	No	Yes	Yes			
Saudi Arabia	Yes	Yes	Yes[2]			
Sudan	No	No			Yes	
Syria	No	No		Yes		
Tunisia	No	Yes				Yes
UAE	No	Yes		Yes		
West Bank, Gaza[3]	No	Yes		Yes		
Sub-Saharan Africa						
Burkina Faso	No	No				Yes
Comoros	No	No				Yes
Djibouti	No	No				Yes
Gambia	No	No				Yes
Guinea	No	No				Yes
Mali	No	No				Yes
Niger	No	No				Yes
Nigeria	No	No				Yes
Senegal	No	No				Yes
Sierra Leone	No	No				Yes
Somalia[4]	No	No				Yes
Asia						
Afghanistan	Yes	Yes	Yes			
Azerbaijan	No	No				Yes
Bangladesh	No	Yes				Yes
Brunei[5]						
Indonesia	No	No				Yes
Kazakhstan	No	No				Yes
Kyrgyzstan	No	No				Yes
Malaysia	No	Yes				Yes
Maldives	Yes	Yes			Yes[6]	
Pakistan	No[7]	Yes				Yes

APPENDIX 3 (continued)

Status of Islam and Sharia as a legal source in the constitutions of Muslim countries

	Islam		Sharia			
	Islamic state	Islam as state religion	The source, of the main source	An important source	A source	Not a source[1]
Asia - continued						
Tajikistan	No	No				Yes
Turkmenistan	No	No				Yes
Uzbekistan	No	No				Yes
Europe						
Albanië	No	No				Yes
Turkije	No	No				Yes

Source: International Constitutional Law (undated) Constitutional Documents,
www.oefre.unibe.ch/law/icl/index.html

1 'Not a source' indicates that these sources are not explicitly named as sources.
2 The Koran and the Sunna are not 'only' the sources on which the Constitution is based, but are the
   constitution. Art. 1 reads as follows: "The Kingdom of Saudi Arabia is a sovereign Arab Islamic State
   with Islam as its religion; God's Book and the Sunna of His Prophet, God's prayers and peace be upon
   him, are its constitution (…)."
3 This refers to a draft constitution.
4 At this time Somalia has no constitution.
5 This constitution is not available.
6 Islam and Sharia are not explicitly mentioned as sources, but there are indications that these are an
   important testing framework. In connection with this see, for example, art. 1: 'the Maldives shall be a
   (…)democratic republic based on the principles of Islam." Art. 16 sec. 2: "every person who is charged
   with an offense (…) shall have the right to defend himself in accordance with Sharia'ah." Art. 23:
   "No person shall be deprived of his property except as provided by law or Sharia'ah." Art. 38: "The
   President shall be the supreme authority to propagate the tenets of Islam."…Art. 43: "The powers
   of the President shall be exercised subject to Sharia'ah and the Constitution. Nothing shall be done
   in violation of Sharia'ah or the Constitution."
7 The preamble of Pakistan's constitution states that Pakistan is a democratic state, based on Islamic
   principles of social justice.

APPENDIX 4: THE BARCELONA PROCESS, EMP AND ENP

Barcelona process and EMP

In the framework of the EMP the EU has signed agreements with the following partner countries: Algeria, Tunisia, Egypt, Israel, Gaza/West Bank, Jordan, Lebanon, Morocco, Syria, Malta, Cyprus, and Turkey. (In the meantime Malta and Cyprus have become EU member states and Turkey is a candidate-member state.) Libya was recently granted observer status. The EMP operates formally on the bilateral level, via the Association Agreements, as well as on the multilateral level, chiefly through a yet-to-be-formed regional free trade zone and financial aid. The EMP is marked by its ambitious security-political, democratic, and economic objectives. Analogous to the Helsinki Process of the OSCE, measures and special oversight mechanisms have been developed within three separate 'baskets'. The promotion of democracy and human rights is at the heart of the first basket for the 'strengthened political and security dialogue'. The second, economic, basket aims to achieve 'a zone of shared prosperity' through the gradual creation of a regional free trade zone in 2010, while the third basket deals with measures to strengthen the mutual cultural and social relations between the Union and the partner countries along the Mediterranean Sea (Joffé 2004: 2).

The Barcelona Declaration of 1995 includes the following statement about democracy, human rights, and economic development:
"The major objective of the creation within the Euro-Mediterranean region of 'an area of dialogue, exchange and co-operation guaranteeing peace, stability and prosperity requires a strengthening of democracy and respect for Human Rights, sustainable and balanced economic and social development, measures to combat poverty and promotion of greater understanding between cultures, which are all essential aspects of partnership'.

The participants undertake to:
1 act in accordance with the UN Charter and the Universal Declaration of Human Rights;
2 develop the rule of law and democracy within their political systems;
3 respect Human Rights and fundamental freedoms, including freedom of expression, association, thought, conscience and religion;
4 give favorable consideration, through dialogue between the parties, to exchanges of information on matters relating to Human Rights, fundamental freedoms, racism and xenophobia;
5 respect and ensure respect for diversity and pluralism in their societies and combat manifestations of intolerance, racism and xenophobia;

6 The participants stress the importance of proper education in the matter of Human Rights and fundamental freedoms.

Under the social, cultural and human "chapter", participants:
7 attach particular importance to fundamental social rights, including the right to development;
8 recognize the essential contribution civil society can make in the process of development of the Euro-Mediterranean Partnership;
9 will encourage actions of support for democratic institutions and for the strengthening of the rule of law and civil society [...];
10 undertake to guarantee protection of all the rights recognized under existing legislation of migrants legally resident in their respective territories;
11 underline the importance of waging a determined campaign agains racism, xenophobia and intolerance and agree to co-operate to that end."

These objectives and basic principles were again confirmed at the EU summit held at the end of November 2005 as part of the celebration of the tenth anniversary of the Barcelona process (see below).

235

EMP and ENP

In December 2003 the Council of the EU adopted its first common European security strategy under the title 'A secure Europe in a better world'. They decided on a multidimensional policy that linked political, socio-economic, cultural, military, and ecological dimensions. In October 2003 the Council decided to adopt the proposals of the European Commission for concretizing this security policy via the European Neighborhood Policy, ENP. The area concerned stretches geographically from the Balkans, Ukraine, Moldavia, Belarus, and the southern Caucasus to the EMP countries. The connection with the ENP means that also on a bilateral level, in technical subgroups, national Action Plans could be established that could introduce a stronger tie between financial incentives and actual progress. Following the example of the so-called screening procedures for candidate-member states, the European Commission prepares individual country reports. Assessments over the situation in the areas of democracy, rule of law, and human rights are also included in these reports. On the basis of these assessments, negotiations are held with the partner countries on concrete Action plans covering a number of key areas, including political dialogue and reform and trade and gradual access to the internal market. The annual progress reports must keep track of the advances in these areas (European Commission 2003: 14-20; 2005: 5).

At the European summit of 27-28 November 2005 in Barcelona the EMP countries succeeded in unanimously adopting a five-year work plan and a code of conduct against terrorism. Together with the Association Agreements and the bilateral action plans in connection with ENP, the work plan forms the basis for future cooperation in areas such as politics, security, trade, the environment, education, and migration. On the other hand, the member states remained divided among themselves on democratic reforms and the Middle East peace process (Ministerie van Buitenlanse Zaken 2005b; Vasconcelos 2005).

GLOSSARY

Ahmadiyya	Muslim movement in Pakistan
Ayatollah	Religious title (Iran)
Baha'is	Followers of the Persian Baha'i faith
Caliph	Successor of the Prophet, deputy of God, leader of the Muslim community (Ummah)
Caliphate	The rulership of the entire Muslim community (Ummah)
Da'wa	Islamic proselytizing
Fatwa	Judgement based on Sharia regarding individual questions (legal advice)
Fiqh	Both the Islamic knowledge by which God's divine plan with society can be derived and the body of rules itself
Hadd (pl. Hudud)	Five crimes set down in the Quran (literally: limit)
Hadith	Traditions and sayings of the Prophet Muhammad
Hakimiyya	Sovereignty of God
Hezbollah/Hizbullah	Party of God
Hizb al-shaytaan	Party of Satan
Hudud	See: Hadd
Ijtihad	Free interpretation, method of legal interpretation
Imam	Religious leader
Jahiliyya	Heathenism
Jama'a al-Islamiyya/ Jamaat-i-Islami	Literally: organization for Islamic rebirth
Jihad	Struggle; the inner, spiritual struggle of the believer or the struggle to defend the religious community
Jinayat	Rules for the application of the pre-Islamic retaliation principle of an eye for an eye, a tooth for a tooth, or compensation with blood money in cases of murder, manslaughter, or assault
Khilafa	See: Caliph
Khul	Divorce by mutual agreement, entails a payment
Loya Jirga	Consultative assembly (Afghanistan)
Madrasa	Religious school
Muddawana	Moroccan code of family law
Mullah	Religious teacher or leader
Pancasila	Five pillars of the state's constitution (Indonesian)
Pesantrens	System of Islamic boarding schools (Indonesia)
Shah	(Persian) King
Sharia	Islamic law; literally: 'path'
Shiites	A minority denomination within Islam (followers of Ali, the cousin and son-in-law of the Prophet)

237

Shura	Obligation of the ruler to consult with the ruled
Siyasa	Authority for rule-giving, granted by Sharia, to the government, which must not conflict with Sharia
Sufi	Mystical order in Islam
Sunna	Acts of the Prophet (source of Sharia)
Sunnis	Followers of the denomination which represents the majority of all Muslims (literally: followers of the tradition)
Tachtsche	The place where the Quran is stored: the highest place in the house (Persian)
Tawhid	The unity of God, monotheism
Ulama (singular Alim)	Those educated in Islamic law
Ummah	The community of Muslim believers
Vilayat-i-faqih	Spiritual leader (Iran)
Wahhabism	Conservative interpretation of Islam that is the official religious doctrine in Saudia Arabia and that dates back to the ideas of Muhammad 'Ibn Abd al-Wahhab (1703-1792)
Zakat	Compulsory contribution of a percentage of one's wealth to the poor (alms)
Zina	Extramarital sex (a hadd crime)